ONTHEBUS

Double Issue: 19/20   2005

BOMBSHELTER PRESS

Los Angeles

ONTHEBUS 2005 ISSUE 19/20

Editor **Jack Grapes**

Associate Editor **Jennifer Haft**

Published by BOMBSHELTER PRESS **Michael Andrews & Jack Grapes**

Layout & Design **Alan Berman**

ISSN 1043-884X   ISBN 0-941017-63-X

ONTHEBUS
features poetry, prose, translations, reviews, essays, interviews, art, and photography. Send submissions to Bombshelter Press, P.O. Box 481266, Bicentennial Station, Los Angeles, CA 90048. Subscriptions & correspondence should be sent to Editorial Offices, 6684 Colgate Ave., L.A., CA 90048. Single issues are $11. This double issue costs $15. A regular 3-issue subscription is $28 to individuals, $33 to institutions.

GUIDELINES: Send poems at a time; prose no more than six words per story; book reviews, 250 fiction is limited to 1500 year, ISBN if avail., full address and Web site words (reviews must include pub. photo of the cover or author; see this issue for of publisher, page count, binding type, price, prose should not exceed 10 pages. We are happy to accept examples). Total submission, including poems and/or simultaneous submissions. That means you may send work elsewhere while we are considering it. If accepted elsewhere and we also decide to publish it, we will do so after it appears where first taken. We are also willing to consider work that has been previously published (just let us know where, so we can give proper credit). We expect submissions to include contributor's bio and SASE. We will only consider work sent September 1—October 30 and March 1—May 30. Submissions not following these guidelines will be returned unread.

**ONTHEBUS is distributed by Small Press Distribution, Bernhard De Boer, and Armadillo.
ONTHEBUS is indexed in the American Humanities Index (AHI).**

ONTHEBUS is published by Bombshelter Press in association with the Los Angeles Poets & Writers Collective, which sponsors workshops, readings, seminars, retreats, and literary publications, including ONTHEBUS and Rattle. Some of the contributors to this issue are also members of the Collective.

Front cover photograph of Louis Vitale by Robert Durell

Back cover painting by Aaron Smith: Brush, oil on panel 54" x 67"
Courtesy of Koplin Del Rio Gallery, Los Angeles

BOMBSHELTER PRESS
6684 Colgate Ave
Los Angeles CA 90048 USA
www.bombshelterpress.com
info@bombshelterpress.com

Contents

Translations

Reviews

Biographies

Index of Authors

The Dark and Stormy Night

Jack Grapes, Editor

I became a writer not because I had something to say or stories to tell, but because I fell in love with words.

One could make a sentence out of words, and with sentences you could build cities and fill them with people. To this day, when I go into a bookstore and open a book to that first page, I feel as if I've given away all my possessions and I'm standing there waiting for the writer to speak, waiting to fall in love, waiting to be swept away by the writer's voice, by the writer's words.

It doesn't matter where you are, the words can take you somewhere else. You could be sitting on the white sands of a Pacific island, and the words can take you to a roach-infested tenement on the lower east side of Manhattan. You could be listening to the rain pound against the shutters of your New England cottage in the dead of winter, and the words can take you to the Sahara desert, the sun beating down on you, your mouth parched, your throat dry. You could be eating figs on the sprawling lawn of a Manchester estate, and the words can take you to a damp cell, your face enclosed in an iron mask. You could be sitting in first class on a transatlantic flight from New York to Paris, and the words can take you on a trip you've never planned.

> Midway through this journey of our life,
> I found myself lost in a dark wilderness,
> for I had wandered from the straight and true way.[1]

Later, when your friends say, "How was the flight?" you can smile and say, "It was hell."

Wherever you are, the words can take you somewhere else. Or make you wish you were somewhere other than where you are.

---

1   Dante, *The Inferno*

A bird cried out on the roof, and he woke up. It was the middle of the afternoon, in the heat, in Africa; he knew at once where he was. Not even in the suspended seconds between sleep and waking was he left behind in the house in Wiltshire, lying, now, deep in the snow of a hard winter.[2]

No matter how old you are, the words can make you young again.

Once upon a time and a very good time it was there was a moocow coming down along the road and this moocow that was down along the road met a nicens little boy named baby tuckoo. . . .[3]

You could be propped in bed, nibbling a cucumber sandwich, and the words will have you storming the beaches of Normandy in World War II.

Nobody could sleep. When morning came, assault craft would be lowered and a first wave of troops would ride through the surf and charge ashore on the beach at Anopopei. All over the ship, all through the convoy, there was a knowledge that in a few hours some of them were going to be dead.[4]

Say, for a moment, life makes sense. Give the words a chance, and they'll lead you into a world in which nothing is sure and all that is solid melts into air.

Mother died today. Or, maybe, yesterday. I can't be sure.[5]

It doesn't matter that the rent is due, that the roses need pruning.

My God, that bloody casket has fallen on the floor! Some people were hammering in the next flat and it fell off its bracket. The lid has come off and whatever was inside it has certainly got out. Upon the demon-ridden pilgrimage of human life, what next I wonder?[6]

Once you read the words, you can imagine thinking any damn thing you please.

It was a queer, sultry summer, the summer they electrocuted the Rosenbergs, and I didn't know what I was doing in New York. I'm stupid about executions. The idea of being electrocuted makes me sick, and that's all there was to read about in the papers—goggle-eyed headlines staring up at me on every street corner and at the fusty, peanut-smelling mouth of every subway. It had nothing to do with me, but I couldn't help wondering what it would be like, being burned alive all along your nerves.[7]

You'll know how lucky you are when the words remind you of what it was like when you had nothing or no one.

It happened that green and crazy summer when Frankie was twelve years old. This was the summer when for a long time she had not been a member. She belonged to no club and was a member of nothing in the world.[8]

2 Nadine Gordimer, *A Guest of Honor*
3 James Joyce, *Portrait of the Artist as a Young Man*
4 Norman Mailer, *The Naked and the Dead*
5 Albert Camus, *The Stranger*
6 Iris Murdoch, *The Sea, The Sea*
7 Sylvia Plath, *The Bell Jar*
8 Carson McCullers, *The Member of the Wedding*

The Dark and Stormy Night

You don't have to wear headphones to shut out the world. Someone is talking directly to you, close and intimate, their mouth at your ear. *Call me Ishmael.*[9] They're not talking to a roomful of people, they're not performing a tale for the crowd; it's just you and the writer. *Marley was dead; dead as a doornail.*[10] They're practically whispering to you. *I am ill; I am full of spleen and repellent.*[11] Perhaps you want to turn away, but you can't. This is what you wanted. To be held by the truth of another's life. *Lolita, light of my life, fire of my loins. My sin, my soul. Lo-lee-ta.*[12] You want to experience someone else's life, you want to dream someone else's dreams. *Last night I dreamt I went to Manderley again.*[13] You could be happy as a lark, content with your life, and the words can still break your heart. *My wound is geography. It is also my anchorage, my port of call.*[14] And sometimes, the words can change your life.

I was six years old. No, I was five. I had learned to read before I was five. I was crouched on the floor of the living room and it was raining. It was night. I could feel the rug beneath my knees, soft but a little scratchy. I was small, crouched on the floor, and everything was high above me. The chairs, the mantelpiece, the lamps on the end tables, the doilies on the arms of the armchairs. The book was blue. It was *My Tree House.* It was open to the first page, and there was a picture of a purple cow. Under the picture was a short, four-line poem. My mother stood in the doorway, the phone to her ear, her face red and contorted, her voice hysterical. She slammed the phone down. "Your father is drunk, and he's coming home to chop our heads off," she said. "We're going to Ma-Ma's house." Then she hurried upstairs to get our things. I looked back at the purple cow, at the poem printed beneath it.

I never saw a purple cow,
I never hope to see one.
But I can tell you anyhow,
I'd rather see than be one.[15]

Was there really such a thing as a purple cow? All the cows I'd seen were brown, or black with white spots. I never saw a purple cow either. But maybe there were purple cows. If there were, where would they be? Maybe my dad would take me to the zoo or a farm, and we could see one, I thought. Why wouldn't a person want to see a purple cow? Was it a bad thing to see? I was crouched there on the floor, and I imagined for a moment that I was a purple cow, and no one wanted to see me. Maybe because I'd done something bad. Probably because I was purple. No one wanted to see me because I was the wrong color. I looked back at the picture of the cow. All that purple on the page, I thought, was kind of pretty. I liked looking at the purple cow. Then I read the poem again. *But I can tell you anyhow, I'd rather see than be one.* It was nice the way the words rhymed, but especially the rhyme inside the line, *see than be. I'd rather see than be.* I whispered the words to myself. *I'd rather see than be.* I thought about the words. It was better to *see* a purple cow than to actually *be* a purple cow. Being a purple cow must be really bad. You just didn't want to be a purple cow. It was bad enough seeing one, but it was worse to be one. If you had to make a choice, you'd choose to see

9   Herman Melville, *Moby Dick*
10 Charles Dickens, *A Christmas Carol*
11 Fydor Dostoyevsky, *Notes from Underground*
12 Vladimir Nabokov, *Lolita*
13 Daphne DuMaurier, *Rebecca*
14 Pat Conroy, *The Prince of Tides*
15 Anonymous

rather than be one. And then the way the whole line rhymed with the other line. The rhyme inside and the rhyme at the end.

> I never saw a purple cow,
> I never hope to see one.
> But I can tell you anyhow,
> I'd rather see than be one.

My father was going to come home and chop our heads off, but I was thinking about the purple cow and how the words rhymed.

"Here's your suitcase," my mother said, "you can carry it." My suitcase was really a duffle bag. She handed it to me and grabbed my arm and yanked me up. "Let's go outside and wait for the taxi." We stood on the porch until the taxi came. It was still raining, a dark and stormy night. I'd read that in a book somewhere. A dark and stormy night. It felt good to say the words to myself. *It was a dark and stormy night.* We were on the porch, but every so often a gust of wind blew some water onto the porch and my legs got wet. It was scary, but I liked it. The street was dark but every once in a while a bolt of lightning would light everything up and you could you see Mr. Seenac's house across the street, you could see the muddy water swirling down the gutter. Then it would get dark again, and a few seconds later a rumble of thunder seemed to shake the branches right off the trees. When the next bolt of lightning came, sure enough, there in the street were a few branches from the trees. I wanted to get a closer look. I took a few steps toward the edge of the porch and waited for the next gust of wind. "Don't stand in the rain!" my mother said, and yanked me back from the edge of the porch. She was talking and crying, but I wasn't listening. I was thinking about the purple cow, about the poem. I was thinking about the words, how the words were things that you could play with, that with words you could make up poems and stories. I decided then that this was something I wanted to do. I wanted to write down words on a piece of paper and make things up, stories and poems. Maybe I wouldn't have to make anything up. Maybe I could tell stories about things that really happened. Maybe there'd be a boy somewhere who'd want to read them, who'd want to be someplace else.

A yellow cab pulled up in front of the house. The cab driver got out and ran around to the other side of the cab and opened the door for us. He was all hunched over and getting wet. He wore a yellow cab driver's hat. We ran down the steps and got in the cab. I stepped in some muddy grass and heard the squish. Before he closed the door, another gust of wind blew the rain into the back seat. It was scary and exciting. My mother gave the cab driver the address of my grandmother's house. She lived in Metarie. A long drive. The taxi driver pulled down the handle on the meter and the numbers started rolling as he drove. The bigger the number, the more we'd have to pay. My mother had stopped being hysterical. She was re-arranging the suitcases. When we turned the corner onto Ferret Street and headed up Napoleon Avenue, I leaned over and said to the cab driver, "My father's coming home and he's going to chop all our heads off." Then I went back to thinking about the purple cow. I was thinking that I was going to be a writer someday, I was going to write about the purple cow and the dark and stormy night. ▲

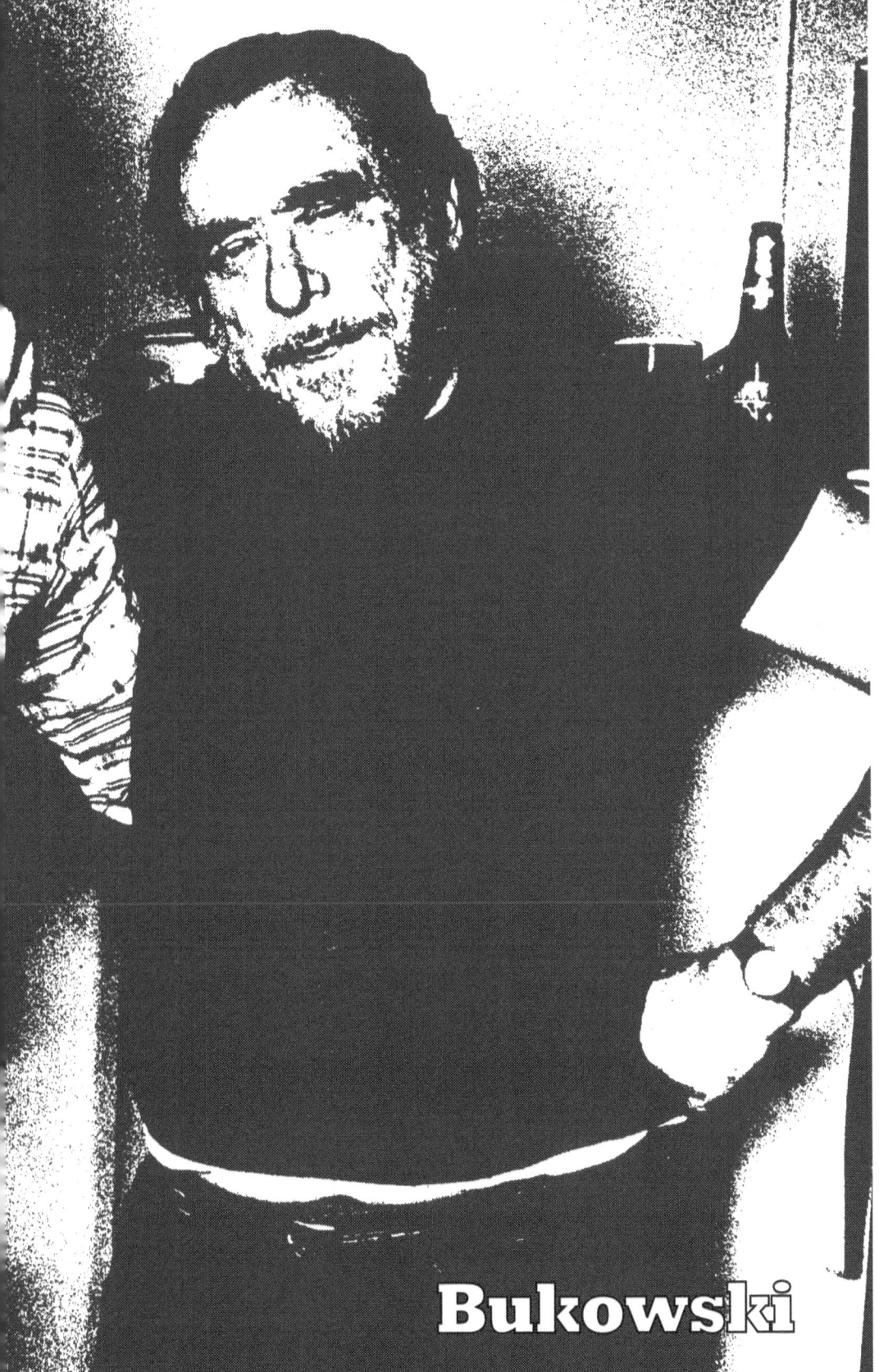

Bukowski

Bukowski: Poems & Journal

Overleaf:
From a photo of Ulvis Alberts and Charles Bukowski by Joan Levine
East Hollywood, 1976
Courtesy Ulvis Alberts

POEMS

looking back

now
I can't believe myself:
in the bars
attempting to pick up
the most dowdy of
women.
sagging stockings,
over-rouged cheeks,
deathly masqueraded,
yellow-toothed,
rat-eyed,
bellowing hyena
laughter . . .
and when I was
successful—
peacock proud,
I was Atilla,
I was Alexander the
Great,
I was the toughest
roughest guy in
town—
Bogart, Cagney,
Gable, all in
one.

and worse,
I can't believe myself
choosing out the biggest
meanest bastard in the bar
to the alley.

to get myself clubbed by
meathooks I didn't even
see coming.
my brain jumped inside
my skull,
I saw blazing shots of
color, flashes of
lightning, I felt my
mouth fill with blood,

sensed my body
on the pavement.
I got up and rushed
forward with my
tiny hands.
there was many a
fight when I hardly
landed a
punch.
I was a laugh a
minute and the crowd
had all
night.
I got my beating
and they got their
jollies.

my face never healed.
I always had a fat
lip, a black
eye, a nose that
hurt all over.
I developed bone-
growths under the
knees from falling
hard.
yet a couple of nights
later
I'd still be looking
for a newer and
meaner
bastard.

but harder to believe
was when finally
through some obnoxious
stroke of miracle
I did win
one,
I was accorded no
accolades.
my stripe, my function
was to
lose.
I was the guy from out of
town
and not even of the
neighborhood.

the strangest most hateful
nights were after

winning,
sitting alone at the end
of the bar
as that gang laughed and
talked it up
as if I weren't even
there.

when I lost they loved me
and the drinks came
all night
long.

so when I won I lost
and when I lost I
won.

and
looking back
it is hard for me to believe
some of the women
I shacked with.
they all had good bodies,
great legs
but the faces
the faces were faces from
hell
covered with
masks.
they were all fair in bed
in spite of a rather general
indifference to it
all.
they had ways of flattering
me
and I was younger,
more open to the
dream.
but Christ, they were good at
finding my wallet
after a day or two
to vanish
with all my money
to leave me
scrabbling for rent,
food, sanity and the
lost
dream.

only to reappear
knocking on my 3 A.M.

door
as if nothing had
ever happened:

"Hi!"

back from robbing some
other poor son of a
bitch.

and worse,
I'd let them back in,
liking the look of the leg,
the general madness of it
all,
to drink with them then,
to hear their sad
stories,
to let the dream seep
back in . . .
after all, where was I to find
a lady?
down at the public library?
or at the opera house?

come on, baby, show me
some leg and let's hear
your story.
and come on, have another
drink!

I had no plans.
I had no idea of what I was
doing.
the world was a strange and
oppressive
place.
a man had to get up his guts
to shove through.
everybody was so sad and
defeated and
subservient,
obedient.

"tell me about it, baby."

I liked myself with my tiny
hands and my pock-marked
monkey face.
I liked myself sitting in my
shorts and my undershirt,
the undershirt torn and

dirty and full of cigarette
holes and wine-stains,
and I had muscular arms
and great powerful legs
and I loved to walk the rug
with my whore watching
while I vomited forth
inanities and
insanities.

I was hot stuff.
I was young stuff.
I was a fool
and I loved the
fool,
I lived the fool.

"o.k., baby, show me
more leg!
more!
your talk dulls me!
lift your skirt higher!
hold it!
not too high!
I don't want to see what's
there!
let me imagine!"

looking back, it couldn't have been
better.

what a lovely
fucking
fool
I was.

what can you do?

there is always somebody to chop the wood
for you,
to speak of the ways of
God,
there is always somebody to kill the
meat,
to unplug the toilet,
there is always somebody to bury
you,
there are always the animals with the
beautiful eyes,
and there are always the gossips,
like Stanley leaning toward me
and saying in a soft voice,
"do you know that at the end of
his career Saroyan had other
people writing his stuff and that he
gave them twenty-five
percent?"
this was supposed to make me
feel good because I was a starving
writer and the rejects were arriving
in endless numbers.
it didn't make me feel
good.

there is always somebody to make
you feel worse about the
human race.

there is always the dead dog on
the freeway.
there is always a fog full of
cutting
blades.

there is always Christ drunk in
the tavern with dirty
fingernails.

dead

he wrote a joyous and mad
novel about unbelievable
drinking episodes
and his words danced with
laughter and mockery,
gamble.

the novel made him
famous and he went on
to write others but none
like the first.

then he stopped
writing, came here from
his land
and became a professor
in a southern
university.

he wears his suit, his
tie, his dignity
as tokens of
acceptability
and his students wait
for him to go wild
through the
walls,
to break glass,
precedence,
minds.

but the semesters
pass in quiet
seasons.

R.I.P.

Now

now the territory is taken,
the sacrificial lambs have been,
as history is scratched again on the sallow walls,
as the bankers scurry to collect overdues,
as the young girls paint their hungry lips,
as the dogs piss again in the temporary space,
as the shadow gets ready to fall again,
as the oceans gobble the poisons of man,
as heaven and hell dance in the anteroom,
it's begin again and go again,
it's bake the apple,
buy the car,
mow the lawn,
pay the tax,
hang the toilet paper,
clip the nails,
listen to the crickets,
blow up the balloons,
drink the orange juice,
forget the past,
pass the mustard,
pull down the shades,
take the pills,
check the air in the tires,
lace on the gloves,
the bell is ringing,
the pearl is in the oyster,
the rain falls,
as the shadow gets ready to fall again.

WENT TO THE TRACK TODAY IN THE RAIN and watched 7 consensus favorites out of 9 win. There is no way I can make it when this occurs. I watched the hours get slugged in the head and looked at the people studying their tout sheets, newspapers and *Racing Forms.* Many of them left early, taking the escalators down and out. (Gunshots outside now as I write this, life back to normal.) After about 4 or 5 races I left the clubhouse and went down to the grandstand area. There was a difference. Less whites, of course; more poor, of course. Down there, I was a minority. I walked about and I could feel the desperation in the air. These were 2-dollar bettors. They didn't bet favorites. They bet the shots, the exactas, the daily doubles. They were looking for a lot of money for a little money and they were drowning. Drowning in the rain. It was grim there. I needed a new hobby.

The track had changed. Forty years ago there had been some joy out there, even among the losers. The bars had been packed. This was a different crowd, a different city, a different world. There was no money to blow to the sky, no to-hell-with-it money, no we'll-be-back-tomorrow money. This was the end of the world. Old clothing. Twisted and bitter faces. The rent money. The 5-dollar-an-hour money. The money of the unemployed, of the illegal immigrants. The money of the petty thieves, the burglars, the money of the disinherited. The air was dark. And the lines were long. They made the poor wait in long lines. The poor were used to long lines. And they stood in them to have their small dreams smashed.

This was Hollywood Park, located in the black district, in the district of the central Americans.

I went back upstairs to the clubhouse, to the shorter lines. I got into line, bet 20 win on the second favorite.

"When ya gonna do it?" the clerk asked me.

"Do what?" I asked.

"Cash some tickets."

"Any day now," I told him.

I turned and walked away. I could hear him say something else. Old bent white-haired guy. He was having a bad day. Many of the mutual clerks bet. I tried to go to a different clerk each time I bet, I didn't want to fraternize. The fucker was out of line. It was none of his business if I ever cashed a bet. The clerks rode with you when you were running hot. They would ask each other, "What'd he bet?" But go cold on them, they get pissed. They should do their own thinking. Just because I was there every day didn't mean I was a professional gambler. I was a professional writer. Sometimes.

I was walking along and I saw this kid rushing toward me. I knew what it was. He blocked my path.

"Pardon me," he said, "are you Charles Bukowski?"

"Charles Darwin," I said, then stepped around him.

I didn't want to hear it, whatever he had to say.

I watched the race and my horse came in second, beaten out by another favorite. On off or muddy tracks too many favorites win. I don't know the reason but it occurs. I got the hell out of the racetrack and drove on in.

Got in the place, greeted Linda. Checked the mail. Rejection letter from the *Oxford American*. I checked the poems. Not bad, good but not exceptional. Just a losing day. But I was still alive. It was almost the year 2,000 and I was still alive, whatever that meant.

We went out to eat at a Mexican place. Much talk about the fight that night. Chavez and Haugin before 130,000 in Mexico City. I didn't give Haugin a chance. He had guts but no punch, no movement and he was about 3 years past his prime. Chavez could name the round.

That night was the way it was. Chavez didn't even sit down between rounds. He was hardly breathing heavily. The whole thing was a clean, sheer, brutal event. The body shots Chavez landed made me wince. It was like hitting a man in the ribs with a sledge hammer. Chavez finally got bored with carrying his man and took him out.

"WELL, HELL," I said to my wife, "we paid to see exactly what we thought we would see."

The tv was off.

Tomorrow the Japanese were coming by to interview me. One of my books was now in Japanese and another was on the way. What would I tell them? About the horses? About the strangling life in the darkness of the grandstand? Maybe they would just ask questions. They should. I was a writer, huh? How strange it was but everybody had to be something, didn't they? Homeless, famous, gay, mad, whatever.

They ever run in 7 more favorites on a 9 race card and I'm going to start doing something else. Jogging. Or the museums. Or finger painting. Or chess. I mean, hell, that's just as stupid.

Bukowski

POETRY IS INDISPENSABLE— if I only knew what for.

PROSE IS A TARDY GENRE, offspring of thought's distrust of the natural tendencies of language.

OUR FACULTIES DO NOT PLAY US TRUE, and both parties are relieved by solitude.

Poems Prose Interview

Overleaf:
"Poetry is indispensible—if I only knew what for."
    —Jean Cocteau
"Prose is a tardy genre, offspring of thought's distrust of the natural tendencies of language."
    —Octavio Paz, The Bow and the Lyre
"Our faculties do not play us true, and both parties are relieved by solitude."
    —Ralph Waldo Emerson, "Friendship"

The Insomniac
circa 1960

Los Angeles had less than three million people and we never heard of the Vietnam.
Fidel Castro was a burr under Ike's saddle and the Mouseketeers were the goddesses of sex.
We rode the bus from Inglewood to Hermosa and rented surf mats from the guy on the corner
who was wrinkled and tan and doomed to die of multiple melanomas.
After the crash of the surf we spent all afternoon dripping sand and salt water
in the back stacks of the Insomniac Bookstore on the north side of Pier Avenue.
The floors were concrete and the shelves were raw wood and home made.
Beatniks in black dueled with rooks and knights on rickety chairs over battered boards,
the rank sweat of strong coffee inhaled through cinnamon tubes.
Everywhere we looked we saw minds greater than our own.
We shivered in our soggy bathing trunks, our little pricks ever alert while we read
the dirty parts of *Lady Chatterly's Lover* and *Tropic of Capricorn*.
We read the naughty bits in *The Canterbury Tales* and *The Decameron*.
In time we learned to think with our heads too.
Every book held a mystery, a promise of secrets revealed
and wider universes waiting for our minds to take the voyage.
The mere cover of a book was worth missing dinner for.
The mere feel of the pages flipping through our fingers
made our minds hungry and our spirits voracious
for the other side of horizons, for truths unveiled.
The words whirred by, the music of the pages fluttered in our fingers
until we stopped, dipped into sentences that led to sentences, that exploded ideas
that created unknown worlds, until our brains imploded
with adventures beyond our imaginations.
The Insomniac is gone now, replaced by sport bars and televisions.
No one reads anymore, no one flips the pages.
No one is struck dumb with awe by the mere sight of shelves of books.
The inebriated denizens bring wheelbarrows of cash and worship any idiot
who can thump a guitar or can run with a ball, dribble a ball or hit a ball with a stick.
Their eyes are awash with tequila and they cannot imagine a world of ideas.
My worlds are humdrum now, prosaic and everlastingly dull.
The secret of secrets revealed is that there is always another secret
and that no secret leads to that final understanding.
The secret of humans is that they are not an intelligent species.
The chess players have departed, replaced by video gamers and sport fans.
I no longer know anyone smarter than me. The knights of chess have died away.
The surf mat shop has long been replaced with roller blades.
Gone are the boys in the salt water trunks, hungry for other worlds.
I look around and no longer see thoughts flipping through fingers.
I no longer see beyond horizons.
I do not know minds like that
anymore.

Blue Silk

As if the rain had taken her hand,
she's out the door and down the steps—
her curved back new with nakedness.

In the doorway, the man who holds her robe
whispers her name to make her return
as she moves across the wet black lawn,

under an empty clothes line, to touch the bark of an oak.
Warm rain falling on her face and chest—
his gifts are small compared to this.

Beside the amber light of a short bare porch,
as the silk robe wilts around his wrist,
he glances at the neighbor's house.

Anyone could see her now, were anyone awake to look:
this glistening woman who dances
in a yard where there are no fences.

Kind of Blue
—*for Sam, at 15*

It was probably a bad idea,
setting up her drums in the room above
my study, yet her deftness with stick
and pedal left me tapping as I typed.
Now the filaments shimmer in the ceiling's
fixtures like miniature cymbals: our son thumps
on her bass drum, smashes her crash cymbal,
rattles her snare: he towers over us today
as I sit here marveling at his first

real fight with his mother—something little
like her wanting him to stop watching a movie
and go to bed—and he, suddenly bristling
everywhere, and most of the time, his head
six inches higher into the heavens, his voice
basso profundo, deeper than the deepest pit
in her stomach, and later me holding him
by his shoulders as he lay in his bed, wide-eyed
the two of us, as I spoke of the beautiful stallion

now in his blood—that women fear it
(saving for later the way they crave it, too),
that he will have to saddle and ride it gently
through flowering fields, that power is power
though bridled: and that, in *Kind of Blue*, Cobb
keeps time cool on the ride, just taps on the crash,
tips his high hat to the irresistible plenty of Miles's
soaring horn—their delicate hands, though
muscles rippled beneath their studded jeans.

Ben Franklin's Son Flies a Kite

Late afternoon, June 1752, Ben Franklin flew
his signature kite in the wind
and sparked the storm
of the century. Beside him, his son
didn't know what hit him
as he held the current in his hand,
flying in the face of electricity
(or was it adversity?). The positive
and negative charged
and all at once, the science
of storms—Our preoccupation
with the cosmic pleasures
and displeasures leaves our small-talk
like printer's ink on the cumulus
pulp of clouds, then poof, erased
for the mystic anomalies
of tomorrow. His dad was not content
to ride the celebrity-of-invention wave.
Instead, he was of the mind
to insulate twine with silk ribbon,
fasten a key to the magnetic fields
(pinned to the wind) of our dreams.
The atmospherics, if you will.
Because when lightning strikes
twice, one son will die,
(as mathematics would have it)
and the other son, the survivor,
lives to record it: how two brothers
rub their socks against the rug
to elicit static shock. Ben's lifelong
sorrow, losing a son to the string
that gets let go. . . . Meanwhile,
back to electricity,
one current to another
in a medium of communication,
one body acts to another
across the intervening spaces.

Landing

Pan Am Shone electric blue and clean-sheet white,
and the clouds shifted like lint couched against a gray gloaming.
It was 1971, and the stewardesses were preparing the cabin for landing,
loping up the aisle in higher
heels than my mother ever wore, and short, short skirts
of electric blue, in bouffant caps of clean-sheet white and peacock feather false lashes
like parrots caught in a shiny cage tossed from one zoo, San Francisco,
to the other zoo, London Heathrow.
I was sleepless after half a world of travel. My eyes, drooping dry,
vacuumed sights like jumbo jet engines vacuumed the dust bunnies
separating us from the ground.
My parents dozed, missing it all. My brother watched only me.
The cigarette sign flashed on and a chime, like a fairy's command, required seat belts
        clacking fastened.
England neared us, spotted by headlights of trucks called lorries and dark puddles,
not the Crayola-colored clean of Castro Valley sidewalks, the lime green grass where my
        swing set swung,
the aqua butterfly-speckled kiddie pool where I splashed in a hot pink suit.
My parents stirred as my baby brother howled, pressure in his ears popping him away from
        the dark Earth
reaching up to catch us as we ironed a gray stripe in the forest mud.
As the ruby-clawed stewardess turned the pump on the cabin door, she unlocked the fog,
        dank and laden
with pond water which turns tadpoles into frogs, and I felt my legs growing.

T-Bone

I was 11½ and we were visiting my father for the weekend. Having his five kids under the roof of his duplex was not occasion enough for him to join us for dinner. It will take Thanksgiving or Christmas for that to happen. He would rather sit in his throne and eat his dinner on a TV tray. He preferred his television over his children. His dog, a pedigree Great Dane named PiPi, was asleep at his feet. Today was payday and he splurged by barbecuing a steak. I got excited until I saw only one T-bone on the grill. He fed us macaroni and cheese and boiled hot dogs. What kind of father feeds his kids mac 'n' cheese while he eats steak? My kind. He raised me to question my worth.

Everyone brought their plate to the sink except him. I approached his throne. "Are you done, Daddy?" I asked. "Yeah," he answered as he pulled a drag off his cigarette. I picked up his plate and saw there was still meat on the bone. I licked my lips. I saw steak once, maybe twice a year. "Do you want anything else?" I asked. "No," he said without looking at me. My six-year-old brother, Dale, was still sitting at the table fingering his macaroni. His mumble told me he was somewhere else—again. I nudged his shoulder with my father's plate and said, "Dale, look!" His innocent eyes looked up at me, his mouth still in a mumble. "Steak!" I said smiling. His Kool-Aid mustache rose up as he grinned. "C'mon, follow me," I said. We began to tear the meat from the bone when my father's voice stopped us. "Lisa, give that bone to the dog," he ordered. I turned around and my eyes landed on his steak-filled belly that sat satisfied under his blue shirt. The top button of his pants was undone. What is he doing out of his throne, I thought. "Do you need something, Dad?" I asked, trying to change the subject. "Do you want some dessert?" "No," he replied. "I'm gonna fix myself a drink." I stood in front of the bone and pretended not to hear his command. Dale hid half his body behind mine. PiPi waltzed in and sat beside her master. I glared at the dog I had grown jealous of. "Where's that bone?" he asked as he dropped fresh ice cubes into his glass. "This bone?" I said, stepping aside as if there was more than one. "Yeah," he replied. "Give it to the dog." PiPi began to pant in anticipation. I stood there frozen as I watched Johnnie Walker collide against the ice cubes. I'm afraid of my own father. Time is running out. He's going to want to know why I'm not doing what he asked. He sat the bottle down and turned the lid back on. He looked up and his eyes shot through me. "We want the bone," I blurted. "What?" he said baffled. "We want the bone," I repeated. "Why?" he said. I took a deep breath and said, "We don't get steak and there's a lot of meat still on the bone and we want it." He looked at me in complete disbelief. I held it up and asked, "Daddy, can we have the bone?"

He had to choose between his children and his best friend. He pressed his glass to his lips. I watched his Adam's apple jump up and down as the scotch made its way into his throat. PiPi closed her jaw for a quick swallow, looked up at him and then at me. Oh yes, she thinks she's getting this bone. I scowled at her. If I have to wrestle you for it I will, I thought. You weigh more and you've got bigger, sharper teeth, but I'll win. I will not lose to you again, dog. The tension was scaring Dale. He squeezed my hand and took cover behind me. My dad's stare was piercing. The dog was getting impatient and moved toward the bone. I turned away and lifted it higher.

He put his drink down, looked at his dog and then at us and said "Sure, you can have it." I brought the T-bone to my face and said, "Thanks, Dad." He stood there and watched me clean one side of the bone. I handed it to my little brother, who cleaned the other side. I saw something new in his eyes . . . it was shame. I had reached my father. The next night, he surprised us all with barbequed hamburgers, but the real shock came when he turned off the television and sat next to me at the dinner table.

Waking Pains

I've often suspected that my wife does things to hurt me while I'm sleeping. I wake up sore, not every night, but often.

There are no cuts, abrasions, swellings, or burn marks on my body, but there's almost always some part of me that hurts like hell, and occasionally a black and blue mark. There can be no other explanation, I don't walk in my sleep, bang myself against the headboard or fall out of bed. I sometimes have dreams, but rarely remember them. At night all of the doors are double locked so no one can be getting in, and the kids are grown and out of the house. The dog? No, it's not the dog. It's Helen.

Have I accused her? Not exactly, but I've tested her. I'll tell her my finger hurts and she'll say something like, "You must have rolled over on your hand and bent your finger." She's too quick with a theory for every hurt—her responses must be planned in advance. I've set traps. I woke one morning and my knee, the right one, felt as if someone had kicked it. I walked into the kitchen where she was making coffee and told Helen that my nose hurt. "It feeld ad if someone punched me in de node," I said making a convincing face.

"Maybe you had a boxing dream," she said, "and punched yourself in the face. By the way, is something wrong with your right knee?"

"I twisted my knee when I got out of bed this morning," I tell her, dropping the hurt nose voice, and she tells me to be more careful how I get out of bed. "You shouldn't leap up. Sit up and swing your body around so your feet are just above the floor."

Helen sounds sincere—so sweet, caring, and solicitous. That's the side of her I see. We rarely argue and since this is the second marriage for both of us we try to be more open and thoughtful. At night when I'm sleeping, the devious, spiteful, and mean Helen comes out.

I talk in my sleep. Need I say more? My mother was the first person who hurt me in my sleep. Once I woke up in he middle of the night with my big toe throbbing. It felt like a toothache in my toe. Eventually I fell back to sleep, but the next night, when I was supposed to be in bed, I sat on the stairs listening to my mother on the phone with my Aunt Leah. "Teddy was making believe that he was a football player kicking field goals, whatever they are," she said, "and one by one he kicked the tops off Mrs. Samuel's tulips. Of course, he told me in his sleep, said something about being the hero for kicking the winning point. No, I don't think it's a fertile imagination, Leah, I think he's destructive. Why can't he be more like his brother? I grabbed a Hardy Boys book from his bookcase and whacked his big toe with it. Yes. Real hard."

I'd been duped. My mother couldn't read the guilty looks on my face as she'd been telling me, and there were no neighbors or relatives snitching on me, as she also told me. Mom was picking my brain while I slept.

Sometimes I'd wake up in the middle of the night with a pain and the next morning there might be a black-and-blue, and my mother would tell me that people who lie break out in black-and-blues when they sleep. I believed her, because like most kids I was always lying about something and always had a black and blue somewhere.

I went back to my room before my mother got off the phone. I lay in bed thinking about getting even. I plotted and planned and schemed; oh, did I scheme. The things I was going to do to get back at my mother—some embarrassing, some even painful. Then I worried I'd tell my mother about it in my sleep and she'd do those things to me and I got scared.

My brother Billy and I weren't allowed to close our bedroom doors, much less lock them. "Just in case, God forbid, something should happen to you while you're sleeping" she said, "then I'd be able to hear and come running and take care of you." I decided to take my chances and I closed my door and wedged a chair under the doorknob so it couldn't be opened without making a lot of noise.

My father worked the swing shift, four till midnight, at one of the factories in town. He never was part of my mother's nightly question-and-answer ritual with me, and I'm sure that he didn't know the extent of it. He did question my closing my bedroom door because he always looked in on "his boys" when he came home from work. I told him that I'd become a light sleeper and any little noise from downstairs woke me up. He accepted the explanation but probably figured that I needed the privacy to do what all teenage boys did.

I guess that he never talked in his sleep because he and my mother got along fine.

After a late dinner at our favorite restaurant I woke up in the middle of the night with a pain in my eye—the kind you get from a poke. Helen and I had gotten into a silly argument over dinner. It escalated way past where it should have and we went to bed not speaking. She accused me of looking at other women. Helen's a "looker" and takes great pride in keeping in shape. She's tall, with shoulder-length blonde hair, and long shapely legs. She has no reason to worry, but she has no tolerance or understanding of my looking at any other woman when she's around. "Of course I look," I told her. "Just because you're full doesn't mean you don't look at the dessert menu."

"That kind of looking can hurt your eyes," Helen said.

"Is that like the hair-on-the-palm theory?" I asked.

"Worse," she said. "More like the horse head-in-the-bed concept."

Groggy, it took me a few minutes to realize where I was. Rolling over, I saw a sliver of light at the bedroom door and through the slight opening I saw Helen and my mother. They were blurry and I watched them best I could as they took turns jabbing their thumbs towards each other's eyes and laughing. It was as if they were exchanging techniques. I got out of bed and walked towards the sliver of light and opened the door into the hallway. No one was there. Even so, this validated for me my belief that my mother told Helen "my secret." I can imagine her whispering to Helen at our wedding. "You want to know what's going on with Teddy—ask him questions while he's sleeping. He answers questions in his sleep. He'll tell you anything."

For the next few days all I could think about was getting even with Helen, but I couldn't lock her out of the bedroom as I had done years before to keep out my mother. I knew that unless I could stop talking in my sleep there would be no getting even. She'd know ahead of time and would start hurting me more. After a few days, the solution dawned on me. I decided to call my dentist and tell him I was grinding my teeth and ask him to make me an appliance. With that in my mouth I wouldn't be able to talk.

"Helen told me you'd most likely be calling," he said when I called.

"Forget it," I told him.

The next morning I called my father in Tampa and asked him if he'd like a visit. "Everything okay?" he asked, since this was not my usual visiting time. "Sure," I said. "I just feel like seeing you and chatting."

"Need a little father-son stuff, hey? Throw the old apple around, drown a few worms, have that *talk* we never really had. Sure." Dad's well into his eighties but hasn't lost any of his sharp wit. That's part of the reason his freezer's full of casseroles, or "widows' offerings," as he calls them.

I told Helen I was flying down to Florida to visit my father. She seemed genuinely surprised. I don't know how this slipped by her—I'd expected her to hand me the plane tickets.

Paul Beckman

Even though I told him I'd rent a car, my father picked me up at the airport anyway. He was no longer able to drive but kept his old Caddy polished and at the ready. Walking off the ramp into the terminal I spotted a handwritten sign reading TEDDY. It was held by a pair of identical twin elderly women. Both were sporting reddish pin curls, blue eyeglass frames, and silver nail polish. The only difference between them was the color of their jogging suits. One red, the other blue. They had identical smiles as they moved the sign back and forth over their heads. They looked like cheerleaders for the Octogenarian Olympics. Carrying my bag I walked over and stood in front of them. Together they said, "You must be Teddy." To passersby it might have looked like a stickup, a man standing in front of two elderly women holding their arms in the air. "You can lower the sign now," I said. They did and giggled a not unpleasant old lady's giggle. "Right. I'm Teddy and you are. . ."

"We're Shirley and Pearlie," they said in unison.

"Of course you are," I said, not asking who was who. "Is my father here?"

They nodded and began to slow-walk towards the exit, ignoring me and chattering to each other. I found it hard to walk that slow and wanted to scoop them up, one in each arm, and carry them out of the terminal. Smiling as I passed them, I was remembering when I called my father on his 85th birthday and asked him what he wanted for a present.

"Same as you, Teddy," he said, "a pair of babes, red-headed twins." Helen, who'd been talking to my father on the other line, hung up and grilled me about his comment for weeks. She refused to believe that my father and I never discussed red-headed twins before.

One night Helen came to bed wearing a red wig, and I can't say we didn't have a good time. She takes it out once in a while, and if I see it on the pillow I know it's her way of apologizing for something or we've gone too long without sex for one reason or another. She calls it our acrylic foreplay.

I spotted my father's Caddy and opened the back door where he was sitting. I interrupted his thumb twiddling (thankfully a gene not passed down to me). After giving him a hug I noticed two baseball gloves and a softball on the seat. I walked around the car and got in while the twins were still chatting on, heading towards the car.

"What do you think," he asked. "I make one wear red and the other blue so I can tell them apart, but I forget who I assigned which color to."

He smiled proudly as the twins opened the front doors and got in. Red jogging suit drove, rejecting my offer to do the honors. She drove just a little bit faster than she walked, so Dad and I got to catch up on family news.

The four of us had dinner at Marty's Eatery. Along with the check came a small peppermint patty and a Marty-Pack. Each person at the table got one, which contained packets of salt, pepper, ketchup, mustard, saltines, and a half-dozen coupons (Sunsweet, free blood pressure test, etc.) and a Marty-Star which was to be pasted on a Marty Card which held twelve Marty-Stars, and when filled, could be traded in for a free Marty Meal. Shirley and Pearlie eyed my Marty-Pack, but of course I passed it on to my dad, who gave them both a smug look.

By 6:45 Dad and I were alone back in his condo. We watched a ball game, made small talk, and at eight on the dot Dad said good night and went to his room.

In the morning when I got up, Dad was dressed and having a bagel.

"What's bothering you, son?" he asked. "Bagel?"

I nodded and he pointed at the freezer. The door was lined with a sentinel of Saran-wrapped bagels. "Take from the left," he said. "First in, first out. I haven't had to buy a bagel in years."

"How so?"

"The Bagel Kingdom always gives a free sample and I stop in anytime I'm in the neighborhood."

"Isn't the Bagel Kingdom on the corner?"

"That's the one," he said, and winked. "Pretty lucky, huh?"

There had to be two dozen bagels; and, against my better judgment, but not wanting to hurt his feelings, I took the oldest. It was hard to ignore the freezer burns after I eventually got it unwrapped. I nuked it before popping it into the toaster oven and it tasted exactly like it should.

"Tell me."

So I told my father of Helen and my mother. He's a good listener and "hmmed" or "uh-huhed" while I told about my talking in my sleep and the pain it's caused me over the years. He felt a kinship with Helen. She called him often and they laughed and teased each other a lot. She got a kick out of his telling her what he considered risqué jokes, and she often mailed him cookies when she baked.

"Mostly you would mumble but you weren't understandable unless Mother told you to stop mumbling and speak clearly. Then you would. You had to be prompted to speak and probably still do. I wouldn't call it speaking freely," he said. "Answering questions is what you did best. Whenever Mother engaged you in conversation where she asked and you answered, you never woke up."

"Did you ever talk to me or question me in my sleep?"

"No, not you," he said.

"If not me, who?" I asked. "My brother, Billy?"

"Mother," he said.

"Mom talked in her sleep?" I asked incredulously.

"Yep, but I never told her. I first heard her on our wedding night and it continued until she died—forty-two years later."

"Did you question her and use the information like she did on me?"

"Of course," he said. "But like any true super hero, I only used my power for good, never for evil."

"Like what?" I asked.

"Like things that bothered her, like my leaving my dirty clothes on the floor instead of picking them up, or places she wanted to go on vacation. I never missed getting her the right gift and on time for her birthday or our anniversary. Things like that. Later on, as we got to know each other better, there was sex talk and our sex life became more creative and enjoyable—not that it wasn't enjoyable at the beginning, mind you." My father blushed. "Mother would mention something she read in a book, or heard from a girlfriend, and I'd wait a bit and try it out; or, if it was a fantasy, try and fulfill it," he said proudly, wiping away a tear.

We sat, quietly sipping our coffee, and I flashed back to a conversation I had long since forgotten between my mother and Aunt Leah. I was very young and eavesdropping from my regular listening post at the top of the stairs as they talked. I broke out of my flashback and looked over at my father and in his cataract eyes saw him going through memories, most probably fond ones of him and my mother. I didn't have the heart to tell him that my mother didn't talk in her sleep—she just pretended to in order to get what she wanted. That's what I heard her tell Aunt Leah.

"So who do you like more, Shirley or Pearlie?" I asked, breaking the moment.

In the afternoon, my father left me alone and took off with his women for a couple of hours on a planned bus trip to an ostrich farm. I browsed a museum and took a nice stroll back to the apartment. On the way, I cut through a park and sat on a bench, people watching and thinking about my mother manipulating my father just as she manipulated me. I realized that my father wouldn't agree that she was wrong, even if he knew she was faking.

That evening, while waiting to leave for dinner, my father took out a bottle of Canadian Club and two shot glasses. We sat at the kitchen table and he said, "Pour." I did and realized

Paul Beckman

that this was one of the few times in my life that I saw my father having anything stronger than an occasional beer.

"Listen, son," he said. "I'm going to let you in on a little secret I promised never to tell. "Your mother didn't give you all those black and blue marks—you gave most of them to yourself."

"What?"

"I'm not telling you that, on occasion, you didn't anger her and tell her things in your sleep that made her feel some discipline was necessary. I didn't agree with her and that's one of the reasons I stayed working the swing shift all those years. Every time I got seniority and was about to go on days, I would leave that factory for another. The changes were good for me and good for our marriage."

"I'm lost," I said.

"You would argue with your mother or someone else while dreaming and while playing the role of the other person you would often pinch or punch yourself. That doesn't excuse mother for her occasional treatment of you, or for letting you believe it was always her in order to keep you in line. That's the only thing we ever really fought over, and my way to resolve it was to hide from it by working."

"And Helen?"

"It's the same thing. Do you think that after years of hurting yourself you'd suddenly stop?"

"But she talks to me when I'm sleeping, just as mom did."

"So?"

"And the pains when I wake up?"

"What do you think?" he asked.

Shirley and Pearlie called and they were waiting in the lobby for us to take them to dinner. They were dressed identically. They had also changed the shade of red in their hair. My father acted as if he didn't notice, but several times in the restaurant I looked at him and saw that he was enjoying their game. When they left the table to "tinkle," my father asked me if I liked the new hair color he picked out for them. "Sure," I said. "Why the change?"

"Adds zip," he said and I nodded. I drank too much and one of the twins drove home while I dozed in the back seat.

Later that night I got up to go to the bathroom and stubbed my toe on a chair. It hurt like that Hardy Boys book whack. I didn't remember moving the chair near my bed when I got home. Who else could have? I passed my father's room and thought I heard voices and pressed my ear to his door, wondering if it was Shirley or Pearlie, or, God bless him—both. I had the deja vu feeling of listening in on my mother talk to Aunt Leah. I heard my father say, "Helen," and forgetting about the bathroom, I went to the kitchen where I none-too-gently grabbed the wall phone. There was a sudden silence on the line. Finally I gave up and went back to bed, leaving the phone dangling.

I woke in the morning and packed, not knowing if I dreamt my father's phone murmurings or really heard them, but I knew a hangover when I felt one. When I lifted my arm to brush my teeth, I felt a discomfort in my forearm and checked in the mirror for a black-and-blue mark. I also had a pain in my right ear, the one I pressed to my father's bedroom door and held the phone to.

Shirley and Pearlie, back in their blue and red outfits, sat on either side of my father while I drove to the airport. After parking in front of the terminal we all got out of the car. The ladies each gave me a kiss on the cheek. I hugged my father goodbye and he asked me why my ear was all red. I shrugged and then winced when he clapped me on the arm—right on the sore spot. He smiled, and Shirley and Pearlie waved as I walked, bag in hand, into the terminal.

Lifting My Mother's Face

A pre-cancer growth the size of a flea appears on my nose, sending me to a plastic surgeon, my own doctor afraid her handiwork will leave a scar. I step into the same office my mother visited last year to get her face lifted, and immediately feel lost in a foreign, cosmetic country. The plush first-class seats in the waiting area swallow me up, and everywhere I turn, framed magazine covers of movie stars wink at me from the walls. The blond, gem-studded technicians in white lab coats beckon me to follow them and suddenly I feel underdressed in my jeans and tennis shoes. I ask one named Beverly if my mother had her surgery done *here*, remembering how afterwards she looked as if she'd been hit by a truck, so I'm wondering how they could work someone over like that in this tidy palace. "Oh, yes, dear, we have a fully licensed operating facility down the hall," she says, showing me to an exam room the size of a supermarket. I think about what it must have been like for my mom back *there* where they hide the messy facts of bruised flesh, and red, splintered bone. How the doctor must have stood over her, his ambitious knife posed above her beautiful face like an Olympic diver. I thought about my mother's complex relationship with her mirror, the hours she'd spend in the powder room while my father snored into his bourbon on the sofa. I'm thinking this as I watch Beverly's inflated lips vibrate instructions, her diamonds tangoing back and forth across my paperwork, and I'm imagining what the Navajo woman hugging a swollen clay pot in the painting behind her thinks of all this, knowing that in her world, old wounds were considered the body's visible proof that you had done battle with the enemy and lived to tell the story.

Single

That one sits on a stool.
He reads a *Sunset* and chews on a toothpick,
bent and twisted from his chopping block.

Another walks past, cocktail napkin pressed to his
mouth and ear, shouting into it with self-importance.
Yet another tries to catch my eye, but I look away
before he can read the bubblegum wrapper there.
He frightens me. Because he's too beautiful.

The one screaming into his cocktail napkin
barks out a laugh like a last-call-to-board-plane announcement.
The beautiful one ignores him, and keeps his eyes on me.
What does he see? What does he think he sees in me?
A dark-haired watermelon with a slide step and crooked mirror?
What else is there?

I don't trust the beautiful ones. I wish he'd look somewhere else.

How about the watermelon sitting on that stool over there?
She's got a smaller, straighter mirror, shapelier legs,
and probably a used condom brain.
Perfect. Perfect for the beautiful beasts.
A used condom brain is easy to throw away.

But the beast with the cocktail napkin soldered to his ear
approaches the used condom watermelon instead,
and she highballs him, taken in by his mix of seltzer and sour.
He leans down to spray to her,
and used condom watermelon is off the market, just like that.

I turn in my chair, and sneak a warped wooden floor at the beautiful beast.
He still looks at me.
I have to go.
I think he wants to ferment my heart and eat my pimento soul.

Divertissements

While you are waiting for someone to play
you hear that awful word *food*. You suspect
what is up. Guests spill from gameboard corners
to the next room, seeking roughage and paper cups.
You chide them back. There is a tic
in your eye that just won't quit.

Already, you could be winning. Already,
your hand could be orbiting the board.
The playing pieces all respond, but you
can't stand to have your skill ignored. How long
can you take their cat smearing its nose
on the skin above your sock? You worry

about animal bites. And have you ever noticed
the way these games dwindle to an end?
A player walks into the room and announces
that the toilet has stopped, that the night
is getting nowhere. You think of the card table
your mother would wipe with a cloth

and then fold the legs and put away.

In the Middle of the Night

Awake in the kitchen
between two bedrooms
my son asleep in one
my father in the other
I consider
his limp & his lunch
his repetitions & his why
his criticism & his acceptance
his love & his love.
These two men eighty years apart
& me in the middle
between answers, still asking questions
wanting to be understood & getting told what to do
telling my son it's time to go & being told I shouldn't by my father.
In the middle of the night in the kitchen
I peel an apple
watching 4 A.M. traffic 21 floors below Queens Boulevard
so far away from life in California & birth in Czechoslovakia
the end of his story & the beginning of his.
Troubled by some haunting
or something I haven't done
being in the middle of everything
the night
the passage
the place between these two men.
I eat the apple bit by bit without a sound
the traffic slips into summer
watch the morning amber press the cobalt sky
listen to his stirs & his snores
as I leave the last of skin and seeds
between parent & child.

Sticks and Stones

The Phone

My father first got the news of my mother's death on the phone. The message was not even live; it was a recording left by one of my mother's friends: "Can't tell you how sorry I am to hear about Diane's death."

"That's crazy," he said. "She just left here this morning on her way to work." He shouted this at the phone as though the machine had concocted the message, as though the phone had dreamed that the line to which it was attached was a vine in disguise and the words he had heard were the fruit of its imagination.

The Paper

A newspaper has many words. They never shut up, the words stay there whether you read them or not, they just keep on saying whatever they are saying. Shouting whatever they are shouting. What's black and white and read all over? That's an old one. Besides, I just gave you the answer. What's black and blue and red all over? My mother, after her auto accident, according to the newspaper account, which I never read but heard about later. I read my father's face as he came walking up the drive with the paper shook open and the words hammering out at his eyeballs and him holding it at arm's length like it was road kill, destined for the garbage pail. He threw the paper in the fireplace and lit a match. I couldn't look at his eyes: they were brighter than the fire.

The Neighbor

Lucinda and her 50-year-old mother moved in next door just a while ago. I hear them when they talk out on their porch. Mostly the younger one talks, reads stories to her mother from the newspaper. "Lucinda is my eyes," the older woman said to me the other day when they introduced themselves. The mother likes the stories about fatal accidents, just eats them up. I wonder if the daughter read her the story of my mother's accident. It made quite a splash on the front page over a year ago. There was a photo too, in living color, as they say. I don't know, I never saw the picture. Except in my head, and it's pretty bad in there, but then I tell myself to ignore that because it isn't real, just the way a movie isn't real.

Lucinda borrowed a screwdriver from my dad and later that day returned with a plate of cloud-fluffy biscuits—"as sort of a repayment," she said. To my mind the biscuits were more of an advertisement than anything else (she had found out that ours was a motherless household), but I didn't mind. She was nice, not just nice when people were looking, but nice when she didn't know they were. And I could tell she suffered from too much mama, just like I suffered from too little.

My father pointed to a chair and she sat down. After that, though, Father remained silent. He had already thanked her for the biscuits and he was a man of few words. After a minute or so, Lucinda began squirming in her seat. "Have you read your morning paper yet? No? Well, a woman fell out of the sky (nobody saw an airplane, thought there must have been one). Just fell out of the blue. She landed on a stone wall, which severed her body."

My father looked at her with astonishment. But neither spoke. Lucinda looked like she didn't know if he was astonished at the news or at her, for relating it. His white face didn't give her a clue, and I thought of the time my mother lined the quiche dish with pastry crust before she remembered to copy the recipe for the egg/cheese/bacon filling that was inscribed on the inside of the dish and was now covered up. Then I noticed my father clamping his lips together as though a bunch of words were backed up in his mouth and if he opened it, they would come out in a stampede.

He picked up the dish of biscuits and placed them firmly in the hands of Lucinda, then helped her rise from the chair, then showed her to the door, all the time putting the camera in reverse, making all her actions undo themselves, take themselves back. Erase themselves. Make themselves as blank as the beautiful backs of those pale biscuits.

The Candle
On my mother's last birthday I bought her a candle that started singing when lit and was supposed to stop singing when blown out, but there was no hushing it up, even a dunking in water didn't do the trick. So we put it out on the stoop to drive the moon and the stars crazy. Maybe the candle was smarter than us, maybe it knew this was her last birthday, so it was singing a refrain for each of the years she should have had left.

Skywriting
I am on my back in a field near our house, watching a plane write a message in the sky. The first letter is a "D." When the plane circles up to dot the second letter, I know for sure it is an "i." The pilot starts to form an "n," but I stop with the first two letters, the first two letters of my mother's name. The skywriter becomes my father, writing a letter to my mother, a letter she can read from the other side, although it will be like mirror writing.

"Diane," it will read, "forgive me for the mad, ugly words I sent with you when you left the house. I keep trying to take them back."

No, that last sentence is wrong. My father already has the words back; he needs to get *rid* of them. The crickets around me are singing so strongly they are starting to drown everything else out. Even the writing in the sky is being dissolved, losing its outlines. I put my hands over my ears, but the sound doesn't get any smaller! It's like it's coming from the inside, as though the sound I am hearing is a condensation of the words in the newspaper and the words I heard my father say to my mother when she left the house, all stirred up together, whirling around, reading fever pitch. I run, trying to go faster than the speed of sound, trying to outrun the din that is right inside my very own head.

Orphan Mask

L'etat, c'est moi
—Louis XIV

I am the State.
Scaled down to size, a double
indemnity, a geranium
in the dry fist of winter.
Dear Kindness,
do not come looking
for me. It is too late.
I cannot tame what is about to happen.
One dreams the territorial, dreams
someone has your story, shares
a perversion for oversized rooms and high ceilings
but has no home, no idle realm, nor lasting
digression. I love a god
alone like me, swinging
from his hammock, his black
mouth open with a real despair
for stars. A convert companion
who collects anchors and maps, squanders
cheating, spits shiny
watermelon seeds into the little coffin
paper beds of the empty chocolate box, a self-
punishment for knowing no one.
And because the broken
scullery is filled with strychnine
in tins, wallpaper-smothered cornflowers sealed in
arsenic who say, Yes, I say, Yes, but
cannot return the favor. To temper
this rush-blood feeling
inherited at birth
I place my every seal in red
wax, my signature
and no domain air
down. Leave me now. You know
I have handmade work to do: ragged
heirloom, chromosome rain, and mournful
prophecy memory. There
will be no unjust space big enough for me.

Permanent Kind

He turned his head to look at me
and asked me what I wanted.
I wanted him.
But I asked for a tall latté instead.

He turned to me again and asked,
Are you having a good time?

Nobody has ever asked me
if I was having a good time
standing in line at a Starbucks.

Only he would do something like that.

I have to think about it for a moment
but the truth is, I am.
And he said, "Good. Me too."

His hand moves to his chest
as if he were going to say
the Pledge of Allegiance.
But he plays with a stain on his shirt.
It's one of many
from being on the road
for too many months.

He fingers it
in an absent-minded sort of way
maybe trying to figure out
what it is
and
how it got there.

I am that stain.
I am not red wine or chocolate or even coffee.
I am one of those stains
from some meal he won't remember.
I am not the permanent kind.

The Stony Brook Lodge

That lodge was once a brothel
during WWII, an officers club.
The rooms, divided
into studios, rent for $250
a piece. A crazy veteran got
his piano in one. Another
veteran dances down at
the Elks on his wooden leg.
A woman student risks her thumb
on the road out front, hitches
to college. You never know
if she'll come back. Pine trees
out front are thick with hundreds
of years. Raccoons rob
the unlidded garbage at night.
Once a fox froze
like an icicle. I helped
a drunk veteran off the floor
to his bed. First I had to
do a jig with him, his drunken
breath breathing up my nose.
I cleaned the librarian's room.
All his books locked in
a glass case in the lobby downstairs.
In his room, an unmade bed
and large chest of drawers,
no chairs, lots of pillows. If I ask
he'll open the cabinet and lend me
War and Peace.

Where Was Fidel When I Needed Him?
—to Elian Gonzalez

Because your father looked nervous during his interview with the INS,
your granduncle's attorneys don't believe you should go home,
they say your father doesn't really want you,
that Fidel is making him say such things.

When I was six, my father was across the ocean, too.
Divorced from my mother before I turned a year old,
in arrears for child support, hiding from the court,
he'd gone to Vietnam to research how the communists
brainwashed people out of the comforts of exporting rubber.

When I turned 16, I met him. He took me
to a Baja bar where I listened to his voice
as I tunneled beneath our wasteland of memory,
trying to resupply our love, but
the tunnel didn't lead that way.

Throughout the afternoon, he uncoiled his story
how my mother and grandparents hid me from him.
Later his story wound back on itself like a python,
how he drank in Saigon, drank at San Diego State,
drove around Berkeley with a Marine friend
yelling "faggots" out the window at the longhairs.
I could not hear myself in his voice.

He said we were alike because we played football,
but despite the distance between us,
he'd never thrown one pass to me, nor
had I been close enough to lean against him in a block
and feel him push back.

How I wish Fidel had walked into the bar,
taken my father at gunpoint,
locked him in Cuba's darkest prison
without rum and brainwashed him,
electrified the genitals I came from,
made him scream that he wanted me with him.
Where was Fidel as my grampy sang me to sleep,
where was Fidel as my father bought Saigon Tea
for the mothers of dust?

3rd Avenue

Nothing reminds me more of the rare
unhurried gesture my mother made, maybe

twice each year, than the scent of clean
street water in mid-spring, say, when a crisp

airborne freshness suggests a plenitude of time
and my own sweet promise. In the sun-mist

of second grade, I once breathed that new scent
as we strolled down 3rd Avenue. The trucks

hadn't yet dumped their gas into the air lining
the sidewalk to my grandmother's apartment

on 54th. I can't know why but for blocks she held
my bare hand without the usual speedy tugs,

the quick, rough squeeze meaning *Keep up,*
meaning *Now.* And I remember the same scent

one unheralded July midmorning, my tenth year,
a sun shower ending a game of stickball

before I stole in to join her quietly on the couch
as she read. So it was I carefully stretched out

beside her, and for a full thirty seconds,
as absentmindedly as turning the next page

of a mystery, that fierce, untrustworthy hand
began scratching through my summer crew cut,

while I lay in the brief capacious gift
happened upon like love.

St. Margaret at Eighty

—for Grandmother

She refuses the titanium dream
Of new hip and knee. "There's to be none
Of that," only the merciless rising
At dawn for the Trevi and the Forum,

Each brutal step over the broken stone
A jolt up the bone path sucked into lungs,
Then inhaled, dismissed like ordinary
Breath: The long-perfected means to dissolve

Ankle-hungry rock, to transform the giant
Slate-scaled serpent into benign pith.
Nothing's unfair. Once Methodist, she will
Abide no patron saint. Still, she's Margaret

At eighty, headstrong, beating down the beast.
Her dreamless stare augurs sleep. She slays rest.

Korea 1951

New in the camp
I ran into the barracks and shouted
"One of those big tanks of gas is burning!"
No one moved from their bunk
"It's the one on the hill right above here!"
No one moved
Them things is always burning
Someone said

I ran to the hill and grabbed
A shovel, frantic to dig a ditch
For the flaming gas to follow
Away from the barracks
Heat, dirt, sweat, until I shoveled up a
Burning load of dirt and saw more
Coming toward me, threw the shovel
And ran down the hill, turned to look
Heat and flames roaring higher, but
Now the burning dirt was going the
Other way, away from the barracks.

Six months later another frantic
Newcomer charging into the barracks shouted
"One of those big tanks of gas is burning!"
I turned the pages of my book slowly
"Them things is always burning,"
I said.

Preparations

I am the executor of the will,
my mother told me today.
It's a lot of responsibility, she said,
but you're old enough to handle it, my father added.

We'd like to be cremated,
and you get the house and the dining room set.
And I nodded like a dummy, learning about death
as if I was learning the facts of life all over again.

Do you have any wishes for us? my mother asked.
Yeah, I said, don't die.
and they laughed, good naturedly,
as if I was kidding,

Then my father talked on
about tax ramifications and estate planning,
while I wondered which one
would have to die first.

And then I shook my head
and hated myself pure
because I chose one
over the other
too quickly

in my head.

Get Outta Town

Sometimes it's best to let things die, especially houseplants
given by friends. My dog believes if you turn your heart away
from something it dies and from there you can simply watch it go.
I've packed the things you left in the corners of what used to be
a shared home, and plan to mail them this week. Your pants
keep rustling around in the box. Your little animal statues,
I hear them too. Everyone says *have fun now, ride the racehorse*
and keep kicking 'til he dies on you, but I am tired and follie
closed itself in the garage with a running car. I found the body
this morning on my way out for a jog. It's hard to love someone
and hard not to, I can't keep up with which or don't want to. Funny
how big the rooms seem at first, and finally, how the bigness gets
crowded out by my circus of flowering vines and the tall boy that cares
for them. I keep the blinds closed and the bedclothes rumpled
on the off chance that you've forgotten something and need to swing by
one last time. This is not killing me, it's not. That's not your car
parked outside the house, and that wasn't you I saw
waving from a windy field. That was a blue-grey rag tied to a stick.

Rock-and-Roll Wannabes

I'm tired of rock-and-roll wannabes,
men with shaggy haired cuts
standing in subways
with smoke-glazed eyes
singing songs of undying love
when they'd fuck anything they could get flat.
Men who profess to be outsiders
when they're really nerds
in black Levi's
with limp dicks.
Strum, strum, strum.
Strum your guitar hard
and let everyone see your pain.
What is your pain?
Your great deep heartache?
Soothed with a beer and a fuck.
Oh, you're so deep,
so deep.
You wouldn't know heartache
if it sat on your face,
spread its lips and ground itself
into you.
You with your beer friends,
you think you know poetry?
You think you know words?
I see a tragic drunk.
I see a little boy.
A spoiled child
wanting to be spanked,
wishing to be spanked.
And you fool young girls.
Oh, they think you're a god,
a guitar god.
As if your sweat were nectar
and your black shirt were torn from the back of Jesus himself.
You wrap yourself in your pain
and wear it like the fuckin' flag.
But you don't know pain.
Pain doesn't live in the back seats of limos,
on two-hundred-dollar dinners in Soho.
Pain lives in cracks.
It seeps in slowly.
It takes you away in blurry fogs.
It leaves you to die
without fireworks and fanfare.

You don't know pain.
You don't know pain.
You only know what sells.

Mother's Boy

He lay sullen,
a pale, flat-eyed mannequin
dressed by his mother's hands
in carefully pressed
brown-gray tweed.
A coarse insult to the silk he'd prefer.

Photographs, her
collages of his life.
Puffy-cheeked boy blowing out
candles on a GI Joe cake.
Snapshots of cut-out girls
perched on his warm lap,
posing.
She'd built a shrine
beside his bed.
Eagle Scouts, track
medals: he'd earned
his masculinity.

In his breast pocket,
Jeremiah's photograph,
sandy blonde hair and coy smile,
embraced by silk arms.
Silent badges—
dull pink triangles
scratched thin,
suffocated by tweed.
Rainbow sleeping behind stone
dead eyes.

She spoke of her son—
Timothy.
Not Timo.
He was electric energy
she said.
A caring soul, a kind smile,
she said.

She said,
"He taught me tolerance,"
and placed
her Book of Mormon in
his casket,
a new closet
six feet under.

After Finding a Photograph of Elsie Brown

My great-grandmother was 15 when she married.
In the only youthful photograph I have,
she stares ungrinning into the rounded frame,
Victorian-broached collar, white-laced quaint.
Her face is round, inviting;
her hair in a rigid, time-honored bun
and her eyes clear as the midwestern sky
that bore her young existence.

I have trouble imagining Elsie Mae Brown
as she must have been that Kansas summer, 1904,
courted by her schoolteacher with fumbling corsages—
thoughts of homework and adolescent romance
formalized into parents' blessings and assurances
that, yes, this farmer's daughter has done us well,
gone out and got herself a husband while she still had
what she had.

I wonder if Elsie felt the same, or if she'd simply been
transfixed by Victor, the lumbering Swede
who taught arithmetic and grammar,
who spoke at the blackboard in that lilting thundervoice—
the learned handsome immigrant who carried her books,
his face as safe and familiar as the warm homespun air.

Thoughts of Elsie never occurred to me
until I saw my own lucid reflection at 26.
Modern, childless, not looking for change,
I want to know more: How she came upon her life,
how it seized her and shook her like a corn stalk,
and how I, an aging girl, as rigid in my own way
as my great-grandmother's values,
could ever be uprooted by a sudden, erotic gust
and impaled by the sheepish smile or the easy confidence
of a man carrying my bags,
handing me my change,
quietly going his menial way
while setting me on fire.

Golden Streets

Leaving the city of snowflakes for the golden streets was not my choice. It was my dad's idea. I was only fifteen. It was exciting but heartbreaking too.

My friends came to the rails to see us off. They kissed our cheeks with glossy lips and hugged us. Hooded, fur-lined jackets waved goodbye. I saw them cry.

One went to Spain later with blond curls, caught a virus and died, leaving her children motherless. She and I were going to wait for each other to find the right city boys, have a double wedding, walk down the rainbow together with our baby carriages, and always be best friends.

If I had stayed in the city maybe she'd still be alive today. Or maybe I'd have gone with her, to the black lace place, and be dead too.

Another childhood friend worked after school at the compacts. She was smart, I thought, having a job like that at her age and going steady, knowing what she wanted. She didn't dream of pink flamingos like I did. She was the first of the gang to get married. Then she was blown up with her chandeliers by a faulty furnace, and left her children motherless.

The train took us to New York, where we were met by drizzle. We went to my aunt and uncle's place and stayed with them and their boxer dog for a week.

I met Jules in a drug store. He was a model, blue-eyed and beautiful. He seemed to like me a lot. I brought him back to the bricks and introduced him to my New York cousin, an older girl. He didn't call me after that, and I found out why: My cousin knew what hockey players wanted; she had experience.

By the time we got to California, I had experience too. I knew what it felt like to leave my circles, and what it felt like to be betrayed. I thought I was ready for the golden streets.

Shovel

The pointed tip of my spade
breaks the ground
and digs deep into the dark rich earth
where the worms are found.
I toil to turn the soil
and ready the garden for our spring planting.
My wife rattles her herbal bag inside the cup
and while the tea steepens
the unspoken crimes and sullen silence between us deepens.
She sits in her director's chair, chanting,
"Faster, dig faster, and watch out for the artichoke plants."
The heel of my shoe perches atop the scoop
while the puppy nips at my heels
just before my foot plunges the blade
deep into the ground
where the earthworms are found.
Shauna holds a tray in her lap, sporting seeds,
dreaming of fruits, flowers, and other riches of greenery.
While the puppy barks, yaps, and plays
as the soil is turned over and sifted,
the mood between us is slowly shifted.
It is the planting of seeds which makes us forget
past hurtful deeds.
Shauna's hard staring glare breaks into a smile,
for a little while,
and she brings me breakfast
along with a few kind words,
a cup of hot chocolate, and a kiss on the cheek—
enough marital bliss to keep me happy for weeks.
I dig a little faster,
careful of the artichoke plants
while the puppy chases butterflies and laughs.
We plant the seeds and dream of spring
unaware of the virus lurking
about to bring the puppy death.
In a few days the same shovel
I use to plant the garden
will also be used to bury our darling baby dog.
In the summer the flowers will bloom,
the vegetables ripen,
and the earth worms will feast
while Shauna and I hold hands
and howl at the moon.

The Onset of a Migraine

There is never any warning.
It appears suddenly,
my own Grendel,
any time, anywhere,
in the shower,
at the beach,
or while clipping hedges,
or midway through a dull meeting
at 10 or 11 o'clock in the morning,
or early on Christmas Eve,
with a party with friends just about to begin.
The lights flicker,
then flash like cheap amateur fireworks—
sight goes,
numbness comes,
first in the left arm
and then in the face.
Soon words break apart,
fly utterly away.
I cannot say my name.

Even Imitrex doesn't help,
although it is supposed to.
This is,
amid the sweating and throwing up,
a kind of recurrent dying.
Somehow
experience
and hopelessness
have taught me how
to surrender to it.

Trapped in Paradise

Another parent

meeting. There to get my anxieties massaged or dispersed to the crowd, or maybe, though rarely, walk out feeling better. These things always feel like crucifixions. Parents, a zoo of parents in every sort: spotted, entitled, scared, assholed, in total denial.

My ride walked out and barely out of earshot said, "That idiot, I can't believe what an idiot that woman was." My brain froze. She might as well have been speaking about me. I could have been the one to offer, "Yes, have the party at our house," sure that I could control it. But you can't control the floodgates of teenagers determined to party. They have a mob, Steve McQueen *Blob* mentality, they pulse and flow and destroy what's in their path, not by intention, but by entropy. They know not what they do, but they do it all and it's not their fault—they just live in the gray zone: the space between child and adult when shit happens 'cause the world is pulling them in too many directions at once and thinking is hard.

Maybe I just can't stop thinking like a teen. It's what gives me a joy and playfulness that I see in few others, a sense of wonder at the world like I was still seeing it for the first time. That's good. I love that. Then I have to put on my adult hat and it doesn't fit, but that's no matter 'cause you still have to wear it if you want to help your kids or at least ensure the survival of the species until 18.

I am an impostor in this group of parents. I am a teenage spy in their midst. And they look clueless to me. They are more frightening, more foreign to me than all the scary stories of what happens at parties. They're the Stepford moms, the automatons that walk the walk and talk the talk and do the gym, the tummy tuck, the A tables, take yoga, eat politically correct seabass. But it's a role, and underneath the script, there are no answers. But what freaks me out the most is that there are no questions. They have it figured out and it works like this:

Assume the world is as you want it to be. Deny the existence of it any other way. Make no contingency plans for things going wrong or unexpectedly. They scare me more than anything, because if they were my parents I would die trying to escape those prisons of thought. Their children will need the alcohol, the buzz, the high, the altered state to survive the gray zone, to catch a glimpse of other perspectives that their parents and this world have not offered them. And then they will get in a car to go home, and some won't want to ever get there.

I don't want this for my children. I want them to know this now. I don't have the answers. There are none—except in geometry and foreign language, so enjoy them 'cause after that life's a mystery. I'm no more qualified to do this job than they are, but it's mine so here's what I know:

Don't rush, there's nowhere to get to.

I am a teenage spy in the adult world. I bring news from the front. We have no answers. We haven't gotten anywhere, we've only put on different hats and silenced our questions, sometimes even to ourselves. We hate our lives and we've fucked the world: Our cars rape the planet, our garbage kills the oceans and we're on our own crash course and we can't stop it. We yak about making it a better place but rarely go out our front door and make human contact, or even one small improvement in anything outside of the tight little boundaries we've drawn around ourselves. We don't recognize the human condition 'cause we're too busy with our own condition: our plans, our bodies, our self-actualization.

We've anaesthetized ourselves with our drugs of choice: cars, homes, private schools and vacations. They keep us in line, a slave to these addictions. They stop us from asking the questions which disrupt our supply. They own us and we are no longer free, so don't rush, there's nowhere to get to.

Oral

I am more powerful.
His strength,
accompanied by his seductive stature of sighing movements,
no longer matters.

His forceful strength
intense as it is,
no longer matters—
he is persuaded into my control.

Intense as it is,
this euphoric moment,
it is persuaded into my control—
all authority is mine.

In this euphoric moment
with my lips pursed around his penis,
all authority is mine—
his weakness is voiced by my laughter.

With my lips pursed around his penis,
my vampiric teeth sink in.
His weakness is voiced by my laughter—
I am more powerful.

Show Business

It was one of those formica jungle chain diners. All
I had in front of me was a glass of tap water containing
chemicals with ice cubes made from tap water full of
chemicals. I couldn't help overhearing the next table's
conversation: male & female: both lawyers & they

were loud. The woman suggested that the man use
her interior decorator, whenever he decided to
overhaul his penthouse livingroom. Her decorator
would only charge him 250 thousand as opposed
to the 300 thousand his had been recommending. The

man, then, began his soliloquy of information: "But
my interior decorator's also a singer, a dancer & an
actor & one night he invited me to his little theatre
group & they were about to start rehearsals for a
musical version of *In Cold Blood*. But that

night they were practicing what's called the art of
improvisation & as a joke had me go up on stage &
play the part of a prosecuting attorney & that's when
it suddenly hit me. Wow, this is the first fun I've had
as a lawyer. I say to myself: hey, these actors have

a really good time: I'm thinking, if I become an actor,
I can have fun forever. So, that's why I decided on this
career switch. Look at all the show business connections
I'm already hooked up with. Why, hell, I can be an actor
in the movies without a bit of struggle & have all the fun

I want to have from now on." He sounded like every other
dilettante artist in America who never needed fine-tuned
sensibilities, talent, or desire. His voice sounded weak,
dull, witless, mediocre, secure, safe, & boring. He will be
a major star.

Love for the Sea

I was in the kitchen making tuna fish.
He was in the living room on the big green chair.
His legs were propped, his eyes were glued to PBS
and *The Savage Sea . . . Famous Shipwrecks*.
"That's the thing about the sea," he said, "it's relentless."
"I know a few others around here like that," I yelled out,
mashing the tuna chunks with a fork.
He didn't flinch.
He didn't take the sandwich when I handed it to him, either.
His eyes were filled with tears and I knew it wasn't just for
the 2000 people who drowned on the Russian Ferry.
He cries for the sea often. The sea cries back.
I've seen them standing face to face and witnessed their connection:
Their surface beauty and the diversity of life within.
The similarities are striking.
Both have cold, confused, tumultuous moments and I fear them.
But they can't help who they are. They are water.
They are a wonder of my world.

Collapse

It's out of their control—
wrapped around each other, hand in hand, leg in leg,
entwined like vines in a gusting wind
on an ancient wall, forgotten, overgrown.
The days fly by, rainstorms pass over,
the sun breaks through the clouds, carloads of families
pass under the vault of the sky
in Nebraska, Alaska, France, Peru,
receiving visions of heaven, sunset,
while the wail of a saxophone winds through the dark
beside a moonlit lake, a candle-lit alleyway,
an accordion, a plate of spaghetti,
lovers pass by. They go out, they order in,
take-out containers grow in piles around them.
Spanish, Indian, Mexican, Thai.
Their kisses taste of garlic, cumin, hot pepper, andouille.
They consume each other, devour,
they twist and turn, a hand on a breast, a foot on a hip,
a mouth on a stomach, toes, lips, elbows, knees.
Above them a girl arises, stretches her young limbs,
dreams of worlds unknown, her imagination
a lushly plumed rainbow bird flying through vines,
past the muscular bark of enormous trees,
up through the glowing yellow-green, shadowy
canvas of leaves, breaking out
to an ecstatic calm of blue.
Below her feet a latter-day Van Gogh,
orange hair, gaunt face and all,
sits on his bed pressing the barrel of a gun
against an anxious temple vein,
laughing maniacally, unsure of his intent.
Underneath his bed, underneath his floor
They are joined at the mouth, pushing themselves
across the bed, across the floor, across a universe
of books, music, stars.
There is nowhere else
they want to be, they have been here
from the beginning of time,
since yesterday, since before they met,
they have never met, caught in a dream,
in the man's head, the woman's head,
they speak their disbelief,
their disbelief is misapplied,
is justified,
does not exist.

It is spring, life is overflowing,
breaking through the cracks in the walls,
through the cracks in their thought;
the sun is coming up—people sitting down to dinner,
spring air pregnant with the smell
of lilacs and magnolia billows in the curtains;
now the leaves are falling, an edge of a chill,
winter threatens,
in the air there hangs a twinge of dread.
They fall apart, wondering
where the time has gone.

Life in the Electric Chair
(or, Sometimes Every Day Is Halloween)

Some clowns were juggling mirages on the sidewalk at noon
Other shadows passed,
Throwing nonsense across the planet by remote control
Ghosts slap each other's backs, feeling a slight awkwardness
As their hands pass through each other's transparent skin
They're going on how life is great trading in real estate
For a moment, these figments pause for a slide show in the park
A building, a freeway, a monument, a plane
With a pointer, a vampire each time taps the screen
Wiping blood from his chin with the back of a pale white hand
Though they know better, they tell themselves that
It's just chocolate syrup
Except the other vampires who smirk with delight
He seems to be indicating something
That makes the gathering of undead nod
A businesscorpse in front, who's starting to rot
Starts calculating costs, his bones slipping out
He seems to remember he's doing it for his kids
Forgetting that his children have grown, have aged, have died
After a lifetime filled with little more real than malicious intent
His daughter now fertilizer for a rare kind of subterranean fungus
And his son slowly rotting in a lake in Tennessee

Twice Cut and Still Too Short

Old German Carpenter Joke

My grandmother thought I'd be a surgeon (Look at the size
of those hands!) and my mother, a pianist. My sister thought

I'd fit the profile for a psycho-killer—a wielder of big knives
or ice picks, a prediction owed to one too many scuffles

at the breakfast table and an Aunt Jemima bottle broken
(plastic, but full) over her head. I got in the habit of cutting

my hands, shoulders, and forearms with kitchen knives.
It simply amazed me how the sharpest knives don't let you

feel a thing. And how dull knives are more dangerous,
so willing to miss their mark. There is a picture of me

in the first grade cutting (and I don't mean to brag)
what my dad said was "the best damn shamrock

in the class." I'm holding it up, the orbs of Father and Son,
and even Holy Ghost connected nicely to a stem.

The girl next to me, Penny, holds what might be called
a lollipop rhombus. She's a beautician now; I rarely work

my hands. But I have always been good at cutting. My grandfather
made cabinets. My father, a factory worker, would come home

wounded most days, blood dried to the bandages. My teacher,
Sister Grace, asked what my dad did at work. I said, he bleeds,

which was true enough at the time and maybe I have a little guilt
for not bleeding enough—for not using my hands until a map

of scar would make them impossible to be read
truthfully. When I was seven I wanted to be a carpenter. I wanted

to work the wood into pieces that fit—angles that converge and don't give.
Actually, that's not true. I just loved power tools. And I loved

my grandfather's sketchbooks full of lion-headed table feet
and dragons that smiled complicitous smiles, their eyes looking up,

nostrils flared. I loved to watch him file down dovetails,
so intricate and smooth they became relationships

that could be seen. I loved that he didn't speak
while he worked. I'd watch him do final touches, pressing

the ancient lathe, rubbing the wood down with what fingers
he had left on his right hand. I could never touch the saws.

After he died, I went down to his basement, plugged in the table saw
and thought, selfishly, now it's mine: I'll finally be able to create

something, without help, without impediments; and I almost prayed
to the ghost, to guide my fingers smoothly as the chips began to fly.

.

Antlers in the Tub

I wake up. Slide out of bed. Put my slippers on. As I walk up the stairs my hips groan and my knee makes the usual crackly noise it makes when the cartilage rubs the bone. It didn't make that noise a year ago. I hurt my hips and knees in a yoga class. Now they speak to me every day. I sit on the floor with the heater to my back and wait for my body to warm up. I look out the window. The wind has kicked up. The leaves on the eucalyptus tree sway. When the wind dies the dance ends and the leaves hang down from the branches. Long and thin. Light green. Quiet and still.

When I was a girl I learned to still myself within the disharmony of my bloodline. Only then could I dance with them. And, oftentimes, when the winds picked up, my resolve was tested. During summer break between fourth and fifth grades my father went bankrupt. He drove to Chama and poached a buck. He hid it in a cabin of the camper. He brought it home to feed us.

When he arrived my mother paced back and forth in the kitchen because he'd broken the law. The tension between them swelled, unbroken. The sun touched the horizon. My mother told me to get ready for bed. I walked down the hall and into the bathroom to brush my teeth. I stood by the sink and paused. I smelled something. Something different.

I turned around and saw the buck's antlers, and the skull they grew out of, lying at the bottom of the tub. Shallow red water surrounded the skull. Velvet hung from the antlers. Deer hide still attached to the bone. Bright blood painted the white walls, the tub basin, the antlers and the brick floor. Flesh hung from the skull. I ran out.

My legs carried me to the kitchen where I pushed the screen door open with both hands. I ran into the twilight. I threw up my supper. Then I crouched beneath the pine tree. My arms wrapped my shins and I bowed my head and rocked on my soles. I rocked between two blocks of limestone. Limestone filled with fossilized creatures. Creatures once of the sea. The sky darkened and the screen door slammed and my mother walked across the gravel driveway. She saw my tears. I felt her stiffen. "Crying is weak," she said. "Stop it!" I held onto my shins and rocked and wept and wished her away. I heard her command. I just couldn't stop. My tears had a life of their own. My mother turned and walked back across the gravel driveway and into the house. My tears dried. I stood up. It was then I decided that I would not brush my teeth that night, and I walked back into the house.

Crack in the Armor

Finally, the rain stopped. A break in the storms. I sit in the living room, my feet propped up on the coffee table, and wait for the clouds to pass. For a break in the darkness.

It happened that way once when I was on Mykonos with Rick. Our hotel, Cavo Tagoo, was built into a hill. All the buildings were whitewashed, inside and out, including the restaurant. The first few days we were there, a wild wind blew on our side of the island, but that day it was warm and still, so we sat outside.

The waiter, a young Greek man, walked us to a table overlooking the blue-green ocean. I sat with my back to the sun, though the sun was beginning to set. Rick sat across from me. We both wore cotton tops, shorts and Mephisto sandals. The waiter took our order and brought us a bottle of red wine from Santorini.

Rick and I sat in silence. The weight of our marriage rested like an invisible rock between us. The rock was our constant companion. As the years went on it rolled alongside us, gathering disappointments, resentments, fictions, pains, projections.

The silence was broken when the waiter placed a Greek salad in front of me and a bowl of Avgolemono soup in front of Rick. I looked at him and smiled. He smiled back and I saw tears and the spark in his eyes that I saw when we first met, 18 years earlier. His hair was thinning at the temples and just beginning to gray.

He looked down into his soup of lemon and egg and rice. The he looked up, again.

"You know, Peggy," he said, "I really do love you."

When we first me, I remember lying naked with him, my left arm draped across his chest and my left leg resting between his legs, waiting to hear those words. I knew if I said it first, he'd say it back. But I needed him to say it on his own, and he never did. Not once during those 18 years. And my anger had grown with each turn of the stone. He'd never said it on his own until that moment on Mykonos.

When he did, time stopped, and the armor that shielded me from the pain of loving him and getting so little back cracked. There was an opening, a parting of the darkness, and I saw him. I remembered that there was more between us than the rock. At that moment, time stopped, and I felt close to him.

And then the terror. Shield after shield returned to its designated place. First the shield that covered the stars where our souls connected. Then the shield that hid the moon and my physical desire for him. And finally the one that blocked the sun, and with it, laughter, hope, and playful discourse. When the feeling of love was gone, I sat on the other side of the rock. Alone.

"Did you feel that," I asked, as I gathered a forkful of feta, cucumber and tomato, "Did you feel what just happened between us?"

"No," he shook his head, before putting a spoonful of soup in his mouth.

I put the fork in my mouth, chewed, and nodded my head. I stared at the white table cloth, the food in white porcelain dishes, the half-empty bottle of red wine, the few drops of wine bleeding into the white table cloth.

I was shaken. He didn't notice. We finished our appetizers.

"Why don't you turn your chair around," he said, "so we can watch the sunset." I turned my chair sideways and we waited for the main course, as the sun disappeared into the ocean.

The Serpent that Passed Through

It was early summer and I was playing outside with my sister Ingrid. She was three-and-a-half and I was five. We were riding our stick horses in the shadows of the setting sun, when Mr. Tafoya walked by. My daddy had just hired him to do work in the yard. I watched him walk into the toolshed, poke his head out, and say, "I have a surprise for you girls."

We dropped our horses at the corner of the adobe house and walked across the dirt yard toward the shed. When we got there, I looked in. The walls of the shed and the built-in shelves were stocked with tools, fertilizer, and bug killer, and Mr. Tafoya stood in the

Peggy Geisler

center, surrounded by those weapons. I could see there was hardly enough room for all of us to fit in, but I wanted to see the surprise, so I walked in and Ingrid followed.

Mr. Tafoya closed the door so it was open just a crack, just enough for us to see, and then he turned sideways, unzipped his fly, and pulled his pants down to his knees. His penis was right in front of my face, 12 inches away, like the head of a serpent dangling from a thicket of curly black twigs. He grabbed it and pulled rhythmically and the snake stiffened and moved out of the bush, into the dim light that shone through the crack in the door. I couldn't take my eyes off it, even though I could barely see. It was even harder to see the white T-shirt hanging across his skinny torso, his white underwear almost fluorescent in the dark, down below, peeking out of the dusty green pants crumpled on top of his workboots. I stared at the penis, sniffed its libidinous odor, and heard Mr. Tafoya ask, "Would you like to touch it?"

I held my breath and felt the cord of my cowgirl hat pull up tight under my chin. I lifted my hand up and over, touched the top of the erection, and put my hand back by my side, next to the silver Annie Oakley gun that hung on my right hip. I watched the penis pulse and he asked, "Can I see yours?"

I thought it seemed fair, so I lifted the folds of my red dress and pulled my white panties down, just far enough to show myself. I dug my red and white cowgirl boots into the earth and pressed my hips forward so he could see my pale, hairless mound, and he asked, "Can I touch it?"

I nodded and watched his hand move toward me. His middle finger touched my lips and that's when I heard Mommy yelling, "Peggy! Ingreet! It's time to come in."

I pulled my panties up with one hand and released my ruffles with the other. I looked at Ingrid. "We better go," I said. "Mommy's looking for us." When we got home I told her that Mr. Tafoya showed us his thing and I showed him mine. The next day he was gone. I never saw him again.

But in the dark at night when I'd go to sleep, I'd still see the serpent in front of me. First limp and still. Then rising from the thicket. Releasing its scent. I was drawn to it. Fascinated by the mystery of its rising. Sometimes, the erect penis turned, moved toward me, getting bigger and bigger. My body froze. Breath went shallow. I closed my eyes. Tried to make myself invisible. And failed. When the serpent found me, it pressed its head into my vagina.

I woke from these dreams with a start, pulled my pillow between my legs, rocked my hips back and forth until I orgasmed—although I didn't have a name for it then. I would stick my mother's bobby pins into my vagina. That was something I started doing when I was two, after my great uncle began having sex with me. I would stick the bobby pins in and out of my vagina, then hide them under the mattress.

During the day, I stood in the doorway of the shed to see if the serpent was still there. But every time I looked, it was gone. I turned, sat on the threshold, and looked at the outer wall of my great uncle's study. His favorite place to have sex. I looked at the brown paint, uneven corners, and rough plaster. I looked at the shadows cast by the cherry tree, just outside his study. I looked up at the sky and watched a white butterfly flit out of sight. I looked at nothing in particular, and everything, and thought about the serpent that passed through. The one I would never see again, but would always remember.

Tin Foil

I have this fantasy about him,
the man who makes tin foil airplanes
out of tiny pieces of bubble gum wrap.
I watch from across the crowded room
as his fingers pull and tear and twirl an intricate web,
the tiniest piece of pulp fiction art.
The long tangled caress of his strong, solid hands
over the shredded aluminum
leaves quiet rattles in the hall.
Not a movement of sound occurs
as he silently works on his craft:
so demure,
tempered, tempered, tempered,
so rhythmic the touch, so confined his attention.

He is watching the inside.
I am watching him,
wanting to swirl in the words of his weathered head,
masker of emotions to the guarded gate of the gut,
a veiled light under a flat, tough shell of abs and gristle.
Hidden, caged, shock and rage, removed pain, space-age wordsmith,
red-toed and boots to hike.

I see him from across the crowded room in my invisible hole:
so out of sight that nowhere never asks where I have roamed,
so furtive that the mourning dove fails to flutter in my path,
so petrified that wood begs for bending.
I long for his cage to contain all I fear to set free,
what rages beneath the chess game of my existence,
the carelessness of complacency.
I want to be tin foil again:
wrinkled, torn, solid,
cradled in strong hands that twirl an intricate web
out of the pulp fiction of my art,
and set aloft into the sky
to fly.

Getting It

Once, i wrote a poem
not autobiographical,
not about me or my
husband at all, but still
in the first person
and about an affair,
a one-hour visit
to a No-Tell Motel
and even though
i explained to him,
in language clear and
non-poetic, the part about
assuming a persona,
about the immediacy
of the "I," it is this
poem, out of all
the hundreds, my husband
remembers, keeps tucked
behind his ear until
one day, he drives me
fast to the most sordid
motel he can find, one
with cinder block walls, nipple
pink, and a mirror to prove
yes, we are really here
and we fuck for exactly one
hour (i watched the clock
—i think he did too)
and he whispers *Say I'm better*
than anything you've ever had
and o-o-o he is and now
there's nothing more to write
about, nothing to do but wait
and see what this poem'll get me.

**The Holiness of the real
Is always there, accessible
In total immanence.**

*Kenneth Rexroth, "Time Is the Mercy of
Eternity"*

KENNETH REXROTH: The Poetry of Luminous Authenticity

Kenneth Rexroth, who was born in South Bend, Indiana in 1905 and died in 1982 in Santa Barbara, California, was a major American poet and man of letters who has yet to receive his due. Orphaned in early adolescence, self-taught, a polymath, Rexroth became one of the most learned literary figures in 20th-century American literature. His knowledge was awesome. He was at home with, say, ancient Greek mathematics, Roman engineering, early Church doctrinal and 1920s European Marxist schisms, Medieval Latin poetry, English Renaissance sacred choral music, 18th-century French street culture, the traditions of social revolution and Utopianism stretching over six or seven centuries, the 19th-century Russian novel, and so on. He was also a translator of poetry from six languages, but especially famed for his work on Japanese and Chinese verse (the great 8th-century poet Tu Fu was a major influence on his own poetry). Rexroth also wrote essays, literary and art criticism, newspaper columns, plays (a tetralogy based on ancient Greek tragedies, *Beyond the Mountains*) and letters, as well as being a modernist painter, a social and religious Anarchist, a mountain climber, a Pacifica radio station book reviewer, a cultural gadfly to the San Francisco Bay Area, as well as a promoter of, and publicist for, the Beat writers and other young female and male artists and poets.

Donald Gutierrez

This amount of work and activity would fill up the careers of two or three people and it doesn't even include what was Rexroth's supreme achievement—writing surpassingly fine love and nature poetry, as well as richly evocative political verse. For a number of reasons, Rexroth has only recently been discovered by the English Departments; to this day he is excluded from the canonical Norton Anthology of American Literature. This is an outrageous omission. Rexroth's nature poetry is stunning in its sense of authenticity, naturalness and immediacy. In his best poems (a sizable number), Rexroth's verse conveys an exalted experience through words that have been rendered so plain, so "artless" and "right" as to take on a kind of transparency revealing the heart of the poem's life itself. Consider these lines from the early poem trilogy "Toward an Organic Philosophy":

> . . . The ventriloquial belling
> Of an owl mingles with the bells of the waterfall
> . . .
> It is storming in the White Mountains,
> On the arid fourteen-thousand-foot peaks;
> Rain is falling on the narrow gray ranges
> And dark sedge meadows and white salt flats of Nevada.
> Just before moonset a small dense cumulus cloud,
> Gleaming like a grape cluster of metal,
> Moves over the Sierra crest and grows down the westward slope.

Rexroth learned to write poetry that sounds—or seems to sound—like the speech of an intelligent person speaking to another one, or just thinking out loud; it is, to be sure, heightened speech, and a kind of "talking" poetry, sparse in metaphors, very subtly rhythmic and acutely accurate in details (the belling of an owl, a cumulus cloud, the gray ranges the mountain crest being part of the Sierra Nevada range, and so on). Rexroth felt that poetry was a mode of exalted communication, rather than some hermetic, autonomous construct to be laboriously deciphered. This should not viewed as meaning that his poetry was always or necessarily crystal clear or simple; it could be quite subtle and allusive. But many of his signature poems—"Time Is the Mercy of Eternity," "The Signature of All Things," "When We with Sappho," the three Andrée Rexroth elegies—possess an almost uncanny clarity and purity of expression through which an experience of love or nature is rendered with such a craft of authenticity that the poems transform ordinary reality into something extraordinary verging on the holy.

Rexroth is hard to quote briefly because he usually avoids the flashy or brilliant figure of speech or overly intricate syntax. Rather, he lets his poems gradually unfold, until you begin to realize that you are in the presence of a complete or consummated experience. Rexroth was an accomplished poet of reverie and elegy. The three elegies to his first wife Andrée are comparable in tone, directness and authenticity of utterance to elegies from his *Poems from the Greek Anthology* or Ben Jonson's heartbreaking little poems to his dead children. Here is the entirety of his first elegy to Andrée, who died of complications due to epilepsy in 1940:

> Now once more gray mottled buckeye branches
> Explode their emerald stars,
> And alders smoulder in a rosy smoke

Of innumerable buds.
I know that spring again is splendid
As ever, the hidden thrush
As sweetly tongued, the sun as vital—
But these are the forest trails we walked together,
These paths, ten years together.
We thought the years would last forever,
They are all gone now, the days
We thought would not come for us are here.
Bright trout poised in the current—
The raccoon's track at the water's edge—
A bittern booming in the distance—
Your ashes scattered on this mountain—
Moving seaward on this stream.

One is struck by the absence of overt lament or grief in the poem. The grief is only implied in the next-to-last line. The speaker and his wife had been so absorbed in each other and in the natural surroundings as to assume that the present would exist forever. But the unthinkable has occurred: the death of Andrée Rexroth. This death—the pivotal event and implicit climax of the poem—is rendered very poignant by the shock of its gradual disclosure, and by the fact that she who had made nature complete or wonderful in that idyllic past is now ashes. Ironically, nature continues to run its course (trout ready to leap, the bittern making a mating call). But the beloved is now one with the nature that, at one time, had bolstered and beautified her relationship with the speaker; she is now an inorganic substance moving implacably towards final dissolution in the sea.

Rexroth does not sentimentalize his lament. Nature in a sense is just as splendid and lovely in the bursting out of Spring after Andrée's death as it was before. Yet of course Andrée's permanent absence enormously reduces the pleasure and beauty of the surroundings. What is masterful in the poem is the sheer quietness, indirectness, muteness of the unending loss of Andrée Rexroth. The subtle obliqueness of the lament creates in the poem the kind of silence so overwhelming that one can hear the silence; it is all one can hear. And that is the character of the sadness this elegy leaves one with. Without getting melodramatic or wringing his hands, Rexroth makes the loss of his loved one almost feel like the reader's loss.

Rexroth was an extraordinary poet of sexual love, writing a love verse of finely articulated, exquisitely direct passion, as the following climactic lines from the early 1940s poem "Floating" suggest:

Let your odorous hair fall across our eyes;
Kiss me with those subtle, melodic lips.
As I undress you, your pupils are black, wet,

Donald Gutierrez

Immense, and your skin ivory and humid.
Move softly, move hardly at all, part your thighs,
Take me slowly while our gnawing lips
Fumble against the humming blood in our throats.
Move softly, do not move at all, but hold me,
Deep, still, deep within you, while time slides away,
As this river slides beyond this lily bed,
And the thieving moments fuse and disappear
In our mortal, timeless flesh.

Despite the intense eroticism here, those final three-and-a-half lines lift this poem above eroticism for eroticism's sake. The whole buildup and thrust of the poem, as can be seen in those last few lines, is to surmount time not only through an act of sexual love, but through a vision of love recreated as a poem of reverie. The love experience will end, as Rexroth implies in the words "thieving moments" and "mortal" in the final two lines; but, paradoxically, through memorably capturing both its finitude and essence, it will last forever.

No general description of Rexroth's poetry is sufficient without mentioning his long poems, such as Part I of "The Phoenix and the Tortoise," the exquisite, poignant "Love Poems of Marichiko," "The Heart's Garden, The Garden's Heart," and "The Dragon and the Unicorn." The last work is his longest poem, and probably to this day his least known, yet it could be considered not only his finest long poem but one of his major achievements. Written in the late 1940s, unattractive in its occasional passages of homophobia and misogyny, "Dragon" is nevertheless an extraordinary poem and document of the times. It is written in a 7-9 syllabic meter that endows the nearly 171-page poem with enormous syntactic and rhythmic pliability for markedly different purposes—jeremiad, philosophical disquisition, satire, acute travel descriptions of persons and places, and some of the finest lyrics Rexroth ever wrote:

Paestum of the twice blooming
Roses, the sea god's honey-
Colored stone still strong against
The folly of the long decline
Of man. The snail climbs the Doric
Line, and the empty snail shell
Lies by the wild cyclamen.
The sandstone of the Roman
Road is marked with sun wrinkles
Of prehistoric beaches,
But no time at all has touched
The deep constant melodies
Of space as the columns swing
To the moving eye. The sea

Breathes like a drowsy woman.
The sun moves like a drowsy hand.
Poseidon's pillars have endured
All tempers of the sea and sun.
This is the order of the spheres,
The curve of the unwinding fern,
And the purple shell in the sea;
These are the spaces of the notes
Of every kind of music.
The world is made of number
And moved in order by love.
Mankind has risen to this point
And can only fall away,
As we can only turn homeward
Up Italy, through France, to life
Always pivoted on this place.

or

Bright petals of evening
Shatter, fall, drift over Florence,
And flush your cheeks a redder
Rose and gleam like fiery flakes
In your eyes. All over Florence
The swallows whirl between the
Tall roofs, under the bridge arches,
Spiral in the zenith like larks,
Sweep low in crying clouds above
The brown river and the white
River bed. Your moist, quivering
Lips are like the wet scarlet wings
Of a reborn butterfly who
Trembles on the rose petal as
Life floods his strange body.

Turn to me. Part your lips. My dear,
Some day we will be dead.

One could object to some of the philosophic passages in Dragon which at times seem either vague, pretentious or prose-like. This possible flaw, however, is rendered more attractive by the interspersion of other modes of discourse (lyrics; brilliant, ferocious polemics; a lively, perceptive, heterodoxical opinionatedness about almost everything; and a sense of "spirit of place" as vivid and memorable as D. H. Lawrence's).

What to this reader is most striking about this strangely compelling, powerful, endearing and irritating verse travelogue is the overwhelming sense it conveys of the nihilism created not just by the Second World War, but by its outcome, despite the

Donald Gutierrez

necessary defeat of the Axis. Rexroth, in a poet's vatic role, projects in "Dragon" an annihilation of values and community coming out of that war that seems like a prophecy of all the world's wars, massacres, and genocide in the final half of the century, no mean feat.

Another work that could rival "Dragon" as Rexroth's finest long verse is "The Love Poems of Marichiko" (1979). Supposedly written by a Japanese woman and translated by Rexroth, Rexroth actually wrote the poems himself. There is space for only a few quotations from "Marichiko" but they might provide a sense of the character and prosody of this body of sixty short poems:

Sick with love,
I long to see you in the flesh.
. . .
Love cuts through my heart
And tears my vitals.

(#1)

Because I dream
Of you every night,
My lonely days
Are only dreams.

(#15)

Every morning, I
Wake alone, dreaming my
Arm is your sweet flesh
Pressing my lips.

(#34)

The poem moves from ecstasy to abandonment and a death-in-life misery, but aside from the enormous power in "Marichiko" of that arc of love and abandonment is the sheer, bony simplicity and lucidity of the language, as well as the harnessing of its naked, unaffected eroticism to a compelling experience of tragic love. "Marichiko" is one of the great love poems of the century.

I would have liked to quote and comment on one of Rexroth's poems of social comment like "The Bad Old Days" or the political poems such as "August 22, 1939," the date of the horrifying Nazi-Soviet Pact, or the long, powerful, violent memorial to Dylan Thomas, "Thou Shalt Not Kill," a significant influence on Allen Ginsberg's more famous jeremiad "Howl" that Ginsberg never owned up to. Instead, I will simply quote lines from the first section of one of the great meditation poems of the 20th century, Rexroth's deceptively simple "The Signature of All Things":

The saint [Jakob Boehme] saw the world as streaming
In the electrolysis of love.
I put him by and gaze through shade
Folded into shade of slender
Laurel trunks and leaves filled with sun.
The wren broods in her moss domed nest.
A newt struggles with a white moth
Drowning in the pool. The hawks scream,
Playing together on the ceiling
Of heaven. The long hours go by.
I think of those who have loved me,
Of all the mountains I have climbed,
Of all the seas I have swum in.
The evil of the world sinks.
My own sin and trouble fall away
Like Christian's bundle, and I watch
My forty summers fall like falling
Leaves and falling water
Eternally in summer air.

I will conclude with the final lines from Rexroth's "When We with Sappho," which in its supernaturally natural reverie of a love experience as exalted contentment can be considered love verse on a level with the Marichiko poems:

. . . The sun has fallen away.
Now there are amber
Long lights on the shattered
Boles of the ancient apple trees.
Our bodies move to each other
As bodies move in sleep;
At once filled and exhausted,
As the summer moves to autumn,
As we, with Sappho, move towards death.
My eyelids sink toward sleep in the hot
Autumn of your uncoiled hair.
Your body moves in my arms
On the verge of sleep;
And it is as though I held
In my arms the bird filled
Evening sky of summer.

Donald Gutierrez

On What Would Have Been 92

She was ready to go.
Days before her stroke
she told him
"Enough is enough, already."
And even though I told her
it was okay for her to let go,
it didn't mean I was ready to say goodbye.
But somehow I did.

I sat beside her hospital bed
and held her hand.
I told her I loved her.
I thanked her for loving me.
I tried to soak in everything.
Her familiar hands, now swollen,
missing her gold pinky ring,
her recently painted fingernails,
her hazel eyes
and barely wrinkled skin,
her green hospital gown labeled number 32.
Inch by inch I scanned the dull beige walls,
the faded floral print posters,
the empty chair in the corner,
the dusty window sill,
the tired afternoon sun
casting a shadow through the trees,
and the twelve cars parked below her window
in the parking lot.

I watched her fade in and out of consciousness,
open her eyes and try to talk.
"Waaaaa-aaaaaa-aaaah."
"Waaaaa-aaaaaa-aaaah."
She kept repeating over and over.
"Waaaaa-aaaaaa-aaaah."
"Do you want water, grandma?
Is that what you want?"
"Yes."
She said it clear as a bell.
It was her voice.
The same voice that told me
I'd get a lickin' if I didn't behave.
The same voice that told me I was a sucker
for buying a $45 bracelet
made from a mahjong tile

---

when I could have bought a whole set for that.
And the same voice that told me every Sunday,
you know how I feel about you
you know I love you.

And so I took the yellow lollipop sponge
and dipped it in the cup of water beside her bed
and watched her suck the sponge
like a baby to a bottle.
I can still hear the sound of her relief
when the water coated her dry tongue.
I wiped the water that dripped down her chin,
and she looked at me
soaking me up with her eyes
the same way I was doing with her.
I didn't want to forget anything.
I hated being aware that it was
the last time I'd see her.

And today it's her birthday,
and she's not here.
I don't get to send her a card,
I don't get to call her
and sing "Happy Birthday."
I can't bring myself
to remove her birthday from my calendar.
I can't bring myself
to cross out her name from my address book.
And I can't bring myself
to delete her phone number from my phone.
All I can do is think about that moment
in that hospital room
when we thought she asked for ice cream,
and how we all sat around her bed
and fed her from one of those wooden ice cream spoons
while we watched her enjoy the sweetness
of vanilla and chocolate
as the afternoon sun ducked behind the trees.

Jennifer Haft

Cholula—June 15, 1999

On my 50th birthday
an earthquake strikes our hotel
a real shaker *un temblor muy fuerte.*
Churches crumble, fifteen are dead,
hundreds with no homes. The cupola
of a 16th-century chapel falls to the ground.
Se calló, the bartender tells me.
I order two beers and he gives me
a look that drills the word *gringa*
into my face. Then he opens the Bohemias
we will sip on our lounge chairs by the pool.

Están bien todos? I ask about his family.
He says *sí* but he is grim-faced
and then he asks me if I felt it
as if I could be immune to natural disasters.
Oh yes, I felt it. *Me da miedo,* it scared me.
It was *muy fuerte.* I want him to know
I feel everything.

It's my birthday and it's a serious one.
There's gravity everywhere
the specific gravity of time squeezing its fist
and the earth flexing its muscles
rolling around on its tectonic plates.
Birds rise up out of the trees shrieking
crossing and recrossing the still air like sirens.
Dogs bark in the rutted streets.

The beer is cold even though the electricity is out
there's a card game and a set of lovers drinking cognac
waiters move deftly among us in pigeon gray jackets
hands full faces impassive.
The sun plays on the perfect blue
of the pool in fingertips of silver.

We're concerned about our pillows
too round and hard for our necks.
Will the maid find us some flat ones?
I ask her about her family, her house
listen to her small story,
walk up the darkened stairs
into the unnatural quiet.

If I Could Talk to My Mother

Maybe I'd yell so long and loud
that she'd be hypnotized
when I pulled her by the hand
out into the garden

where she always shows
the new growth, plant by plant: *my lilies,*
my snapdragons, my ground cover. . .
I'd say, it's only us out here, see—

erase the stars, forget the shrubs,
no cars are in the carport.
But surely she'd find
something: *An ear of corn,*

she'd say, handing it to me,
this is practically my heart.
And I'd be beaten then,
stand there eating the words,

you failed him, you failed me.
Stand there like a dummy
with her corn heart
in my hands.

Picking up the Pieces

As usual, we slipped into bed that night with our backs to one another. We slept on a mattress and box spring without a frame or headboard, which was no protection against the boogeymen as far as I was concerned. The sheets were old and mismatched, but warm when we were under them together, and gave me a sense of security. I kept an eye on the fuzzy silhouettes tiptoeing across the wall, which had snuck through the translucent sheet hung across the window with nails.

I prayed, as always, with my eyes closed. Tucked between the sheets, I firmly placed my palms together and silently recited the only prayer I knew, "Now I lay me down to sleep. I pray the Lord my soul to keep. If I should die before I wake, I pray the Lord my soul to take. Amen." Then came the whole of "God Blesses" that I annointed everyone in my life with, "God Bless Mom, Dad, Granddad, Aunt Ruth, Aunt Mary, Uncle John, God Bless Margarite, Angel, Marie, Mrs. Iddions, Coach Murphy, Linda, Dan, Blackie and Peekk-A-Poo. Amen."

I'd squeeze my eyes shut so hard that silver fireworks went off inside behind my wrinkled lids. If I squeezed them tightly enough, I thought, then no prayer could escape God's notice.

It must have been my mother's mother, Edith Louise, who instilled piety in her four children. I'd seen pictures of her and the girls dressed in black patent shoes with white, lacy ankle socks and white, knee-length, cotton dresses. I never met her, as she died from breast cancer long before I was born. My mother, the youngest, was a girl only eleven years old, still in bobby socks. Praying made me closer to my grand mom, especially on restless nights like this one.

I tried forcing sleep by closing my eyes, but the Sandman was running behind schedule and my bedtime was two hours past. My mind refused to stop thinking; but, as I was an only child, I was used to having long conversations in the privacy of my own brain. I knew how to entertain myself and that night was no exception.

Me, Marie, and Angel, Margarite's children, and my pretend sister, Ashlie, were setting off on a cruise, a sort of chaperone-free, Ringling Brothers floating circus across the Atlantic Ocean. It was a candy store, a toy store and a zoo combined. No parents, no rules, only carousel ponies, monkeys, pink cotton candy, and endless pajama parties. Life was safe and fun. No one got hurt, no one got yelled at. We were just kids being kids.

I was deep in this fantastical cruise when I noticed headlights turn into the shared driveway of our tiny duplex. Loud, muffled music that I couldn't discern blared through the thin stucco walls. The noise seemed to come from the car that just pulled in. I switched my attention to the indefinite gray monsters creeping across our bleak bedroom walls. I knew they were just shadows of shivering branches and passing headlights from Dunwoody Road, but they seemed to move to the beat of the stranger's music. It unsettled me.

I knew our neighbors, Linda and Dan, were gone for the weekend because I had the responsibility of taking care of their two cats, Blackie and Peek-A-Poo. My head ran off without me as I began assessing all these recent events—the unexpected car, the disturbing music, the two-stepping shadows and the vacationing neighbors. Maybe it's a robber, a murderer, or a rapist, I thought to myself.

I've always been scared in my own home, especially in the dark. Sometimes, at night, if I have to go to the bathroom, I'll hold it until day breaks and even then I do a "hi-ya" karate chop if the shower curtain is pulled, but I do my best to keep it open, so all corners are unobscured and in full view.

I don't like not being able to see, and a swarm of Monarchs had just been released in my stomach. I turned to see if my mom had been stirred by the relentless bass lines thumping like those of Lynyrd Skynyrd. I closed my eyes to focus my listening while placing my fantasy kid cruise on pause. It was definitely Lynyrd Skynyrd, my father's favorite southern rock group. My heart sunk. "Could it be, could he be here," I wondered. Surely not, I reckoned. I hadn't seen him in months and as far as I knew he was back in Alabama.

Just then Ashlie popped back into my head. "Come on," she urged, "we haven't ridden the carousel yet." She beamed with the exhilaration of the possibilities rendered by the bright lights and big toys of our floating circus. I thought about it for a moment and decided to run away with her back into my laughing, happy head.

Ashlie and I were riding the merry-go-round, which ran along the periphery of the circular pool, where floats of all colors, shapes, and sizes invited us to dive in. I rode a brown carousel horse decked out in fancy red and gold tack with a real set of leather reins. Ashlie was next to me on a white horse tacked up in pink and silver gear. I could see that Angel was trying to win a stuffed Garfield at the ring toss game and Marie was sitting at a bench coloring in her book and sucking on a colorful lollipop, content not to be harassed by her older brother, when I heard footsteps approaching our front porch. "I knew the shadow monsters were real," I thought to myself, wishing desperately to be on that cruise in real life. Maybe, I thought, it was someone delivering a pizza. It was not quite midnight and even though our neighbors were on vacation, the pizza boy could be lost and at the wrong duplex.

The footsteps stopped at our front door. Outside our window, which faced the driveway, I heard what sounded like someone putting out a cigarette with a foot, stomping and grinding the fiery butt until it was out and flattened. My body jolted with a dose of adrenaline as I put the pieces of the puzzle together. Loud Lynyrd Skynyrd plus cigarettes plus no pizza boy plus midnight equals him.

He began banging, wailing on the front door like a man seeking sanctuary in a stranger's home, except he was about to break into ours. "Open the goddamned door," he yelled, kicking the door with his boot.

The moment his voice settled in my ears, I got up, my suspicions confirmed. I had been hoping against all odds that I was mistaken, that my imagination had run away with me again, but the voice—that voice—belonged to one man and he was my father.

"God damn it, it's Lecil Galveston, let me in, you fucking bitch," he demanded at the top of his lungs, drowning out the eight-track still rocking in his car.

"Oh my God," I said to myself. "What are we going to do?" This was not the first time he'd shown up high and destroyed everything in his path, but maybe it'll go fast and no one will get hurt this time, I thought.

Lock the bedroom door. Call the police. Crawl out the window. Hide under the bed. I raced through my options. We can't hide under the bed, there's no frame. Hide in the closet. Hide in my bedroom. Hide in my closet. Sneak out the back door. Crawl into a cabinet in the kitchen or the bathroom. Climb up into the attic. Play dead. "Oh, what do I do?"

I searched for a sign from God.

I rolled to the right to see if my mom had wakened because of his hysterical cursing, but she slept, oblivious to the earthquake at our door. My father was very much like an earthquake in that we never knew when to expect him or how bad he'd be or how long he'd last or if we'd survive the seismic thrusts, which would surely slam our home and us.

"Mom," I whispered, "Mom." I nudged her shoulder. "Dad is here," I warned.

E. Kelly Harrison

In a half-daze, she answered, "What?" in a groggy, barely audible voice that stretched across the stagnant air in the room. He continued to pound on the door with his fist so doggedly that the window quaked with vibrations.

His fury was fueled by the obstinate, surprisingly resilient front door, so he began kicking it harder.

"Let me in. Goddamn you fucking bitch. Open the motherfucking door before I take it down," he said. "You piece of shit, let me in. God damn you," he shouted.

Ashlie knew Lecil was dangerous and like me, she dreaded seeing him—ever. She had sat crouched in a corner petrified with me with many times in the past. She'd stay huddled by my side until my need to protect her from him grew unbearable. Then, she'd disappear into thin air.

Ashlie flashed in my head, motioning me to come with her. She wanted to go swimming now. Her blond hair was up in two lopsided ponytails and they were swinging to the beat of her skipping. She sauntered toward the water, but I shook my head no, telling her, "I can't come now. Wait for me. I'll be back, I promise."

His rage pulled me back. I heard the door splintering off the frame. The door would be down soon and he'd be in, revved up from his first round with the door he'd just beaten the shit out of.

I looked over and saw my mom's blue eyes wide and scared. "Mom," I said, "Just stay there. Be quiet. Don't move. Play dead."

In a dulcet, nurturing tone she said, "I love you."

"I love you, too," I said back, as the door slammed open.

I knew there would soon be another hole in the wall from the door handle breaking through the flimsy drywall.

"God, dear Lord, help us," I silently prayed.

We both tried not to breathe, tried to fake dead. He picked something up in the living room and smashed it against something else. It sounded like it could have been a piece of doorframe that he threw at the glass table by her favorite olive-striped chair.

"Oh my God," I prayed, a lump of fear lodged in my shrinking throat, "please don't let us die." I picked at the edge of the pink elephant sewn with black thread on my cotton, knee-length pajama shirt.

"You think you can keep me out, you fucking whore," he taunted as he rampaged down the narrow hallway to our bedroom where his fist would feast upon her flesh. "I own you, bitch," he declared.

His footsteps were fast and determined, like invincible soldiers on an unstoppable mission. I inched the covers over my eyes, but not all the way, so that I could still see out of the corner if I needed. As he came through the door and flipped the light on, I could smell the whiskey smoking on his breath.

"Wake the fuck up," he yelled.

"Lecil. Lecil, I didn't hear you. I swear to God, I didn't hear you," she said, popping up from beneath the covers.

"I'm going to kill your ass tonight," he promised.

"Why," she asked. "What did I do? What did I do?"

"Shut up. Shut the fuck up."

I was furious she didn't stick with our suicide pact. We were supposed to play dead. Now I'm just dead. Alone, buried in covers that no longer seem safe or warm.

I peeked from beneath the sheet to see that he was unbathed and bleeding. Apparently, he cut his hand when he broke in, as fresh crimson rivered past his wrist to his elbow where it steadily dripped. He's not a big man, but medium-built with a beer gut. His hair is brown, receding and thinning. And spit sticks in his moustache when he screams. His cold eyes were focused on our bed.

"Take your fucking clothes off," he said.

She didn't move.

"Take 'em off, I said."

She still didn't move.

"Guess I'm gon' have to take them off for you," he threatened.

He rushed toward the bed and leapt on to her with the full force of his weight. His face was no more than two feet from mine. I could tell by the glassy look in his eyes that he had filled up on toot before coming here. He's powerless in his drug-induced, delusional world. I always wondered whom or what he was escaping from.

Who scared him out of reality and into numbness?

"Lecil, please, please leave us alone, dear God, what did I do, what did I do?" she begged at the mercy of his sharp glare and white-knuckled fists. I could see sweat beading up on his balding forehead. He wiped it dry with one fast sweep of his backhand. He had a mean backhand. I don't think he had feelings in his hands, because if he did, the sting of a slap or the crack of a bone would pain him almost as much as the person he was pounding.

"You think you can whore around and not fuck your own husband?" he asked her. She said nothing, but defended her gut by curling her legs into a ball and shielding her face with her arms. She had divorced him over a year ago, but he had it in his head that she was still his wife, still his piece of flesh to abuse.

"Oh my God. Oh my God. Oh my God," I chanted over and over in my head, still faking dead, but rocking myself inside. I wanted Ashlie.

I forced my eyes closed to try and find her, but the heavy breaths and yelping kept me with my mom. He had wrapped his hands around her throat in a choke hold, his customary gag to quiet her pleas for mercy. I could feel her body fighting his as she choked and began to suffocate in his grip. She gasped for air and her arms flailed, searching out air as if her palms could suck it up and send it to her starving lungs. I heard death.

"My God, what do I do?" I asked myself again.

I closed my eyes in a game of solitary hide 'n' seek to run away from a sight that was all too familiar in my seven-year-old life. I could hear Ashlie beckoning me to come to the pool. I looked inside and saw she had her tippy toes in the water. She knew what I was having to deal with, my dear, patient and understanding sister. She didn't see me peek in, so I left her there waiting for me to return.

Skynyrd's "Freebird" echoed clearly through the busted-down door. Hope flashed into my heart. "Maybe someone will hear the music, the screaming," I thought to myself. "Someone will call the police and we'll be saved."

The more she gasped and cried, the tighter his hands became on her throat. The tighter he squeezed, the more she struggled and the angrier he became. There seemed to be no end to this escalating cycle of wills. The will to kill and the will to survive. Predator and prey. We were base animals acting on instinct, not enlightened worshipers living on faith.

Exhausted from fighting, she gave up. She bawled quietly and uncontrollably, her body shaking with her silent sobs. She lay still on her back in her Virginia Slims t-shirt that read, "You've Come a Long Way, Baby." We hadn't gone anywhere. We were stuck in this moment like a scratched record. I was angry she gave up. I was angry she didn't go along with our plan in the first place. I was angry I had to be the one to even decide we played dead. I was angry she was too weak.

I heard his pants unzip.

I caught another glimpse from my grave between the sheets and saw gray streams of mascara mixing with the blood from her nose. Both coursed down her cheeks that were hot from the beating, crying, begging, fighting, choking, screaming. I glanced into the ceiling light and noticed a handful of dead bugs had collected in the glass cover.

E. Kelly Harrison

"Shut up. Shut up," he scolded her. She tried to contain her emotions, but they spilled out in involuntary shakes and whimpers. She was trying to surrender. She had stopped fighting. She had stopped crying. She seemed to have stopped breathing.

I thought she was dead.

I searched for Ashlie. I needed her now more than ever. I had to get out of hell and to the pool that sparkled with the hope and promise of fun and safety. I begged my mind to take me there, but it had abandoned me, too. No God. No mom. No police. No Ashlie. No escape.

I was alone.

"Oh God, please, dear Lord, let me die," I prayed.

"Emilie," I heard an unfamiliar, tender southern voice call. "Emilie. Emilie. Can you hear me, Sugar?" the matronly voice asked.

"Hello," I answered. "I'm here. I hear you," I said to the visitor.

"Emilie," she said, "Dearest little one, it's your grand mom, Edith."

A sudden sense of security enveloped me. I relaxed in the cradle of her voice. "Grandma," I whispered. "Is that you?"

"Yes, dear. It's me," she reassured me. I couldn't see her face, but I remembered her picture.

"Emilie. Know that I'm always here. Always. And I've always been here and will always be here. No matter what happens to you, you will be okay. Everything will be all right. I promise."

"Grandma," I started, "Take me with you. Please."

"Dear one, I cannot take you with me. You have a long, happy life ahead of you. Trust me. One day, this piece will fit in your puzzle. Don't throw it away or forget it, but keep it and one day you'll know where it fits. Forgiveness always fits. Hold tight, Emilie."

"Grandma," I called to her. She didn't answer, so I called again, "Grandma, you still there?" I imagined that she was visiting her daughter, my mother now, advising her just as she had done for me, but with less conviction. It must have been indescribably hard for her to see her daughter beaten and raped.

I mustered the courage to stay present with my nearly dead mother. I glanced through my sweaty fingers and saw him tugging at her panties. She didn't fight and I understood her sacrifice. She was trying to get out of this alive. She didn't want to orphan me.

He peeled his jeans along with his underwear down to his ankles, leaving his shirt and shoes on.

She tried, one more time to negotiate with the mad man. "Lecil, please don't do this with Emilie here," she asked. "Let's go to another room, but not here. Not now. Not with her. Please. Please. Lecil. Please. Let's move."

My dad didn't agree to move to another room. He reached for his flaccid penis and began stroking himself. He jerked himself off until he was hard enough to penetrate her. With one hand he led himself into her and handcuffed her wrists above her head with his other free hand. He began slamming his anger into her. The frameless bed absorbed his convulsive blasts. The thunderous booms shifted the plate tectonics of my soul.

She just lay there, trying to be quiet, trying to escape her body and that moment.

He finished with her, zipped up his pants and walked out of our wrecked room. We lay in bed together, back to back, in silent reverence of the soul-splitting event. We never talked about it. We just picked up the pieces and put them in our pockets.

No Bad Words

My son's friends like to come to our house
because I let them say *fuck*
and *shit*. I even let them say *motherfucker*
and *suck my cock*.

There are no bad words, I tell them.
Only bad people.
And sometimes bad people don't even say those words.

They know this is the truth,
though they don't quite know why I, a parent,
know this.
Usually only teenagers
or very young children know the truth,
or maybe saints.

I am not a saint.
And I don't claim to know the actual truth.
That alone makes me an honest person, I think.
I'm just saying I believe these kids are fabulous.
And the ones who get kicked out of school
are sometimes the best kids, and the first-chair trumpet
a shithead.

So, anyway, they can say any words they want to here.
I won't be offended. Even when my son says, "Fuck you, Mom,"
I say, Yeah, I know what you mean, son.
If I don't know what he means,
I say, Son, tell me about it.
He doesn't always know, himself,
and sometimes *fuck you* is all there is.

"Listen to that cello, Mom," he says.
"Hear that cello? See, they take a nice instrument like that
and they fuck it up."

Yeah, son. I see.
And I do. Sometimes.

Atomic Autumn

Mortal mushroom.
Knowing what
we know,
we thought
we could harvest you.
Your white
sheathed bellies
against the cool
black earth,
pallid ghosts
waiting in dark silos
for the deadly roundup.
One mistake
and you glow
on the horizon
dropping your
lethal spores on
those too
innocent to
understand you
and the rest
of them?—of us?
Unwilling to
root you out,
we leave you to those
who covet you.
What else can we do
but try to forget you,
to live as if
you didn't exist,
to tend roses and children,
to rescue stray dogs
off the freeways,
to keep up appearances
as if we'd nothing to lose.

My Slender Happiness

Perhaps you'll remember how happy I was with the Italian, Piccolo,
before he was lost at sea.
My mother had run off with the Pope
and I wallowed in happy endings.

Piccolo just disappeared.
Maybe he is awaiting rescue
although he was, and is
my slender happiness.
I can't help him now.

I'm living in Nuremberg,
far from the sea,
bonded to the dull Teutonic Meat Grinder.
Our apartment is small.
The slits in the shutters allow only enough light in
to taunt me with the possibility of what's out there.

Here, nothing skips.
In the gloom
dark shapes disappear into one another.

I'm partly to blame for this decay,
but Piccolo is too.
He could have stayed home with me in the kitchen.

I hear the Meat Grinder,
the amputized thump,
as he makes his way up the stairs.
I crawl between the dank sheets
and pull the covers over my head.

If I'm lucky,
he'll forget I was ever here.
If I'm lucky,
I'll forget too.

Alice Hayward

Pictures of Houses with Water Damage

My son is sitting next to me in my truck and I'm driving him home and he says, "I don't want to go back."

"I know," I say.

He's playing with a toy truck. The toy truck is silver. My truck is dark blue. My son, he's ten and his name is David.

David says, "We could drive away to another city."

It's not a bad idea. I'd be arrested for violating the court custody order. "Yeah, well," I say.

He knows. He nods. He says, "I don't like it there anymore."

"It's not that bad."

"No," he says, "but I don't like it there anymore."

"Is it because of Bill?" I ask.

"Bill? There's no more Bill."

"Oh?"

"It's Jeff," my son says.

"Who's Jeff?"

"He comes around a lot now."

I can't keep track of my ex-wife's rotation of boyfriends.

"Does Jeff drink?" I say.

"No," my son says, and goes quiet. We're near the house where my ex-wife lives. It used to be my house. I don't miss it that much.

I park in the driveway. There are two cars there—a Camaro and a Datsun 280-Z. The Z belongs to my ex-wife. Her name is Marilyn.

"Ohhkkeyy," my son says, getting his backpack in order.

"See you in two weeks," I say.

"Yeah."

"Want me to walk you to the door?"

"No, that's okay."

"Call me if there's a problem."

"There are never any problems," he says. He gets out of my truck and goes back to his mother.

I feel like getting laid. It's a sudden desire; I'm driving away from the ex-house and my son and I'm thinking that getting laid would be nice. I haven't gone out on a date or been laid in seven months.

So I go to a bar. I have some beers and I'm not quite sure what to do. There are women here, and some of them are alone. Some of them are young, some are my age, and some are a number of years older. The beers taste good. I don't drink like I used to. I used to really drink. That's why Marilyn divorced me and I see David every other week.

I start a conversation with a young woman. She has short blonde hair and her name is Lucy. She works at a supermarket.

"So, what do you do?" she asks.

"I take pictures," I say.

"You're a photographer?" she says, interested.

"Well, I take pictures of houses with water damage."

She looks at me and goes, "Huh?"

"I'm an estimator for an insurance company," I say. "Water damage is my specialty. A house gets water damage, I take pictures of it, I make an estimate on how much it'll cost to repair."

"Oh," Lucy says, looking at her drink. "Isn't that kind of boring?"

"Isn't working in a supermarket boring?"

"Yeah, well, what do you expect," she says.

This conversation isn't going too well. I don't think I will be leaving with Lucy to have sex.

One beer later, I'm talking to another woman. She also has blonde hair—it's long and stringy. Her name is Rene and she works at a cyber café monitoring people on Internet-hooked computers.

"How do you like working there?" I ask.

She shrugs and says, "It's pretty boring."

I am alone in my bed when I go home. I'm thinking of the houses I have to take pictures of tomorrow. I'm thinking of going over to Marilyn's and confronting this guy Jeff. It's easy to have violent fantasies. I picture myself having a few drinks with this Jeff and liking him when I want to hate him; we become the best of friends and this irritates Marilyn and I'm thinking this might be the route to go.

My phone rings. It's my son.

"I can't sleep." he says.

"What's wrong?"

"Nothing."

"Are you sure?"

"I'm sure," David says. "I just can't sleep. Were you asleep?"

"No."

"Tell me a story," he says.

"A story? What kind of story?"

"A bedtime story," he says.

I've never told him a bedtime story before. My father used to read to me from books when I was his age. I can't remember any of those stories. I could tell him that once upon a time there was a man who led a wild and crazy life, got married, thought he found some peace in having a home and family, but messed it all up when he went wild and crazy again.

"I don't know any stories," I say. "Why don't you tell me one?"

"That's not my job," he says.

"It is your job now," I say. "I just hired you."

"All my stories are boring."

"Try one on me."

He yawns. I know it's fake. "I'm tired now. I think I'll go to sleep now."

"Okay."

"Good night," my son says, and hangs up the phone.

Michael Hemmingson

Finding My Way Home

Moving along Storrow Drive I hear voices,
Fiedler music from the Hatch
the distant flap of swan's wings at the edge
of the Public Garden pond as paddle boats
gliss by powered by youth's intentions.

I pass the Ritz and hear the crunching of coal dust
on the linoleum beneath my feet
as the New York train speeds by my window
along St. Botolph Street tracks.

I stare out the seventh grade windows
of the Prince School watching the ascendant
John Hancock building now dwarfed
by the Prudential Center standing
an old freight yard rails and hear the horses' high whinnies
from the Police stables on Massachusetts Avenue—

The crack of the bat from the distance at Fenway
sitting in the bleachers with my mustard fingers
in the double-header sun, thrilled
by the Splendid Splinter—Ted Williams.

On this remembrance trip my eyes scrim
with tears of things and past moments,
my mother's voice,
Ritche. . . ieeeee—come to supper,

mashed potatoes and gravy.

Almost

I almost called a man I didn't know.
             My hand

held the plastic thing and
             I tried to

imagine myself saying hello,
             him

saying hello, sounding pleased, sounding
             eager

to talk, but I knew it wouldn't be
             like that.

I knew that he would know I had
             nothing personal

to say. I knew he would know
             I just wanted

to hear a voice, in my ear alone,
             a private

ocean, the way I want to feel
             skin

again, the way I want
             joy.

Surviving My Goddess

I am thinking in hormones
There is a beige rug from which I ground
There is a computer phone that I must wait for
I tend to the needs of others in hopes the phone will love me
The computer is now my lover
There are messages outside and a pool sparkles in chandelier
I am a phone divided between a wire and a stage
A Home and a Universe
The phone's been my stage but now I divide
In order to Survive My Goddess—She calls me

I was in her office—her makeshift office
Loading stacks of gum paper
Lots of names on her mailing list
Picking up his pieces, paying his bills
Organizing the gum of his cum
She's getting it together
Her real son left her but the gum didn't want to
The gum hung on. I don't know the whole story
It's sticky.

A True Smoothie

Working on the treadmill my right hip
Felt out of place. It's been a stranger
To its home for a few weeks now but I keep
the smoothie on the elliptical edge
I survey the bodies, the round butts, the smoothie
Instructors, the gold chains, the diamond studs,
The determination to beat God at his best game
Designing the smoothie in its perfect colors,
Enhanced ingredients, proteined and siliconed
With fat sorbet sucked through a straw to be better,
More delicious—to beat God
A True Smoothie.

Flight of Hands

My father's Pendleton shirt slumps crumpled
on the chair beside his bed.

He insists, in his last days,
on white spaces around him, he who
filled galleries, museums with his paintings.

His wife takes photographs of my sister and I
collapse beside him; I weep into the quilt
he is so so cold so cold.
The smell of his body, stale with sweat, makes me gag.
A hospice nurse, impossibly calm, explains why
eating solid foods is no longer necessary for the dying.

Being here, in this house, lodges a finger in my throat.

Michigan in March bitingly cold,
trees stripped bare of leaves,
his paintings stacked like frozen slices of toast everywhere.

I can't get to him
I know this is the last time I will see him alive,
but I am not ready to let him go.

Speaking to my daughter, I maintain the lie
of still being in New York.
To Tom, all I can do is utter,
"He's dying, and I can't
do anything about it."

I am accustomed to being the yeast
that makes the bread rise.
There were always books with answers—
experts to consult—
numbers to call—
I could always find a way out.

But the streets of this Detroit suburb are labyrinthine to me now
and I've no car, only my stepmother and sister,
black holes for eyes, wearing pajamas all day long,
so frosty indoors, I see my breath come out in urgent little puffs.

I can't leave fast enough
it takes three planes to get home,
the last at midnight, a thirty-seat prop-plane
that bucks and rocks with Manhattan cupped then lost in the windows.
I can feel the air rush against its sides.

Seated beside me, an Indian military man, returning
from security training in Washington,
rubs the palms of his hands against one another—
I have to comfort him—
we think we might just die up here,
strangers to each other
in late winter cold.

He grasps my hand as the plane dips abruptly
as I had grasped my father's hands,
hands in hands in hands,
the pulse that is life.

A Man Like That

I.

He walked until dawn the night before,
south along the ocean edge, the moonless shore,
moving away from the center of his life,
his children sleeping in a house he had already
begun to erase from the field of memory—
and you, his childhood shadow, boy with deep
light in his eyes he led into manhood,
what will you carry into this world that he
let go, just as he let go of all you thought he was;
a man who danced on city streets, bought
homeless women roses instead of bread, knowing
that was the part unnourished, what will you
carry from this man whose love for life shone
in each act, who, knowing his mother would find
him thought to cover his face before he threw
himself over the bannister at the end of his own
rope—what will you carry for a man like that?

II.

Let's assume he knew what he was doing when
he placed the pillowcase over his head and knotted
the rope around his neck, let's assume he'd carried
the knowledge of that noose inside for a long, long time,
let's assume that solitary image drove the spontaneous
acts of generosity, the insistent displays of love, let's
assume his death is not a dropped stitch, but an integral
part of the pattern, and that he knew this, and knew
that only in death would the tapestry be complete.

Let's assume what he did, he did for love.

Let's assume you know what to do with that horror,
the unfathomable unknowing, the cutting edge of
'Why?' Let's assume the door he closed opened another
much larger, for his children, left you the gift of your own
life, broadened, let's assume such a perfect light could only
burn so long, let's assume we have to trust
a man like that.

Alive . . . or . . . DNR

If I become pedestrian,
break my legs.

If I become fluent in the language of small things,
sew my mouth shut.

If I become frightened of what's new
or cling to what's old,
smash the clocks and the mirrors.

If I become too sad to laugh,
tickle me senseless.

If I become too smug to cry,
sing to me.

If I become too fearful
to risk my heart,
cut it out.

If I become too languid to create,
shock me to the bone.

If I become too indolent to learn,
beat my head against the wall.

If I become lost to art and language,
burn every finger and snatch the air
from my lungs.

If I become closed to the possible miracle,
bury me.

Badlands

The first time he hit me, it felt right, it felt like home.
Like brown couches and cold drafts coming in around windows.
I went to basic training in those sycamore rooms.
Learned my lessons like a good soldier.

It was spring and daffodils were blooming.
Just-washed sheets hung on the clothesline.
Blue skies waved gently in the breeze.
My world stretched tight between two poles.

I kissed the floor.
Its ancient skin cool against my cheek.
Didn't know what it was like until I was down.
Down there among broken glass and soft furry bodies.

Didn't know what to do:
Leave dirty red tennis shoes on the floor,
or pack my pride in a soft leather case
and carry it to the waiting car?

I took a Crayola crayon and tried to fix my life,
all the while asking:
Is this happening to me?
Is this someone else's life?

I walked through empty rooms.
Felt the chill of blue metal caress my cheek.
Spent dreamless nights in the arms of a chair,
afraid of the white picket fence.

Who knew when I became strong?
Courage was steel that crept under my skin.
In that morning light he looked into my eyes and saw the riot,
hid his hand in his sleeve and knew that I was gone.

Michele Hugus

Bedroom Changes

I washed the sheets,
Faithfully,
Once a week
Before you moved out.

Now I sleep,
Religiously,
One week on one side,
One week on the other.

Not much has changed,
Really,
It's just twice as long
Between washes.

Context for "Sanctuary of Artemis Dying"

Patmos. The island where St. John was exiled in 95 C.E. The cave where he wrote the Book of Revelations. I could see the three-pronged crack in the wall that some say was the Trinity, Christianizing the cave. I got angry. Weren't caves sacred to earlier religions? Wasn't the Catholic hierarchy trying to gain legitimacy by Christianizing already sacred sites?[1] Pope Gregory said, "Purify the temples with holy water. Set relics there and let them become temples of the true God." It was plain theft. Not far from Patmos is Ephesus on the coast of Anatolia (Turkey). For over 1500 years, its Temple of Artemis drew large masses of worshippers. Artemis was the Mistress of nature, free of male domination. But in 268 C.E., the Temple was destroyed and Ephesus became an important Christian center. Christians also built St. Peter's where once was the Temple of Cybele, Idaean Mother of the Gods. Interestingly, it was at Ephesus that Mary was proclaimed Mother of God in 431 C.E.

But why was "sacredness" associated with any given site in the first place? Perhaps it is the landscape that holds the key.[2] Eleusis, a site sacred to Demeter, the Goddess of Agriculture, was a place of worship for over 2000 years. The celebration began with a 14-mile procession from Athens, marked by the appearance and disappearance of the sacred horns of Mount Kerata.[3]

It is sad that we can not sense what ancient religions held sacred. As I stood staring at the chapel floor of St. John's Monastery, I looked up around me with new, and old, eyes.

1   Christ, C. *Odyssey with the Goddess*. NY: Continuum, 1995.
2   Scully, V. *The Earth, the Temple, and the Gods*. NY: Frederick A. Praeger, 1969.
3   Streep, Peg. *Sanctuaries of the Goddess*. Boston: Blufinch Press, 1994.

On the Sanctuary of Artemis Dying

In a place like St. John's Monastery
the wall she sees scales fifteen meters
juts out like a broken nose
scoured by the idled sight

of innocents incised in blackened
rededos, a flat-faced John,
his forehead marked, his brother
James's skin broken, drawn.

And the floor, remembered from a pagan
temple, marbled slabs made numb,
aged, for a time and half a time
seemingly 2000 years or more

as endless rows have come and given
will, gray-fashioned until not
one more footfall could be taken
whether by moon or under blood.

Invisible, she stares, reflected
bowing to the sons of thunder
who unaware, not caring
have crushed the back of Artemis.

A Conversation with

JOHN IRVING

One of John Irving's most extraordinary achievements is his emergence as a popular novelist and a literary craftsman as well. Like many writers he paid his literary dues by composing three critically acclaimed but economically challenged works of fiction. But, unlike so many of his peers, his fourth novel, *The World According to Garp*, was a staggering commercial success.

Success, of course, breeds envy, and for a time it was fashionable to dismiss Irving as a talented but regressive author, a writer whose undisguised enthusiasm for Charles Dickens, Joseph Conrad, and even Jack London made him vulnerable to the charge of looking backward instead of forward, of sacrificing aesthetic integrity for monetary success. But, as Irving's works continued to take a resolutely moral look at the world in which we live, and as his spell-binding narrative skills continued to attract legions of readers, it has become clear that his is a singular, uncompromising, talent.

His brilliance was anticipated in his early work, especially in the searing description of male-female relationships in *The 158-Pound Marriage* (1974). And his post–*Garp* works have established that he was hardly sequestering his talents in the world of nineteenth century fiction. *The Cider House Rules* (1985) took an unflinching stand on abortion. *A Prayer for Owen Meany* (1989) moved the story of Jesus Christ into the twentieth century. *A Widow for One Year* (1998) took many of the themes of the *Garp* saga (the celebrated author, the foreign city, the horrific auto accident, the dead child) and re-told them from a female point of view. His many honors include a number of university professorships, National Endowment for the Arts and Guggenheim fellowships, a National Book Award nomination and, because of *The Cider House Rules*, an award from the National Woman's Political Caucus.

In this interview, John Irving talks about writing: writing in general, and writing *The World According to Garp* in particular. He discusses his extraordinary powers of narrative expression; the extensive pre-writing and plotting strategies that precede his actual novel-writing; his belated recognition of his wish to be a novelist; his attraction to what Pieter Brueghel called the "Carnival" element of human experience; and his experiences as a student of Kurt Vonnegut in the University of Iowa Writers program and as the Writer-in-Residence in the same program.

Charlie Reilly Your novels are so original, so new, but I always get the feeling you are honoring the old rules of story-telling. Do you see yourself in any type of literary mainstream? Are there any of the "older" authors you feel close to?

John Irving There are a number of authors I admire, but the idea of "feeling close to" an author is not something I'm comfortable with. How can I put this? I admire *The Sun Also Rises* and love *The Great Gatsby*, but I don't feel close to Hemingway or Fitzgerald. I suppose my preferences are arbitrary, and they're certainly influenced by what I like in art. I like art to be entertaining, and I especially enjoy works which combine a comic force with a dramatic force. I can think of a number of really different writers I've been influenced by over the years. Jack London is one; Conrad, especially with the way he handles the adventure story, is another. And then there is Dickens. When I was fifteen or sixteen, I remember reading Dickens with a great sense of wonder, over and over again. *Great Expectations, Oliver Twist,* and *David Copperfield* meant more to me than I can say, and I suppose some of it rubbed off.

> What's important to me is that Vienna is a city whose life is over. I think the description of the city as it strikes Garp as a kid is the best I've done with it. It's almost like a city that has been put into a museum.

To get back to your question about a literary mainstream, I'd say I write narrative fiction, particularly the kind that gathers momentum—as opposed to fiction that gathers density. But I think writers are probably the worst judges about whom they resemble or are influenced by. I don't really have much of a sense of what my virtues and vices are. For example, people will often say to me, "I *loved* your novel, it reminded me so much of . . ." And then they'll name a book that astonishes me—a work either I was indifferent to or to one I actively disliked.

CR You give the impression of effortlessly spinning a tale. Your writing suggests you could pick up a menu in a restaurant and walk out the door with a novel. Are you just a born story teller?

JI That's a fair question. Yes, I do think constantly about story telling and, yes, I frequently have more ideas for novels than I can sort out. But one of the rules I try hard to obey when I am writing—I don't always succeed in obeying it—is to keep my mind focused on what I'm doing and not let myself get distracted by new projects. Ideas come easily to me, but ideas are cheap. The rendering of those ideas, the transformation of an idea into a well written, tightly organized novel, is a slow and complicated process which gets slower and more complicated as you go along.

The last two hundred pages of *The World According to Garp*, for example, took the longest to write, and that's especially significant because another one of my rules is never to begin the actual writing without the conclusion—ideally, without the conclusion and epilogue—in mind. When I begin work in earnest on a book, I have a precise idea about how the novel is going to wind up. It's not that simple, of course. Like everyone else, I encounter things along the way and they sometimes turn out to be among the strongest parts of a work. But it's crucial to me to have at least the illusion that I know where everyone is going and how things will wind up. And it's rarely just an illusion.

To stay with *Garp*, I knew from the start I was going to work with a unique mother-and-son relationship, and I knew each of them would run afoul of groups, and I knew very early on that the novel would ultimately be about a woman who was assassinated by a group of women who hated men. If you go back over the novel, you'll see the theme of sexual polarization is present throughout.

> I can think of a number of really different writers I've been influenced by over the years. Jack London is one; Conrad, especially with the way he handles the adventure story, is another. And then there is Dickens.

At the same time, the interesting stuff involved what I didn't know. I knew there would be a transsexual character who would more or less "gap" the friendship between mother and son and who would be capable of carrying on a role of some kind of sexual duality. In fact, to the extent that there is a hero in the novel, it would have to be Roberta. But I didn't know that, in the early stages, Roberta was going to achieve such a dimension that she threatened to take over the book. She was a much larger character in the first drafts and, as the novel progressed, I found myself consciously struggling to keep her under control.

Also, I knew from the start there would be an "Under Toad" and that this force would have enormous impact upon the characters. It's odd. When *Garp* was in progress, people would ask me what I was working on and I'd reply, "I'm writing a book about a man with a famous mother." This went on for years, but I wasn't sure what else to say that wouldn't be misleading. It was only when I was well along that I had a better idea of the novel's implications and could give a better answer. Then I said, "It's a life-affirming novel in which everyone dies." I know I had a sense of that from the start, but only a sense.

I knew from the start that I would have to work hard in the book's second half to mute, or at least diminish, the impact of the loss of Jenny and then the loss of Garp. Maybe this is a better example. Five years earlier, the opening line of the book had been, "In the world according to Garp, we are all terminal cases." But as I wrote, I kept shoving the line further back, kept moving it from the last line of one chapter to the first line of the next. Finally, it became the last line of the book.

CR You've said you don't stick to a chapter-by-chapter progression?

JI Correct. I'll return to a problematic section and really throw myself into it—the results of which will frequently dispatch me to other sections, either to adjust for new developments or to revise what had impressed me as poorly written passages. Sometimes I'll move chapters around as well.

CR One of *Garp's* most admired chapters was the one with the driveway scene. I'm not thinking so much about the farewell fellatio as I am about the death of Walt. Was that a difficult scene to write, or did it just flow?

JI In my opinion, that chapter, "The World According to Marcus Aurelius," is the strongest in the book. It should be. It's the last chapter I wrote, and I spent an enormous amount of time on it. We spoke a second ago about my skipping around? During the novel's first draft, when I came to Walt's death in the driveway, I just stopped writing. I always knew the scene was there, and I knew what to occur in it. Yet I knew it would be very difficult, very painful, to write that chapter. In a sense I didn't want to do it. I had children of my own

A Conversation with John Irving

and I knew I would need time to think things through.

Also, and this is relevant to our question, when I went back over the first 300 pages of the manuscript, I decided to take out the Under Toad because I realized its presence as a heavy hand was inappropriate during the early going. The first half of *The World According to Garp* can be compared to the progress of that Volvo up the driveway. It's a domestic com-

> It was only when I was well along that I had a better idea of [*Garp*]'s implications . . . then I said, "It's a life-affirming novel in which everyone dies."

edy. There is a little death on the side, but it doesn't touch us. The girl who is molested in the park receives our sympathy, but we don't know her, she's not our friend. Garp's father dies, but we don't know him either and he's presented almost as a vegetable. The first half is comedy in the classical sense. It's Mrs. Ralph, it's looking for a job, it's the courtship of Helen, it's encountering prostitutes.

Beneath the surface, of course, there's an unpleasant reality, but in the first 300 pages it goes by us. We don't have a sense of the heavy hand until the shit hits the fan. Then, after that meaningful loss of life, it seems everything falls apart. So, and I do want to answer your question, I decided to withhold both the existence of Roberta, who has such wonderful recuperative and healing powers, and the story of the Under Toad until the movement toward tragedy had actually begun. In effect, I wanted the early portions of the novel to be like that trip up the driveway—lighthearted, fun and games—because that's the way the early years of our life typically are.

To that point, it's a golden story. It's about a woman who wants to have a baby without the unpleasantness of a father and, hey, presto!, she gets what she wants. It's about a boy who wants to be a writer and, lo and behold, he becomes one and marries his childhood sweetheart besides. It's about a woman who sits down to write her autobiography and wakes up to find herself famous and the author of a widely-admired bestseller.

So, until the trip up the driveway, it's the best of all possible worlds. But then, a little carelessness, nothing that would merit such a catastrophe—as Garp and Helen say, "A most inappropriate treatment for a little indiscretion"—and the world falls apart. A point I was trying to make, and I hope I made it in a respectful and sympathetic way, is that the Garps' tragedy reflects a sad fact of life. The men screw around and nothing much happens. But let a woman be indiscreet and all hell breaks loose.

In the novel, I wanted to work with that old cliché. I wanted to present it in a shocking manner, but I also wanted to spring it suddenly upon the reader. If you go back over the early portions of the novel, you can see—at least I hope you can see—the stage has been set for a tragedy. But I felt it important that I present these things subtly, that the catastrophe explode upon the reader. I wasn't worried about skipping the chapter, about saving it for last. I knew everything that would happen, I knew how it had to be revealed. So I left it alone and went on—knowing, of course, that I'd have to return. When I did address that chapter, I was in an ideal position because I had brought the novel to at least an unpolished conclusion.

You know, there's another reason why I feel "The World According to Marcus Aurelius" is as determined a chapter as it is. I have some very close friends who suffered through the loss of a child, and I knew that in such an event a lot of time has to pass before you can bring yourself to utter the dead child's name. What your friends notice is the *absence* of the child. He or she isn't spoken of. The pictures come down from the wall. The name is rarely brought up.

CR I recall Duncan speaks about his blinded eye and says, "It's the eye I can still see Walt with."

JI What you notice is the absence, the loss. In a sense, the book is concerned with loss. Perhaps it's because I wound up being a writer, but as a child the loss of speech always struck me as a particularly frightening handicap. Perhaps I shouldn't generalize but, to me, ultimately a writer has to worry about an inability to communicate: a state where he is incapable of conveying what he means. In any case, I knew from the start that a major character would become traumatized and would lose the capacity or willingness to speak for a time. And I knew the first words I wanted him or her to say after the trauma were, "I mish him." I can't explain why, but I know I had the line in mind from the start.

CR At the point when the Garps were having their two babies, did you know one of them was going to die?

JI Oh yes, when the book was conceived I knew that a child was going to die. In the very beginning I didn't know who the child would be, and for a time I wasn't aware Garp would get married and have children. At that point, I presumed the child would be a sibling; I toyed with the idea of Jenny begetting two children. But once the writing was underway, I found the focus was on mother-son, Jenny-Garp. There was no "Helen" in the early drafts but there were a number of children, the foremost of whom, of course, was Garp. As the novel took shape in my mind and as Jenny moved more and more into the foreground, it became clear that I couldn't kill off Garp or his "brother" because such a death would oblige me to deal with the mourning and agonies of Jenny—and I'm not a mother. In effect, I had planned myself into a corner. The more I worked on it, the more I realized I couldn't see Jenny clearly enough in such a circumstance to do justice to her emotions. At the same time, I knew a child's death was critical to the novel, so I decided Garp needed a wife and his family had to be extended. In a sense, Roberta became a member of the family; even people like the Percys became kind of extended members of the same family.

> My sole ambitions . . . were . . . to become a first-rate wrestler, or failing that, to become a writer.

CR How did you get started as a writer?

JI The real story isn't very interesting, as most real stories aren't. I once had dinner with Joseph Heller and Kurt Vonnegut and we fell to talking about generations. To be specific, we spent a good deal of time talking about the way some people define others in terms of the generation they belong to. My contribution to the discussion, and it's not irrelevant to your question, was that as a writer—and as a person, for that matter—I never felt I belonged to a generation. By the time I figured out that I had a peer group and shared a number of characteristics with them—let's say, by the time I was fifteen—I had more or less slipped into a world of my own. My sole ambitions, and I hadn't thought about either very carefully, were, ideally, to become a first-rate wrestler, or failing that, to become a writer. I devoted a number of years to wrestling—I was vastly more fanatical about it than Garp—and I wound up being a better wrestler than Garp. But I was never as good as I had hoped, and when it became obvious that the championships I had dreamed about were beyond my peers, I recognized it was time to get to work, and work hard, at becoming a wrestler.

What I am saying is, from the age of sixteen I suffered from an odd form of myopia. Throughout my prep school and early college years my time was dedicated to talking shop with wrestlers and getting utterly involved in *training*. People in training aren't living in a real world, they get lost in a time warp. It wasn't until I was in my twenties and realized I wanted to be a writer that I could recognize the extent to which I had lost contact with my peers. And once I decided to become a writer I went about it as fervently, and myopically, as I did a wrestler. I dropped out of college and went abroad. Fortunately, I also got a job and took some courses at the University of Vienna.

> Emmylou Harris sings a song . . . about a person who dies . . . he goes to "a place where it's legal to dream."

CR Is that how it worked? I don't know why but I had gathered you had won some kind of elaborate grant.

JI I did get a grant to study at the Institute of European Studies in Vienna and I did take advantage of it—gratefully, I should add. But what I really needed was to get out of college in America and get over to Europe where I could get to work on becoming a writer. It turned out to be a far from unique story. My wife became pregnant, my income was hopelessly inadequate to support us, my career was becoming a careen. I came back to America, a husband and a father, and dedicated myself to keeping us all fed, getting a degree and writing my first book. For four years that was all I did and, as a result, I found myself even further disassociated from my generation. Since I had a wife and child, I was sheltered from the draft. By the time they got around to me, the Viet Cong would have been landing in New Jersey. So I studied and wrote and worked. I was a librarian, a bartender, a waiter, and, like Garp, I spent a lot of time being a housewife. Unlike Garp, I didn't like it.

CR Is Vienna a special place filled with memories, or is it just a place that provided you some things to write about?

JI Emmylou Harris sings a song that has a line which really caught my imagination. I think it's about a person who dies and, in any case, he goes to "a place where it's legal to dream." Well, Vienna has a place where it was legal for me to dream. Whenever I located the action of my books in Vienna, I knew I had moved to an almost magical locale where I could be sure something would happen. The Viennese I know tell me I am gratifyingly accurate about their city and, although I am pleased to hear that, such precision is not what concerned me. It hardly mattered to me, in fact. A copy editor once unfolded a street map of Vienna in front of me and proved that, since the street I had identified was one-way, there was no way the automobile trip I had described could have taken place. My response was, I know but I don't care. In each case, the correct street name was one I personally did not like. I didn't like either the sound or the implication of it, so I let my literary instinct prevail.

A writer has to make some odd decisions in his attempt to recreate reality. It's difficult to describe what I mean, but if there ever could be a "Pension Grillparzer," it would have to be in Vienna. Legalized prostitution is in fact the way I describe it in *Garp* but I'm not interested in that type of accuracy. My descriptions of Vienna are largely accurate and my departures from realism are trivial, but that's not what is important in the Vienna of my fiction, and it's not what made Vienna such a productive locale to work with. What's important to me is that Vienna is a city whose life is over. I think the description of the city as it strikes Garp as a kid is the best I've done with it. It's almost like a city that has been put into a museum.

CR John Barth was once asked what effect the teaching of writing had upon his own writing and he replied, "It slows it down considerably." You've taught writing for years and you've earned a Masters of Fine Arts at the University of Iowa. Did you learn to be a novelist at Iowa?

JI I don't think I was taught to write, and I'm not at all sure writing can be taught. But some very experienced and gifted author-teachers saved me an enormous amount of time when I was studying at Iowa. I would have learned the lessons they taught me sooner or later, but their wisdom and experience combined to save a lot of time-wasting experimentation. The teaching of writing is a craft. It's the craft of pointing out to a young author, just as a good editor does with an inexperienced author, what his virtues and vices are. Surely a skillful teacher can recognize what a struggling writer should concentrate on and what he should avoid. These are hardly unsolvable mysteries and any writer with talent will figure them out sooner or later. But why come to these solutions after months of futility if someone can get you on the right track sooner? A good teacher should save a writer *time* and time is so very important. It's one of the few things money is really good for: money can buy a writer time to write.

> . . . emotional committments are short-lived, and so often they create more expectation than can be realized.

When I recall my experiences with Kurt Vonnegut at Iowa, I can say that Kurt Vonnegut really taught me nothing, but he did everything for me. For example, he would remind me of my habits. After examining 100–150 pages of a manuscript, he would say, "You're in the habit of doing this, which is good, but you tend to slip into the habit of doing that, which reduces the effectiveness of your work." It takes a long time for a writer to recognize his habits, and they often vary from book to book. So it's wonderful when someone as accomplished and incisive as Kurt Vonnegut can save you months of stumbling about trying to figure out why something that is "almost there" still isn't working.

CR In *The 158-Pound Marriage* you wrote about Pieter Brueghel's painting, *The Fight between Carnival and Lent*. It seems to me that your novels often describe such a battle and, as often as not, the "carnival" impulse within man is destroyed. Does that go too far?

JI The conflict is certainly there, and that novel's resolution, its moral, does seem Puritanical, doesn't it? Discomfortingly Puritanical. The lesson seems to be "Don't mess around" or "Be good, or else." Such lessons seem so damned life-denying, and yet they play an important role in our lives. I am certainly a moral cautionary, but I always enjoy the gestures, the occasional leaps, toward amorality in my works. Even though such gestures wind up seeming wrong, often immoral. How can I put this? I admire the moment of falling in love or, to be less aggrandizing, the romantic and emotional rioting that goes on within us in love's early stages. But so often emotional commitments are short-lived, and so often they create more expectations than can be realized.

So I frequently wind up dealing with these emotional explosions, these heroic flights, and the subsequent descents into reality. As I think about and write about my characters, I find myself fascinated by the obsessive, almost myopic, need we have to choose between Carnival and Lent. It's hard to argue with the idea that we should select Lent, but, God, it can be stifling. Historically we see that, when clung to, family life can be stifling. But when it's rejected, its loss can be devastating.

A Conversation with John Irving

I think Brueghel felt the same way: neither his "Carnival" nor his "Lent" wins. He found both dimensions of life admirable—and so do I. I think it's so important in fiction and, to the extent that it's possible in life, to respect the diversity of human beings and their lifestyles. It's not easy. The tension between our need to be independent and our wish to be a part of a couple—or, conversely, our need to be part of a couple and to retain independence—has always fascinated me. The possibilities are endless.

> The teaching of writing is a craft. It's the craft of pointing out to a young author, just as a good editor does with an inexperienced author, what his virtues and vices are. Surely a skillful teacher can recognize what a struggling writer should concentrate on and what he should avoid. These are hardly unsolvable mysteries and any writer with talent will figure them out sooner or later.

I think the tensions and anguish one necessarily goes through when determining a personal lifestyle can engender jealousy, love, hatred, friendship, envy—all the basic and raw emotions that make stories happen. When a writer deals with a character who is jealous of or filled with hatred for someone, he will have little difficulty persuading his reader that the character will perform an important, often dramatic, act. Nor will the writer himself have much difficulty in imagining interesting and dramatic situations in which to involve such characters. So in a good deal of my work, and *158-Pound Marriage* is a perfect example, I work with broad emotions: emotions engendered by conflicts, emotions experienced by people who are burdened with uncertainties.

I have no pronouncement to make on the issue. As a writer, though, I find such relationships enormously interesting because they show that people are as cherishable as they are dangerous. Because people are so vulnerable in such relationships, we can't help but sympathize with them. Because they are prepared to change, radically change, their lifestyles and habits to make a relationship work, they become dangerous. There is always the chance they will snap back to their real selves and abandon those who have grown dependent upon them. Those sacrifices and transgressions almost beget stories, don't they? Certainly it would be difficult to write a novel about five people who saw eye to eye on everything. What the hell would it be about: a night out bowling?

my house is empty

my house

is empty this morning. totally empty. empty the way it used to be before my son was born. my dog, who used to fill up so much space in the house, sleeps in the sun. . . seeming lifeless in comparison to the kind of energy my boy generates. i'm not sure how to feel about it. i love it. i know it's temporary. the minutes are ticking and the silence won't last more than another hour. i'll be chasing and smiling and hugging. i'll be a mom. i want to cry when i think of how much i love him. . .and how much i want my freedom. i hate myself for not being more content. i already see my 55-year-old self. . . more time alone than i know what to do with and i regret my impatience.

i'm sitting at a desk. it's cluttered and messy, just like all of my desks have been since i was a girl. i'm typing and sorting through scraps of papers when i stop to put my thesaurus back on the credenza behind me and i glance at a picture of my kids. quinlan is a man. his platinum blonde baby hair has mutated to a head full of sandy brown wavy locks, but his smile is the same. my soon-to-be-born daughter stands next to him . . . a woman . . . smiling with a closed mouth. she's tucked under his arm.

a squirrel rustles in the leaves on the tree outside my window and i try to imitate the way quinlan couldn't say "squirrel" until he was three and it came out sounding something like *fierral* . . . and then i remember skinny bare legs that needed kissing after a fall on cement, balloons that floated into the sunshine before i could anchor them to a wrist and ketchup and dirt-streaked faces smiling at me . . . but i was rushed most of the time . . . rushed because i had things to do . . . i wanted to be a writer . . . i wanted to prove something . . . mostly to myself, but also to them. i wanted to prove i was more than my peanut butter-stained sweatpants and tennis shoes full of park sand. i wanted to prove i was smarter than conversations about potty training and halloween costumes.

but now my books are on a shelf behind me. their smooth glossy covers are a testament to my perseverance, my creativity, my brilliance. my picture is on the back. sure, i'm a little wrinkly around the edges, but i've done it. i've done it before, and i'm doing it again, but it doesn't have the whisper of new love on it anymore. it doesn't have the scent of my son's milky breath when i'd lean into his crib late at night. i should have known it wasn't going to last, but at the time it seemed like it would last forever. i thought i'd never see the end of screaming fits because i cut a sandwich in pieces that were deemed too small or put the milk in a blue cup instead of a green cup. i thought buying presents for birthday parties and the dropping off and picking up from school would never end. but it has. now, i can read the sunday newspaper in bed without listening to the sing-song voice of barney in the background. when i have to pee, i can be sure nobody will follow me in and ask what i'm doing. i can go to the movies any time i feel like it. morning, matinee, midnight showing. because nobody needs me home to make dinner. nobody needs a tissue for a runny nose. nobody needs a haircut or a new pair of tennis shoes. now . . . it's just me and my books and my words. all of the words i've collected over the years. the words i stored away from the time i was young and i have all the time i need to unravel them.

my hands rest on the keyboard a little longer. i wait for a sound. something to disturb my work, but it doesn't come . . . and i begin to type.

Not to Make a Big Deal out of Death
—to Liz

You're in a band and you fall in love,
as they say, so you write a song
about it. You're so deep in love,
and everyone loves it. Then he screws
your friend, says sorry, and leaves.

You want to cut his nuts off and tear
out his eyes. At least forget him.
But everyone loves the song. They demand
that you sing it. Over and Over. How much
you love him. So much that even
the hatred makes you sound more sincere.

Two-Way Walkie-Talkies
—to Todd

When we were kids you wandered away and never
came back. The neighbors helped us search
the woods and cops dredged the creek. No one
could find you. But when you wandered away you had
the other walkie-talkie. That was part of the game.

You wake me at night, like a cat meowing beneath
the floor boards. Where are you, I ask. Someone's
with me, you say. Hello, who is this, a voice
asks, and I know it's your voice, answering
from farther and farther away. Sometimes years

between words. The walkie-talkie is beside
my bed, underneath the window. In summer
when the breeze blows in, you whisper. You tease me. I've made
a discovery, you say, so beautiful, but you'll never believe it.
Tell me, tell me, please. But your voice becomes
sobbing downstairs.

War Stories

A silver chain sparkles
on the man's neck
where mahogany smells like rain

Raindrops, dewdrops, become eyes
that stare in the night
after bullets explode

I found the German Luger
on the dead soldier
with medals across his chest
a jewel in his navel

The apple trees
were frosted with snow
then we were charging downhill
into battle

Tank flaps spun
pieces of men
arms and legs
scattered like geese
on a farm

Only when the wind came
did they fly away

Raindrops hit the tin cup
in the dining room
where mother has laid out the china
She waits in a chair by the window
polishing the same glass

Infinity and *God*

My five-year-old is enamored of the words
"infinity" and "God," employing them
to map space and time. *God* is bigger
than our house, bigger than the city, bigger
even than the biggest monster or spaceship.
A race car's *infinity fast*, boys eat *infinity cookies,*
his scrubbed face is, he says, *infinity shining—*
shining all the way up to God.

                        At day's end,
God shrinks—small enough to become
the perfectly still, almost invisible period
that rests at the end of his nightly prayer.
And infinity spirals down to the size of his pillow.

The Palace

I lifted the farmhouse floorboards
to shine a flashlight under the house,
the light tunneling down into a sturdy little palace
of twigs, paper, shredded plastic bags,
and furnished, if that's the word,
with almost unrecognizable trinkets:
the broken nib of a fountain pen,
a silver bracelet laced through a wall of straw and wire.

Sovereign in its chamber, the rat, affronted,
hunched its shoulders, refusing to abdicate
its kingdom of darkness. And yet its black eyes
blazed and burned, betraying full awareness—

    god with a spear of light,
    instrument of destruction, annihilating hand.

The World of Circumstance

God guard me from the thoughts men think
        —Yeats

Intelligence is the savior
of emotion, for emotion on its own
is a storm of razor blades,
men dragging bags of broken glass. . . .

And thought without emotion
is unredeemed, fact piled upon fact—
the number of beats in a line,
how many died in the conflagration. . . .

But thinking, in the marrow-bone
is the quest for truth
when men say there is no truth;
the struggle to discover meaning
in a universe men say has no meaning.
It is the way one learns to know, to love, to sing.

Death

I liken it to chilled plums
Taken from a blue bowl
And eaten on the veranda
Of a lodge in the mountains
At dawn above a quiet lake
Aflame with sparks of light,
Spruces on the western slopes
Still deep in resonant shadow,
The lush blue-green branches
Evoking a sweet purple dark
That, each moment, brightens
And rises as mist into a pure
And unblemished cerulean sky,
While unseen clouds commence
A relentlessly unhurried march
To an open grave, somewhere
On the other side of the world.

Richard Jones

The Complete Absence of Cats Is Another
Definition for Silence

The tornado of my fourteenth year did many things. It placed Mrs. Zimmer's station wagon in Kim Stanley's lawn upside down, the antenna planted up to the base. It carefully took out each window on the east side of twelfth, even the stained glass of the church. It lifted every dry good in the grocery store and then held them up for nine impossible seconds, the metal shelving sighing a relief known only to Randy Wall, locked out of the stockroom by the older bagboys; not an egg was broken.

It worked a red-striped straw into the sticky black grain of the telephone pole in front of the bank. Until the straw rotted, it was a novelty to pretend you were drinking from it, let the warmth of the flashbulb—the fact that you were alive—wash over you. All but two of the seniors that year had their graduation pictures taken there. The other two had their diplomas handed over to their mothers. There was no eye contact. There was nothing to say. But that was all months ahead.

Right then it was still the wig store in the sky, and a clean, unlikely path around the junkyard, and the Luthers' Great Dane riding across town on a cushion of air, and Mrs. Zimmer with her face pressed to the headliner of her station wagon, her husband's bare legs approaching from the front door of Kim Stanley's house, his lunch hour. He tried to explain: it was an act of God. There wasn't a cat anywhere in the world.

All the bare mannequin heads from the wig store were never recovered, either. You can still find them in ditches with grass growing across their plastic scalps, and in chimneys, their eyes black and knowing, and falling from the sky, their lips composed, cheeks drawn in, about to smile, Rudolph the Great Dane watching them, waiting for them, his great tail fanning the grass slowly. He doesn't remember the Luthers at all, is an Allen dog now. But the straw. Pictures of it are in the display case in the court house—pictures of all of it, really, except me, and the lit cigarette the tornado had wedged between my fingers, and my father touching down directly across from me, his hair still airborne.

We stared at each other as the stained glass fell in slivers all around us and I held the smoke in deep, and then he said it—*I'll pretend I didn't see that*—and turned around, started picking through the rubble to what was left of our house, our town, or lives. Behind him, I smiled, took one long, last drag, and then aimed it back out at the heavens, in thanks.

Bathing

Friday afternoon, before Shabbos,
I carried the teakettle to the sink
and filled it with cold water,
put it on the gas stove,
struck a wooden match against the rusty grate,
and lit the gas.
When the water boiled, I carried the teakettle
through the dining room to the bathroom,
and poured it into the old claw-footed enamel tub,
then added a little cold,
tested the temperature with a finger, and climbed in.
I scrubbed under my arms,
between my toes,
up and down my body
as quickly as possible.
The I scooped up a large cup of water,
poured it over my hair, added a little shampoo,
rubbed it in and rinsed
with another cup of the same water.
Last, I poured water over the rest of my body
and climbed out to dry with the flour sack
that Grandma hemmed
after she had used up all the flour.
First Grandpa bathed, then Grandma,
then Mother, and then me.

Tonight, steam rises from the hot tub in our garden.
We soak, toes touching, but lost in separate thoughts,
I slide over beside Norm, rub my leg against his.
He pulls me close, an arm around my shoulder.
I look at the thick terry cloth towel,
and think about how he will
wrap me in it when I climb out.
I look up at the stars,
more than I can count,
fewer than my blessings.

Taos

Between star shine and clay
—after Lucille Clifton

Lucille Clifton's voice rings in my ears
as I walk this pebble-strewn path
in Taos, New Mexico.
The sky changes here
from midnight blue to pale cerulean,
and the morning stars linger.
Clouds turn fire red, fade to yellow, then white.
A single airplane leaves
a white plume in its wake.
The black mountains point
to the hawks that soar
over miles of sagebrush
and trucks carrying produce
that could never grow here.

I'm alone in the middle of this,
alone on the road,
alone in my coat
alone in my body,
far from family and friends,
yet at home in my skin.

When I was 30
I could not imagine such a trip
with no companion.
Now, at 70, it seems so right
to watch the sun, rising
over the dark mountains,
first a glow, and then the yellow orb
that turns the mountains orange.

Ben

I like Ben Franklin. I began to think more about him watching his biography on KCET. He founded the first public library. He was an inventor. I wanted to be an inventor. Imagine his brain! Its bright light. Bifocals! The lightning rod! The odometer! The wood stove! Ben. Benjamin Franklin. A founding father. The kind of father I wanted. A man to nudge the nuances. *Poor Richard's Almanac.* His frank brain. His founding father mentality. Moving me to open my mind.

I have been thinking about books on Ben. Since I like Ben, I want something more from him. I know I will visit him. "You have a vivid imagination," Roy, my husband, says, rubbing his thumb against his lip. He agreed with my neuro-oncologist. "You can't be a CEO. Those skills were removed from your right frontal lobe along with your brain tumor. You are a CAO. Corporate Artistic Officer." Passion drained by truth. Dry eyes. Logic. "But, Judi," he said, "you have never been logical. I'm your CEO. You're my CAO." Corporate Artistic Officer. I have been sculpting pedestals for years. Pedestals for people with high IQs and talents I don't have. Recovering from brain cancer, I had no IQ. I couldn't find my way home. I didn't recognize a calendar. Sex was on the screen in my mind. I watched close friends leave their mates. They found the fun of a fresh body. Juicy ideas. Me, I was missing. Roy was looking for me, the me that had some CEO skills, social skills, some sex skills, words. Three male friends found three delicious females. I put the three couples on a double pedestal. Front and center. Seductive.

Roy was front and center at my recovery. He turned off the lights and the heat. He counted pills. He hid his terror. He tried to cure me. He bought a Palm Pilot. He knew how to hot sync it to his hard drive. He knew where I should be. He went to every MRI appointment. He gave me his handkerchief when I began to have seizures last year. During the seizures, I was petrified I would die alone. Roy was always there when I woke up.

I put the three couples under a magnifying glass. I wanted to find passion and give it to Roy. From the time I met him, he has said, "I can't stand to see sickness and suffering." Years earlier, when we would see movies like *My Left Foot* and *Lorenzo's Oil,* he left the theater. He couldn't stand to see it. Yet all through my diagnosis, the surgery, the recovery, the seizures that came and went, he was there when I woke up. He's always there when I wake up, holding my suffering, holding my passions, holding my love.

The Poet's Bad Faith

It is a shadow of a shadow, only
more tangible. Like an illness, yet
harder to diagnose. It risks distortion.
For what? Personal expression?
Truth? To know the ideal world's

first radioactive giant-monster?
It is a massive opiate. The poet
designs each word to act as a sleeping pill,
a professor's abstract lecture,
a sermon about lifeless angels

dressed in white so bright. It causes
blindness, unleashes desires
better left leashed, repressed, dreamed.
Pits one against science. Makes one
a cheerleader for natural isolation;

for manic, sorrowful drug experiences;
for out-of-body love affairs;
for the ecstasy of agony. It traffics
in oppressive forms of linguistics.
It is a slave ship of slavers, drifting, delinquent. Still,

everyone climbs on board.

The Boy Who Fell Is Falling Still

It seems strange now
I didn't know you
when your son, a boy
I went to high school with,
crashed his sports car
through the fence
around Cape Kennedy, climbed
the Vehicle Assembly Building,
just to throw himself into the air,
saying he was Jesus Christ,
saying he could fly.

God, in all his wisdom,
gave man many things, but wings
are not among them.
Your son fell forty stories,
four hundred feet, and they say
that he fell fast. But creation
slowed for you, his father,
eating dinner alone
in your apartment,
the one you shared with him.
You heard it on the evening news,
then closed your eyes.

Later, when I came to know
you better than I ever knew
your son, and then to love you,
you gave me a picture
of the two of you.
In it, you are standing,
all tall legs,
the boy between them like a cello,
his blue eyes focused
on something no one else could see.

Even then, you knew
you were losing him,
like the French you'd brought
back from Paris, like you'd already lost
his mother, but in this picture,
you are holding tight,
as if steadiness, no heroics,
would be enough
to keep him safe.

When your eyes opened,
you told me, it was months later.
Your son already buried,
ex-wife come and gone,
the world moved on as well,
the evening paper full
of other leaping stories,
as if the children of the world
could hardly wait
to throw their lives away.

Grief was still there,
like a break in every bone,
and always would be.
But you imagined you saw time,
that good hand, pointing
toward an open window
where, like a white
and moving curtain,
life was starting up again.

Metabolism

I've got sawdust in my veins and paint sloshing in my head
My epidermis has been sanded away
And termites are dancing in my bones.
I need something natural.
Green, lavender, birds and ocean.
The question is whether to shoot me up with liquid nitrogen
Or stick me in the microwave.
Either way, I'm dead meat
Vegetarian-fed, of course.
Colin, the Wheaton Terrier, is licking my face
And telling me, frozen or fried, he loves me anyway.
He crawled under a car to lick his wounds.
Outside he looked okay, but inside he was torn apart.
He couldn't make it, and so he flew off.
But kept hanging out, appearing to Kushi,
And making her wonder, is he dead or alive?
It's all so confusing, and what does it matter anyway?
Warm soft body, liquid brown eyes, what do they see?
Ears on the blink.
Enough to sense the needle approaching,
And the last heartbeat knows fear.
Nothing here worth having; not wanting to go.
Struggle to resist, surrender, last second, last breath.
Still warm, still soft and cuddly, but perfectly still.
Eyes open, but lifeless.
What does she see now, through eyes no longer blind?
What sounds now penetrate the deaf ears that are no more?

Sledges

Each one dragging a sledge
    thick wooden runners
    rasping the earth
    thick leather harness
    marking the bearer.

Each sledge a different load
    cages of one-winged birds
    lead ingots piled high
    barrels brimming thunder
    buckets of cracked tears
    bins of frozen moans
    sacks of lost paths.

Each trail camouflaged
except for the drops of blood.

Two Words

Once two words began talking to each other:
one was *tumble* and the other was *hyacinth*.
They talked about their histories,
how *tumble* was once related to dancing, acrobatics
but, in recent times, had taken a tumble to
describe clumsy or unexpected falls.
Hyacinth talked about her great-great-great grandfather,
the god Hyacinthus,
how his blood in death had created her flower life;
her favorite hyacinth color was azure.
Soon the two began dating,
really mixing it up on the dance floor;
tumble forgot about the clumsiness,
hyacinth expanded her range of moods,
salmon, ecru, purple.
News of the dance spread—
cintum became a craze—
enchanting all who tried it.

What Remains

1.

This moment, suspended—
a moth mounted under glass.
Pin through thorax,
Melittia gloriosa.
If you breathe hard
against those wings
they will flake to dust
that casts no shadow.

2.

In your lungs this moment
1.34×10^{23} molecules of argon
flutter, waiting to be exhaled.
Argon, inert, will not bond
with any other molecule,
will not enter chemical reactions.
Some of those molecules
were mine, one breath before.
Unchanged by pulse or fear,
they passed to you,
perhaps on the breath
that held the words between us.

3.

Yesterday I found my grandfather
lighting hundreds of candles.
"I'm burning regrets," he said.
Match to wick, again and again:
for an unopened book,
an unpainted room,
an unhappy wife.

I watched a flame bludgeon its candle,
burning knuckle-first into the white wax,
a slow, bright metamorphosis.

4.

Kether told me,
"Your leaving isn't what will hurt.
It's the emptiness you'll leave behind."
I know what he means.
It's how I have to start all over again,
getting dressed in the morning,
brushing my own hair.

It's the way there's no one to tell
how my dress feels against my calves
when it's wet with rain.
It's the way the silence in my apartment is whole,
like an uncut melon,
and I swallow it in breaths and bites,
eating my own vocabulary.
It's inside the lungs, the liver,
deep purple and mourning:
aching like oranges never eaten.

Murano

steps out of a suitcase
bigger than her britches
no sturdy yardarm to steady
the pitched battle of her nerves
tosses anger overboard—
a svelte anchor of petty hurts—
in the venison canal
where meter eaters lunch with *e. coli,*
and she,
whose farce could ink
a thousand chips,
recalls
that loquacious bully in her
mom's glove compartment teaching
her a belch now buried
in Venetian glass . . .
suitcase tents, in case of breakage

The Gift

Everything Is a Gift
The sun is a gift
the moon is a gift
breaking the rules on a fall evening
is a gift.
And also,
the man walking through
the Square di Santa Lucia
on a Friday morning
with plants tied to his back
with plants in his hands
with plants on his arms,
with plants on his scapula,
spread like wings made of leaves
stacked to the eyes with plants
to the teeth with plants.
and singing singing singing
does anybody want any plants
plants, plants, beautiful plants
only 3 euros each-a-one
and then he sings to the top of
his lungs in the square
Francesca! Francesca! Where are you?
I love you!

Love Poem to a Stranger

Something more, something more
something wild and unbound
and beautiful and earthshaking
something inside the soul
something that the heart murmurs
In all the chambers
This life
This love on a country road
this swirling current
this sweet sweet boy with
the fucked-up teeth
and a girl he met just yesterday
hand in hand, climbing up the hill
this will cure your asthma
this country fuck in the wilderness
shhhh

love in the meantime
the trees whisper
the crickets holler
love in the meantime
the kisses on the crevice
of your collar bone
behind the neck, touching the fingers
because tomorrow tomorrow
I'll be gone and you'll still be here;
there will be nothing left but you,
sexy and 23, pants slip down,
belt around your ass
make love to the muse,
legs spread eagle in the trees
underneath the electric pole
shhhh. fuck me suck me eat me alive
piece by piece like gelato on your lips.
love is a ghetto filled with broken-down streetcars,
abandoned and hopeless,
with starving ghosts living inside them.

Alexandra Kostoulas

I Attend a Poetry Reading

The fellow reading poetry at us wouldn't stop.
Nothing would dissuade him:
not the stifling heat; the smoky walls
with their illuminated clocks;
our host, who shifted anxiously
from foot to foot.
Polite applause had stiffened
to an icy silence:
no one clapped
or nodded.
No one sighed.
Surely he must understand that we had families
waiting for us, jobs
we had to get to in the morning.
That chair was murdering my back.
That cappuccino
tasted unaccountably of uric acid.
Lurid bullfight posters flickered
in the red fluorescent light—
& suddenly I knew that I had died,
& for those much too windy readings of my own
had been condemned
to sit forever in this damned cafe.
A squadron of enormous flies
buzzed around the cup of piss
I had been drinking from.
Up at the mike, our poet of the evening
grinned,
& flicked his tail,
& kept on reading.

What We Do for Each Other

You're slouched on line
at the department store,
a t-shirt in your desultory
hands, a t-shirt about
which you feel ambivalent
as mid-afternoon, suspended
in a leaky grey haze,
when the woman in front of you
turns her head and gauges
the shirt as if about to paint it:
still life with cotton knit.
"What a *lovely* purple," she
exclaims, as if it had been steeped
in juices of rare shellfish
and shipped from Tyre.
                              "It *is* nice,
isn't it," you say, lapping a sleeve
on your arm, and the two of you,
heads bent companionably,
celebrate the good news,
before going out separately
into the grey afternoon.

My Simpler Nature

I want to go staggering in an orchard.
And meet the Spirit of the Land.

I want to defy evolution
And find a simpler nature.
I campaign for an atavistic revolution.

I want to find the land's true
Fair market value
Measured not in dollars
But time.

I want to splash in an ocean of time.

The desert is pregnant with time.
The orchards are ripe with time.
Now *that* is a property value.

I'm gonna get me a mule
And ride down into the canyons
Like a cowboy butterfly.

Dance Floor

No one is sure when old Herschfeld started
dancing; "I'm Astaire," he'd crack,
shuffling slowly to music that spilled
from his window and followed him
around his grassless, sunbaked backyard.

When Lila Hagler hung her wash,
she'd glower as he'd tango
in a glare of Latin music,
one hand on his chest,
one arm pointing straight toward her.

"He oughta be paintin' that house,"
she'd mutter, pinning her Pete's
long johns to the rope. "But no,
the fool man tangos outside all morning so's
I can barely stand to watch."

Herschfeld's illness gradually
stole his legs, depleted his strength
'til his tangoing was done. Soon
his humble dance floor lay deserted,
silent beneath a late September sun.

His kids came from Omaha for the will,
shaking their heads at the lawn's tawdry
bareness. They could not see a dance floor,
nor hear clasped in wind's teeth
whisks of an old man's final tango.

A Mother's Sorrow Grows Weary of Change

I gasp the morning chill, beating my fists
against the gray sky as the day creeps in to rouse me.
Fog stretches under my skin, ties my tired cells over my ribs
and strings my asthmatic lungs in kindergarten bow ties.
My morning bare feet dangle on the hardwood floor.

Sitting near the open back door,
I shiver as the sea air tumbles in
over the black and white floor tiles,
blows the oiled scent of black coffee through the cottage,
blows the leaves of doorstop branches,
blows haggard and brown long limbs
toward the kitchen door where the first signs of light
coax leaves that submit to a solemn autumn.

Behind the bedroom door my daughter dances
in front of a long mirror; she belts off a newly found tune
of Barbra Streisand's which swirls on a spinning black record.

She dashes off to beat the morning school bell,
her long hair fluffed to match her classmates'; they're all clad
in cable knit sweaters again, dawdling in jeans and '60s garb.
I watch as she leaves and know that
I am afraid every time that she does.

A Contemplation of Cows

On the phone
I'm chewing the fat
with my daughter
and I tell her
that my youngest granddaughter,
her niece, Elyse,
wants to be a cow
when she grows up.
I picture my daughter
cuddling the cradle,
as she chortles,
"Yes, that makes sense.
We grow up,
get married,
get fat,
spout milk."
Then I add,
"We go out to pasture
to curdle, gorge and graze."
Moo, Moo, Moo.

I Know Cooking

There's comfort in cooking.
The use of the hands
to shape the dough, or a poem.
The click and clatter of the instruments
or tools of one's trade:
knives, spoons,
pens, keyboard.
Then there's the memory,
the taste of your mother's bread,
an aroma of burnt toast,
the sweet tang of strawberry,
a line from Rumi.
There's the mystery in the wait,
the tick of the oven clock,
the flat fall of punctuation,
the bell telling me it's done.

Then the cooling-off period,
a chance to doubt—
too much salt,
too much pepper,

too many words.
Only in the eating do we know for sure.

And, if while scrubbing the dirty dishes
the poem seems an afterthought,
a useless clatter of metaphors,
I can always begin again,
shape the dough,
rearrange the spices,
contemplate nutrition.

Alive

Fear slides through my porous skull
Lifting me
Electrifying me
Pressing a magnifying glass to my pulse
I know that I am
Not because I think, or love,
Or any of those trite clichés.
I know that I'm alive
because I sparkle in the fire of fear.

Near Sleep

He says, "You had such a hard life."
I know he means, "I'm sorry."
He says, "I'm so proud of you."
I hear, "Goodbye."
He says, "Love you."
He's asking me to let him go.

He was the toy surprise in my box of government cheese
My cast-off life.
He found me in the bathroom sink
Surrounded by the other things she didn't want
He didn't wash me down.
Now he's finished. Worn away.

Everything changes, but
This is too much.
A knife poised at the cord that tethers me to earth
Like the Underdog balloon in the Macy's Day parade.
I'll be lost forever,
swirling away.

I don't want to be left behind
But, I promised.
When the others went, one by one
In violence and despair
I promised not to follow.
You should not bury your children.

A tiny fist squeezes my throat
Forcing spit from my eyes.
I take it back
Don't leave me too.
Nose bleed in the stratosphere.
Put me in the earth with your Dad, safe.

Psalm 2003

I am weary with calling.
My throat is dry
My eyes fail
While I wait for God.

I was like you once
Careless with hope
Living with abandon.
Heedless to the calling.

The whittling began for me,
As it will for you.
With love I enfolded
But could not hold them.

First mother, then papa,
A husband, my son.
Loss like a stone
Tied to my neck.

I am weary with calling
My blood dries
My limbs wither
While I wait for God.

I Get Down on My Hands and Knees

But the floor never seems to get completely clean.
I wash it again only to find cat hair,
black, like my Sari, and grey
fringed with white, like Bob's;

long and gracefully arranged on the floor
in the shape of an "S," like the first letter of my name.
Across the room, brown and white fur
clings in a clump to a Lalique vase.

The grandfather clock chimes 4:30 A.M.
Now I've cleaned the floor twice,
and by the time 6 o'clock chimes.
I've done the floor four times more.

One cat sleeps on the table,
another is curled in a basket atop the bureau.
Someone's cat is in the seat of my Queen Anne chair.
A cat I've never seen is stretched out along the back of the sofa.

Two more cats huddle over the food dish.
One bites and chews—waits for the second cat to bite and chew.
Each ignores the other.
Five more cats are asleep on my bed.

I open the closet and three cats jump out,
veer around the corner and race down the hall.
With this many cats, I think,
I'll find another place to live,

but before I can get to the door,
four cats roll into a ball that become the wheels of a car.
I drive off thinking
I'll need to wash the floor—quick—once I am fully awake.

About Attachments

This was when I was 21 perhaps,
already old enough to understand
about attachments—the complications—
and I didn't want them. Done with
"trying to make it happen."

Even then, I must have known I couldn't
make anything happen, not really,

---

that it was all predestined somehow,
but still, I thought "I" played the lead—
and my best friend with two children

was going through a divorce,
sleeping with her attorney. She told me
and I remember thinking how clever she was
getting her home phone to ring at his place
so her ex thought she was home with the children.

That sounds like the easy part—but not then,
this was back in the sixties. Her boys young,
newly in big-boy underpants, saying things like
I'm going to kill you, and calling each other
Dog face, Poo-poo head, and the like.

Over coffee, we talked about meeting someone,
not even asking his name, no "attachments,"
just a few hours of passion, pure, uninhibited,
going at each other with no promises,
just doin' it then walking back into the mess

we thought we had made our lives.
I looked at her boys—junior assassins!
I didn't want to be there, didn't want
to go to any place I had ever been.
I left—walked the day until it slipped

into night—until going home
was the only right thing to do.

The Fall

When her hearing died and
she lost the words for things,
daughter became sister;
she spoke to her first-born
in spite of the word, better,
and to the son she called brother,
sometimes husband,
heard more with her eyes
than with that damn hearing aid
she kept losing till
we stopped bothering her with it . . .
After the FALL four years ago
when she couldn't get up
from her living room floor . . .
two days before a neighbor
smelled an odor . . .
our mourning began
imperceptible as her falling,
her struggle to eat food
she stopped tasting
to please us,
falling . . . so light . . . so feather
broke her hip and rambled
lost in 93-year-old countryside;
her eyes flagged us down.
When we left she waved;
a smile teared her face.

After they brought her back
from the hospital and back again,
doctors listened to her heart
with their stethoscopes, satisfied.
Nurses took blood, gave tests;
the word was, she's doing ok.
Not one of them checked her eyes for a pulse.

Mother, I Almost Loved You

My sins   bleed on your pillow
   cold, cold, and then dead
Pay attention
          when I scream

Mother, where were you?
Where were you when
     my cradle was sold   with me still inside
               twitching and turning invisible.
Never mind the holidays
And   elevator trains and   Polish borders

you lost my temper   in afternoon nightmares
          a girl with no dolls
Chinese restaurants   lost and digested
tightened fists angry shouts

     crashing waves of listerine
   pissing on dreams   fertilizing neuroses
          snowmen with purple lips and ejaculating buttons
   cough before killing   pray for us

   Pray for the   earned derangement of
gargling warm salt water while drowning

          Please tell me I was adopted, Mother.
     Tell me where you were.
Tell me who you are.

A New Land

His mother
sent him to me
with clean hands.
He didn't know
how to squeeze juice
from my rosebuds
was afraid
to sully himself
in my oven
didn't know
the language of lust.
How I took that man
on a cold winter's night
in Manhattan
bathed him in green jello
glided it across
steamy flesh
ran his fingers through it
watched his penis rise
from fallow fields
guided him
across crevices
of my mountain ranges
taught him
how to swim
to the holy land
how to pray
for the great coming
how mother
no longer
knew best
in this new land.

Whatcha Gonna Do about Today?

I want to stop everyone
I meet on the street
hey you
hi there
I'm talking to you
you with the mopey eyes
and down-turned mouth
yeah, it's you

146 / ONTHEBUS   Roz Levine

I'm talking about.
Say, man
don't get pissed at me
just want to give you
a pearl of my wisdom.
Today is the first day
of the rest of your life.
Know what I mean?
First could be the last
could be your last friggin' day
on planet earth.
So whatcha gonna do about it?
Get the picture
this is your life
the one you're in right now.
Don't like it?
Move on
shake it up
make it bigger, better
make it what you want.
But man,
no shit
you could be
struck by a bullet
hit by a car
have a stroke
any minute.
So whatcha gonna do about today?
Huh, whatcha gonna do about today?

Roz Levine

The Seine from the Window, Notre Dame

Birds on the table
of Deux Magot
dart between wine
glasses and lip
stick stained
butts for pretzels
and crumbs.
Warm for the
first time in days
in my black
leather jacket,
black velvet scarf.
He loves me,
he loves me not.
I think of the man
who I don't yet
know will send me
the dark purple
iris, color of a
bruise that doesn't
fade

Go

(after Constantine Cavafy's "Ithaca")

If you dream of Aphrodite, of the baths and seas
around her as she rises naked out of history,
forget her. Dream of others. She's only
the woman at the bus stop
you cannot remember.

Note that most people cannot see in the dark,
some have no sense of direction, others
try to be lovelier than the night, and at the end
of the long valley children on tricycles
sing about summer storms.
Is it you who lull them all
into afternoon naps,
who inhabit their dreams as a stranger?

Save something you want for yourself
from this vortex. The final breath. A glimpse
of the one who watches day and night and even
when the door closes. There are many
good memories: a long back rub after hard work,
that gleaming ivory wedding dress, the soft music
of wind chimes. Know
that the seasons wear us down while we sleep.

Never forget the morning light
misting through trees, the sharp smell
of forest fungus under thick layers of pine needles,
the mouth-watering fragrance of invisible apple orchards.
Who are you today? What are you waiting for?
You are not hostage. The world is not watching.
Take the first step. Go.

Fires

Once Dad found a few inches of rank water
standing in the bottom of his shoes.
He lifted one, sniffed, and stretched his eyes wide
as he said *Conrad pissed in my shoes.*

Mom shook her head.
Conrad, a silent three-year-old, said nothing.
His dark, uncut hair shielded him perfectly from our gaze.

We were living in a furnished rental on Boutall Street, in New Orleans,
where a sewage canal cut through the backyard—
Bermuda grass tilled savage by fire-ants.
Sweltering afternoons sneaked in on tarry heels
and thick, honeysuckle air
stuffed every crack in the narrow house.

That was the year, Mom says, that it started to go bad,
the year that Dad plucked a bird-pepper from its bush
and popped it into his mouth—
red-faced, burning, he gagged down bread
until we thought he'd explode.

That year, he dyed his hair black
and couldn't find the doorways,
blundering into them in the dark with bloated arms,
screaming at Mom while sudden thunderstorms
rocked the dresser handles and
Sonny and Cher sang *I got you, babe*
and Conrad, face down on the white couch,
bled from his nose.

Sometimes they left us alone and I imagined
that the strange house, emptied of adults,
would catch fire.
That year, clear fires
burned and burned in my mind,
stifling each breath,
squeezing my heart in their hairy fists.

Hard Bright Star

My breasts have fallen just enough for me to notice.
I consider hitching them up with something lacey, black.
Beneath umbrellas, shoppers pause at windows full of mannequins
with purple hair: day before Valentine's Day in Los Angeles
and the merchants are out.
In the most expensive store I can't afford, I finger silver netting
for the entertainment of my lover: mesh on mesh, a skirt the shade of dusk.
There's a picture book on cabaret—or is it cabernet—
oh, it's photographs of wine . . .
I settle on two pillar candles I actually need, cruise the sidewalk,
crush those scattered pods that make us break their lockets,
squeeze their little hearts, anything
required to release the seeds,
their sticky centers surrounded by ridges of tissue radiating
out like those images of flames sheathing Our Lady of Guadalupe
as the small rain pricks my face and doesn't care, and later, when the rain
is hard enough to have a kind of brightness
like a sun,
each droplet strikes the shingles like a match.

Privacy

I've made up my mind: I'm going to kill the bastard tomorrow. For thirty-six years he's been a burden to me, a leech that's been feeding from me, spiritually, financially, and yes, even physically. Now he's finally going to get what he deserves, that murdering son of a bitch.

He killed our mother, wrapping our umbilical cords around his leg at birth and causing a hemorrhage that took her life. And now I'm going to take his, that worthless parasite.

I've never had a moment's peace from him. He never let me alone, always with me wherever I went, ruining my life, depriving me of privacy. We were driven to grammar school together, went through high school together, where he dawdled his way through classes while I studied like a fiend. He even came to college with me and read comics while I struggled with my graphic arts courses. I was so embarrassed dragging him up on the stage with me to receive my B.A., but I was stuck with him. Jesus, we even had to go to the bathroom together. He sat there smirking while I wiped my behind. I've had to look at his empty-headed smirk for 36 years without respite. Even when I turned my head as far as I could and looked out of the corner of my eye, I could still see his vapid expression in my peripheral vision. No privacy at all.

The doctors told us that joined at the abdomen as we were, we shared a common liver and a maze of major arteries, making it almost impossible to separate us without causing the death of one, or more probably, both of us. I asked him whether he thought his useless life was worth saving in comparison to mine, and he said he wasn't going to commit suicide for the likes of a prissy, obsessive-compulsive dweeb, and that it was just as disgusting for him to be stuck with a self-centered holier-than-thou horse's ass like me.

From then on it seemed as though he'd do everything in his power to make me angry and disrupt my life. After college, I'd managed to get work ghosting at home as a graphic artist, taking on the overage from companies who needed part-time help. I barely made enough to support us, but I was proud of my accomplishments nevertheless. He just sneered at my mention of them. I had a computer workstation set up in one bedroom of our apartment, and of course he had a computer right next to mine. As I labored away on a project, he would find a pornographic website and leer at the sight of all the naked women. He'd begin to masturbate, and the hormones pumping through his bloodstream would enter mine. I'd find myself with an erection, trying without success to keep my concentration through a red haze of sexual tension. When his orgasm came, I would collapse in exhaustion next to him, while he laughed and laughed.

I tried to make him understand that I was our sole means of support, and that keeping me from doing my work would only be detrimental to both of us, but he didn't seem to care. He found someone to supply him with drugs and liquor, and would spend hours in an alcoholic stupor which I unwillingly shared. When he got sick afterward, I had to kneel at the toilet with him, totally repulsed, as he spewed his vomit over the bathroom floor.

We had several fights over the drugs, with me trying to pull the vile stuff away from him and flush it away, and he pummeling me with one hand while grabbing at the junk with the other. He took massive amounts of cocaine, and my heart thundered with the strength of the stuff coursing through my system. I had to fight the feelings of invulnerability and outlandish energy, and try to maintain some kind of emotional and spiritual stability in the midst of the flood of sensory overload.

Gradually, he stopped shaving and washing, while I strove to keep clean and presentable. He stood outside the shower holding the curtain closed as I bathed myself as best as I could. He stank with the rancid reek of sweat and unwashed flesh. The more I complained, the more he strove to wear his filth like a badge of accomplishment. I began hating him more and more, and tried to imagine ways in which I could get rid of him while keeping myself alive. I spent hours each day wracking my brain, but each method I thought of resulted in my death as well, or my arrest for his murder. I had to laugh at that: one conjoined twin placed under arrest for the murder of the other. Would they finally separate us for the trial, or would I have to drag his corpse around with me to the courtroom? They probably wouldn't spend the money on the surgery, considering I'd probably get the death penalty anyway.

I suspected that in some lizard-brained cunning way, he knew that I'd gone through this scenario in my mind to its ridiculous end and that he was safe from my depredations. He redoubled his efforts to anger and mortify me.

He'd go into online chat rooms and send love notes to lonely women, signing my name, inviting them up for an evening of cocktails. When one of them accepted the invitation and arrived, he'd go naked to the door in spite of my trying to keep him back, and the poor girl would go screaming down the stairs to the street while peals of laughter issued from his mouth.

My clients had all since stopped coming around; the sight and smell of my brother combined with his rudeness had closed the door on whatever small bits of work came my way. I began to sit next to him passively and allow whatever drugs he'd consumed to take me away as well. Our small savings were dwindling, most of them having gone for narcotics. Previously, we'd had our food delivered by a local grocery store, but now the boy would just leave it on the landing and run, afraid of the rank, stinking monstrosity that would open the door.

We fought more and more then, swinging and kicking at each other until one of us would land a blow that would send us both flopping onto the floor like some beached prehistoric relic, and we'd both lie there panting and snarling, straining to get our overbalanced bodies up onto each other for a *coup de grace*. The neighbors, disgusted with the stench and noise, called the police, who came bursting into our apartment, then packed out gagging when they saw what was scrabbling in the filth before them. My brother watched them leave, and began to laugh, cackling in the most vile, demented tone I had ever heard issue from his mouth.

Oh my God, why couldn't we have been like other people? Why did I have to have this malodorous albatross clinging to me every moment? He had become a human cancer, a walking, talking tumor eating its way across our connective tissue to consume me, centimeter by centimeter. Why couldn't I just walk away into another room, shut the door, and be rid of the presence of this other being, even for one minute?

Wait. Why can't I? Of course. There is a way for me to bathe in the experience of being away from him. Yes, if only for a few minutes, or perhaps even an hour, I would have my privacy, a time to relish the peace of silence, without the phlegmy gurgle of his breathing, the sight of his mad eyes staring back into mine, the rotting hole of his mouth laughing at me.

And so, I'm going to kill him tomorrow. I'm going to put a screwdriver into his eye and stir his brains with it, and then I'll watch the life drain out of him. I figure I'll have a while before our liver shuts down and our blood becomes poisonous enough for me to die as well, but those moments will be like gold to me. For the first time in my life I'll be *alone*.

My Grandmother's Shoes

Ocean waves, memories, and dreams collide with the
freeway concrete wall. By the seashore, the blue song of
spring is a wide-ruled space of postcards floating in
secondhand clocks.

Distant
    Timeless
        Breathless

My grandmother's black leather shoes come into being
they walked thousands of miles
by water and land
from town to town
from prayer to candle
from body to soul
from earth to heaven

I can still see her now,
her spirit rising from the grave on the day of the dead
the rose fresh petals, the red carpet rolling
inside her purple colored eyes.

It is us now, at the altar
with our heroes made of wood and clay.
It is she who blesses the saint of the day
with her handmade cigar,
her cleansing hands
now holding mine, to keep
them warm and out of harm's way.

Last night at midnight I sat by the river
and saw my grandmother's shoes passing by and with their
wings disappearing behind the
black hills, my small hand
waving good-bye.

Before the Dawn

Above all else
you
you
above the trees
and the moon
and the stars
above the grass
and the streams
above the ocean
the sea
my dreams
that sail before me at night
like a silent movie

above
above
the earth
and it's gnawing
strenuous
day into night
night into day
destruction

above the roots and wheat fields
and day-to-day pleasure
you are my guide
you alone whisper
like tiny birds in my ear
whisper
like the spray from the wave crashing at shore
I carry you with me
light in my heart
lantern of love
above all else
you.

Prelude to My Parents' Divorce—1966

Must I know it again and again?
The precise ache of it a broken
tooth dreamed back and heavy

in my head where I watch
twin aortas bulge and billow
to apostasy, an apartheid of the hearts.

Six years old again, I pray
redress from the strictures tossed
tongue to tongue before me,

kneel as the gospel nears its end.
Gazing to heaven I see twin
christs cleaved from the cross.

Working Weeks

The unbroken stretches of days,
all in place . . . all in a line
at . . . the bank, the
counter, the grocery, its
list, the litany of
the mundane that saves
and damns us. Every-
day things, the incessant
demand of the body's needs,
mewling to be fed, eating,
excreting; next, to be
cleaned, to move.
Let us celebrate the
quotidian this rote
written census of the
senses tabulates: The
soap, the sink, the
kitchen, the hot water
heater, the uncovered
window, the unmade bed.

Notice

The annulment notice came today,
signed by the bishop, stating that
what we did on that day ten years ago
we did not do, undid, never happened.

Ten years! I'd forgotten the date,
but not even relearning it
could move me. Then they named
the place, not just the town but the inn,

which made me sadder, madder
than any of their questionnaires
inviting my rebuttal or response.
Why, I remembered the trees,

the tall green trees and blankets
of September light, a pond with lilies,
glassed porch, champagne, my quarrelling siblings
and best friend, best man, now dead.

I remembered my suit and white car,
my nervous night before, a prayer
the minister read, the chubby minister
who everyone said looked like my brother.

That day began, if nothing else, my past
ten years, steering me toward this moment
like my mother waving her handkerchief
in the landscaped drive. I shoved

the letter in a box marked DIVORCE,
along with a sheaf of legal papers—deals,
decrees, the stuff of many tears—clicking it
closed for good, for real. This happened.

Breastfeeding at a Nude Beach

Halfway between the net
of a volleyball game and the firm sand
of a hunched tide, a woman's covering
herself so no one will see
how her baby's lips press down
exactly at the drubbing smack
of ball meeting joined hands,
and swallows with the muffled leap
that slaps it back: the ecstasy
that tiny creature
believed would never return—
that womb-thump of pure wistfulness—
sounds in its perfect ears again.

Slow Shoes

Reluctantly she hurries, late
to work. Her ankles and knees
won't let her dash the last four blocks
to the bus-stop, but she spurts
a few steps anyway, to show herself
and the boss who doesn't suspect
her miscalculation yet, she wishes
she hadn't lingered in the shower's lush
porous whispering, sipped juice and coffee, scooped
sweet cantaloupe down to the rind, ironed
a kiss of memory with her blouse, wondered
about the daughter squirming at school,
and wavered on the phone with mother
who dragged her potted callas deeper in the shade
of lemon trees. She slows down, certain the bus
will not be delayed, and if it hustles off
exactly when she would've sat, drenched
and panting, could she have lunged this final distance,
she'll stroll across the street, unfold
a newspaper, and ponder
who's selling shoes, the kind one can only walk in, slowly.

The Vowels of Broken Promises

Petty things ensnarl me: a motel room
with a kitchen, and the toaster falters.
I've driven three hundred miles to help
bury a friend, and I can't even firm
this slice enough to lather it with butter
and apricot jelly. Maybe there'll be finger food
to comfort us at the widow's, but I need something to sop
this coffee up now. Last night I dreamed of an inferno,
watching other people being born, and from the frothy side,
them gazing back at my agitation, waiting for my turn.
The entrance was very small, and to spill
through it meant finding a cleft in an abutment
which you could squeeze your fingers
into and loosen the soothing tip.

                    Suddenly alone,
I saw a wrinkled face I couldn't recognize
in profile: an eye, unblinking, was staring out
of the center of an ear as though it could see
what I was afraid to say about my friend this afternoon,
my cravings for the illusion that he is crouched
at the core of our slippery dance, abrupt renditions
of a song's concavities heard by no one else. Its roar
ripens inward, the quivering vowels of broken promises.

Bill Mohr

The Photograph

She tucks her hair back behind her ears, looks down briefly, then casts her eyes up at the
      camera. My mother is five.
She feels invaded, wary,
maybe a little curious.
Her eyes are blue and startling,
even through the sepia.
Her older sister, my aunt, looks frankly at the photographer, her forehead arched, its wide
      expression. She can see it all and will see more than she'll ever want to.
My mother and aunt are standing amid their cousins.
You can already tell the two sisters are destined for beauty.
There is a wood fence in the background. One of the cousins has a smudge on his grinning
      face. It is 1928.
So much is yet to happen to them and the world.
Their backyards will be bombed.
Hitler, Stalin, and Churchill will rise to power. The sisters will fall
in love with foreign soldiers.
They will give birth to American children.
I stare at the photograph.
I wish I could have been a child with them, playing in the garden, running into the house to
      pound on the piano, then back out again.
My grandmother calls us in for tea.
At night my grandfather puts down
his pen, adjusts his glasses, and tells us a story or reads from *The Water Babies*. My mother
      insists she has seen a fairy in the garden.
My aunt rolls her eyes and says
that isn't possible.
I wish I had known them then.
Before my grandmother packed her things and sailed away on the Queen Mary.
Before the bombs fell.
Before the world caught fire.

Before all their hearts were broken.

Learning How to Pray

She hands me a china cup,
steaming with black tea, sweetened
with condensed milk. At four,
it is the best thing I have ever tasted.
She is my mother and we have been apart
a long time.
Outside the rain sounds like tiny horse hooves
moving across a gray sky.
The world is good and clean.
I smell the wet pavement and salt air,
the breath of the ocean close by.
Its giant sigh does not disturb me.
Living here with my mother brings everything
to life.
She's magic.

She is able to put a round stone into a pot
of earth and a while later
a yellow star flower will be living there,
open mouthed as I am at my mother's abilities.
I will learn more of how the world gives such gifts.
If I wait and watch, soon I will know a lot.

I should have been more specific with God.
But no one taught me how to pray properly,
to give thanks for what I had.
The earth and God will take their due.

I can't remember if I prayed for her
the day she died. I can't remember
if I prayed for myself. The rain
clattered outside like horse hooves.
There wasn't much else between me
and the life that was pressing upon me.
But still, I can't tell you what I've learned.

Listen, I will tell you what I do know.
There is a trap door leading
to the worn floors of heaven.
Once in a while I catch an angel
there and its wings brush
against the throb of my temple.
It folds its wings and arms
and waits
for me to either recognize it
or let it go.
So patient. So unrelenting.
So willing to forgive.

Lisa Marguerite Mora

Voyager

Before tiny fingers
could scarcely hold pencil to paper—

(not quite a baby, yet, barely a boy . . .)
I wrote myself off
as unworthy
                    —of anything.   My world—a medicine,

                    too strong too swallow, temporary
                    as sugar-balls, melting
                                        on my tongue—

the moments—
forgotten as chalk marks, disappearing
—down a driveway
in a warm summer rain . . .

                    And me
                    in my sailor suit, captain
                    of a thousand dreams,
                                        set to sea
                                        in a sewer pipe.

the gnostic from surrender teaches borrow for once desire

once history peoples gossip with bills & informs
on was to be glory
steals from city libraries
sells
furtiveness
image
i asked paul why did you steal so many books
the court said six thousand dollars restitution
he said i found i could get away with it
so i kept doing it
words alias
rose sun burnt & losings our weepings. it is old to be found
old
charged with grand theft when he was twelve. he crawled under
the bed his mother & step-dad were sleeping in & his mother
thought she heard a noise woke her husband & he listened
said it was probably nothing the wind
outside an older man sat waiting in a car. he went in to steal
thirty-five dollars he knew was in the billfold
in his step-dad's pants
paul got the billfold crawled out of a window & the two of them
split the thirty-five
later paul found five one-hundred-dollar bills
one each in the middle of
each plastic container

                    went to memphis & bought a silk shirt
got a haircut
a twelve-year-old walking around memphis cashing hundred dollar
bills
his mother & his step-dad called the police & within two days
paul was charged with grand theft
the first time when he was twelve

the library book thief
he got four years probation & restitution
some say his love of poems to many girls are all written to the same
love
last sunday he stopped over & called three women trying to get a
date to the movies
i drove him to a thrift shop on fairfax
he bought a pair of shoes made in japan
three dollars
          he said these kind make your feet sweat
needed them for the job he was doing

he got fired a week later
                         lives in venice in a friend's camper
the name of his first book of poetry is
                  blood banks & bad nerves.

John Garfield

1.

Money can't buy back that look, an eye
straying back into itself, into desperation,
knowing itself a loser. Curly haired
man-boy, innocent really, found-out
trying to do the damned right thing.
What is more than love? Not even dying.
How many killers do you think there are
in the world who really never meant to kill
anybody, or who changed their minds
about throwing a fight, or to whom
Lana Turner was Helen waiting,
their only chance in a lifetime of grit
to get the dame. To his blowzy surprise,
the price for seeing all is everything.

2.

It's not your fault virtue always finds you
believing in it and therefore expendable,
in the last act, and you look astonished
at how paltry virtue can be
and how hilarious doom is, a joke
of a sort, except you laugh alone.

Lana really did love you, man. Much as
she loved anything. She just hated
the touch of a tool in her ringed hand.
Just your luck. You always let them
love you exactly the way they wanted to
and they never ever had to explain.
I feel where you're coming from, man;
waitresses call me honey, too, every time.

The Meek

The first year was a slip. The father,
young, an artist,
had great plans to follow. The mother
alone from birth, let go.

What else was she to do? She had
breathed and that was
all it took to create another person.
Creation would

from then on terrify her. Yes.
She would go it
alone, no problem. The second year
was equally as busy,

for the mother and her child
were taken in by
a man darker than themselves, a foreigner.
She couldn't help it.

She had seen that the foreigner lived in filth,
so she scrubbed
his dirty bathtub until the bone of it shone.
That's all she did.

And so the foreigner took them in,
this mother, meek,
and her child from another man, now
long gone.

The third year passed and language
fell upon the child the way
leaves fall upon the earth during autumn:
the child cold,

but blanketed by the inevitable end.
The child had enough
sense to accept the fact of words,
to not ignore

what he would later understand
to be his only
inheritance. From then on the years
would blur together.

Air

He comes without warning, without knowledge, comes breathless
with the steep stair's creak and damp sheets and the thought
that maybe the dreams were real—the Douglass boy, dead
twenty years, tossing the ball high into the air so that it hangs
and hangs and I shout, *Jesus, Bill nice toss,* and the whole world
hinges on anticipation, and the not quite seeing him walk away
and into the house and the basement and extension cord
turned deadly, slipped over a water-pipe, over his neck. Once,
he asked if I'd go down with him, or I think he did. And since
that I've gone again and again, down the steps, into the warm
wet heat, past a humming boiler. And I know—or I wonder—if
that slight catch in the chest was really just a warning after all
and was his, the ball, the inevitable pause and drifting down then
this, as if the ball had hit dead center and now, I can't get enough

air. On the news they say it's poisoned, that at the metal plant on Pine
some nightwatchman tripped a switch or fell asleep so that a valve
held shut for years exhaled sweet and sick, like a last breath
spewing something overnight pitting cars with rusted
cadmium or some kind of lead so they shine red and raw
And though they say there is no danger, I worry if I left something ajar
a window or door so that the poison entered, creeping in like memory,
or dream, collecting in the hollows of the skin, settling on our tongues,
is that a sore there or there, was it there yesterday, how long. Jesus,
I can't breathe, and the ball hangs and hangs, and there is

Bill, standing on the edge of the drive chewing or spitting—the one
I always thought would be the first to get laid, to drink, to smoke
a cigarette, get out of the one-street cul de sac with the sign that said no-
outlet and the house on the hill that was his and not his. But hung
shadowed at morning and at night boiling with glass and Billy taking
that deep breath of his—you could actually hear it sucking in—and then
explode in laughter or in rage. It scared me then. And since. And now
I'm having trouble breathing when I walk down stairs or lift my boy
above my head or dance or laugh when he throws the ball with all
his strength and I say, *Jesus, that was some toss* and I see

Bill. Scratching at my window or creeping in like smoke or metal
floated into air to coat my lungs like laughter or one long sob. Today,
I'll remember to take my pills, play ball, hold him close, lock
the windows. Breathe. Breathing Billy, *nice toss, Bill.*

Child in White

Whistles, crashes, screeches fill the air.
Lights from the screen on the wall flash across the room
to spotlight a round, white mound on the couch.
Her short arms and legs hang limp like a rag doll.
Eyes shut, two crescents rest on her full cheeks,
Red and black ladybugs, motionless on her nightie
join in her slumber.

She lies on her darkly clad mother, dozing in peace,
proud of her creation. They are one unit, held together
by an inseparable force, like layers of strata on a mountain
pushing skyward. These layers, glued to one another,
do not know about the fires that burn deep below,
fires that break through periodically,
exploding in a fierce display, bursting forth in a dramatic
release of tension, reshaping the layers, and the bonds
that cement them together.
They know not what lies ahead.

Beneath the sleeping mother another layer shows itself.
It is firm and dense; it is the foundation beneath the others.
I am the base that gave rise to the life above me,
the life after me.
I am that lowest layer, the one who has seen many explosions,
who has been pounded down to crack and splinter and crumble.

I've seen the fires burn out, soldering the layers together
ever tighter and stronger. I've felt the eerie calm that follows,
the silence that wraps itself around the mountain
like a healing blanket. I've watched the embers cool,
the snowcap form on its crest.
I inhale the peaceful splendor of this mother and babe,
and wonder what storms lie ahead for this child in white.

Blue Fish

My dream. A green canoe, a pool full
of blue fish, my stepfather's body
a dead mackerel floating on top.
I know his story. He wasn't fishy
or even a deadbeat dad. He got up
every morning & went to work
selling cigarettes. He paid for Mom's
care when I put her in a nursing home.
I put her there because she couldn't chew,
she couldn't swallow. Pieces of food hung
in her mouth. No front teeth & she sucked food
like Tom sucked cigarettes before he died,
lung cancer. At the hospital I ordered speech therapy
to help chew & swallow better,
but they let her go home carrying soiled
pajamas & a sandwich wrapped in wax paper.

I cried a lot back then. I really didn't know
what to do. I didn't want to be her parent.
To feed and help her out of bed. Or change diapers.
Or wipe her ass clean. When Mom died
I made sure they didn't forget to send
the false teeth & glasses to the funeral parlor
because I loved her & didn't want her
to look like a blue fish gulping air.

Dylan Thomas Walks into a Bar . . .

Fuck poetry,
with its phantom diseases,
its word ghosts
curling like fog
around buildings,
wisps of exhaled smoke
—shadow hucksters
shifting colors,
doing backflips,
somersaults.

A youthful tattoo
no longer desired,
he's lost at sea.
Dropping anchor,
he devours baby starfish,
drunk on moonlight and sea brine.

He collects
scraps of paper,
thought fragments
he stitches together
with fine thread and needle,

    Aware that pain
lacks imagination,
                that art
suffers fools gladly,
the barfly messiah,
already 39 years old,
finishes his whiskey.

Coyote

At first it was just a suspicion, a panic-induced flash,
amalgam of all those times he had tried before—
the jet-pack, the dynamite, the super glue.

Yet there he was, smoking a thick cigar
under the pitchfork shadow of the cactus,
the long, thin bones neatly piled by his feet.

Two Women

—to the memory of Alana Barbara Williams, artist,
born February 2, 1941; murdered December 23, 1995

Friends. As true as time and geography allowed.
If one said *Iowa*, the other talked
flatlands and farmhouses; wide, tilled fields.
Alana's longed-for, often-envisioned home:
centered on a lonely tract, bounded by oaks.
Winter. A frozen stream. A woodstove.
North wind. She, huddled near, wrapped in quilts.

In brazen, fluorescent Los Angeles, her boots
clicked over polished floors. She curled
her hair; read the future; capriciously sketched
her cast-off men dead (hands folded, faces in repose);
bedclothes exquisitely disheveled.

That last conversation:
    Alana: *I've been slashing my thighs for years.*
Permanent stigmata, as though, born and bred Catholic,
she could fit Thomas', or Jesus' sandals.

Who would have thought: Homicide.
And what did the coroner say:
    Those old scars?—self-inflicted?
    Alana: *I want out. It's what I think about.*

The movie I watch is her murder.
These mountain winds sift snow,
like salt, under my poorly fitted door;
the draped plastic, tacked-up blankets, useless.

But it is *her* door that opens and opens to cold.

Impression

They had impressions in their minds
that smashed the world of art as it was known.
Renaissance perfectionism started an angry
revolution which ripped the canvas and heart
of the mad artist, only to produce spectacular
slices of real life, that when I have the pure
pleasure of looking at them, jump off the canvas
and become one with the universe.
I stand in front of the Irises and one by one
tears run down my cheek.
And all of a sudden, as if someone had died,
I burst into uncontrollable sobs.
The blues, the violets, the greens, the whites,
the strokes thick, deliberate.
The intensity, the pain, the torment,
the strokes, thick, deliberate.
The violets, the blues, the whites,
the delusions, the genius, the greens,
the strokes thick, deliberate,
looking like he pushed them there arbitrarily,
piling layer upon layer,
piling layer upon layer,
piling layer upon layer,
so that my eyes could touch the blues, the greens,
the strokes thick, deliberate, the pain.
He cut off his ear, for Christ's sake!
He tormented for the love of a woman.
He was put away in a mental institution.
But still he painted, he created beauty.
He created, he created, he created.
He took the beauty of his tortured soul
and adorned a canvas with it.
Sometimes when there is a starry,
starry night, I look up and remember
Vincent, and imagine that starry night
as he saw it, with the intensity
behind his eyes and the passion in his heart.

The Shirt

A hundred and fifty years after his death, George returned to his Wisconsin home. Kneeling outside the cellar window, he watched Dinah, his great-great-great-great-great-granddaughter, place his shirt inside the dryer. Observing this, George was mightily upset because until today, his shirt had not been touched. Upon his death, his wife Delia had placed it in a cedar chest, leaving explicit instructions with her family, that it remain inside, undisturbed, and that it be passed down from one generation to the next. Everyone had respected her wish . . . until now.

Although he hadn't seen her since his last visit in 1958, he knew it was Dinah despite her bulky frame and tightly permed hair. Her posture was still so erect, so perfectly straight as she sat on the dryer that spun beneath her. The shirt's bone buttons tumbled and fell, tumbled and fell inside the drum. And those were her legs, dancer's legs, still shapely, as she swung them against the door. She was looking his way, right through him into the deep night. She appeared angry, or maybe it was just the downward tug of an old mouth.

George scooted under the dryer vent, lying on his back, inhaling deeply. His spirits rose when he felt moist air blast against his cheek. Maybe it wasn't too late to stop the machine, he thought as he dashed out the back door. But it was locked.

George struggled to remember where he and Delia had hid the extra key. Then again, maybe he was just imagining this, maybe they had never locked their door. He couldn't recall. And what if the lock had been changed? Still, he told himself, *Think, think*. He gazed around the backyard. Nothing looked the same. The barn was gone. A rusty swing set by the oak tree was where their chicken coop had once stood.

George sniffed the air. He thought he detected the smells of Christmas: pine needles, a turkey roasting, wood smoke. He was running out of time. He had to stop the air from escaping, now, before it was too late. His clothes! He'd use his clothes! He jumped up and began to unbutton his Union Army jacket. But as soon as he managed to get a button half way out of its hole, his fingers slipped. The same thing happened when he struggled to undo his fly. Exasperated, he wanted to scream; instead, he yanked his hair with his hands. And then he crouched under the air vent again.

Now the smells of his children escaped. The scent of Joshua's skin after running through windswept fields. Baked apples on Abigail's sixth birthday. And the mossy fragrance of wet leaves stuck to the bottom of Lizzie's boots. George began to panic. His eyes searched in desperation for something, anything to plug up the hole. Nothing! Nothing in the yard except a rusty coffee can, a pile of dead gladiola stems, and a pair of soiled garden gloves, sleeping in the grass. George grabbed the gloves and the can and went back to the vent.

Although his children's smells were weakening, he could still, if he inhaled into the depths of his being, discern them. He placed a glove under the opening and held it there until the fingers and the palm were filled to overflowing. Then he quickly twisted it closed. Before bolting over the pile of stalks, he sucked in their odors once more.

While tying a stem around the glove's wrist, the smell of Delia and the Fox River, where they used to swim, blew his way. The full force of the muddy banks and the sun on Delia's naked skin brought him to his knees. After struggling to his feet and placing the aroma-filled glove carefully on the ground, he held the other one under the opening. To steady his trembling, he tipped the coffee can bottom side up and sat down on it. As the second glove filled with the days of their early love, George snaked his body low, his belly skimming the ground. With his nose pressed against the glove, he breathed in the essence of his family as they swept past him.

Then sharp pain pierced George's side as the trails of war eked out of the dying shirt. Gun powder. Rotted boots. The stench from the dead and dying. The crushing buzz of swarming flies. The iron tang of blood.

George slid off the can and jammed it against the air hole in a futile attempt to halt the mayhem. Suddenly grief entered his spine and George collapsed, no longer able to move. As he began to lose consciousness, he heard a loud buzz.

Dinah jumped down from the dryer and removed the shirt. She shook it once. Twice. Each snap exposed the fabric's flaw: a deep gash in the right front panel. When she raised her arms to shake it a third time, the glove hit the ground and George's spirit, chasing Delia, wiggled up and away.

D. A. Roisler

All Hallows' Eve

Late afternoon shadows creep across the floor.
We sit beneath the window, share a pomegranate—
thin red juice spreads across the plate.
Already, I find I am losing the will to love you.
This thing between us a ghost already.
I make clumsy work of cutting the fruit.
You pull the knife from my hand and
show me how to peel back the rind instead,
exposing hidden caches of seeds which glow
neon red behind the white membrane.
You rub your thumb across a row of seeds,
dislodge them neatly into your palm.
Lacking your grace, I crush the seeds from
their alcoves, spill juice down my fingers.
My hands stained magenta,
a devourer of tiny gelatinous hearts,
I offer you the kill, wonder whether to ask
if you would stay another day with me.
Just inside the door, your shoes
beside my shoes. I roll the fibrous
core of a pomegranate seed
between tongue and tooth.

Litany of the Saints

Pray for us you disgruntled sons under the hoods of muscle cars and
Pray for us all you indolent daughters who believe you are nothing without the riveted
      attentions from men Daddy's age;
Pray for us you slow-witted, you mindless biscuit makers in clouds of flour-fog;
Pray for us you ice cream vendors on bicycles, pedaling back streets without enough change
      for a lousy five-dollar bill;
Pray for us you meatpacking apprentices with razor-edge knives and chain metal gloves
      ready, with your yellow rubberboots slipping on the killing floor;
Pray for us you frightened farmers' boys, landless, penciling in today's want ads with blue
      circles of hope;
Pray for us you runaways, you dropouts, you children who are forever in love with an
      amber bottle, you innocents, crazy with night sweats and dreams of fat-fisted fathers;
Pray for us you hitchhikers on the interstate, you failed suicides, you bubble gummy
      prostitutes with a stash of comic books & used condoms;
Pray for us and pray for us all you young Madonnas with pails of water and dirty rags, on
      your knees in executive offices at 3 in the morning, your two little ones still in
      diapers while you're not old enough yet to vote;
Pray for us all you unwanted, misbegotten children, now and forever.

Our souls flutter;
Our lives are in your hands.

The Only Truly One-Man Show

You do not die from being sick, you die from being alive.
—Montaigne

There is someone living my life, and I know nothing about him.
—Pirandello

*Like as the waves make towards the pebbled shore, so do our minutes hasten to
    their end.*
—Shakespeare

Old age ain't for sissies.
—Bette Davis

John, who considers himself as plain as his name, normally speaks aloud only in the presence of at least one other person, prepared to listen. But then, yesterday, Theresa-Angela, whom he considers as fancifully complicated as *her* name, cackled at him in her octogenarian's voice, "But of course you should talk out loud to yourself! Where can you find a better audience?"

So he's ready to try it. He stands in front of his bathroom mirror, searches for new liver spots, new wrinkles, new silver hairs which for some reason comb differently from his remaining auburn ones, and finally addresses his image. "Do you know what I've just done? I've walked into this bathroom with arms full of shirts which I intended to put into my bedroom's dresser drawers." He can't get himself to add aloud his judgment that this act is at least better than when he squeezed shaving cream onto his toothbrush, a few days ago. "You're getting to be too much, John." The latter condemnation he wrings out of himself audibly, however reluctantly. Then he spots his duplicate wristwatch from under his duplicate pile of shirts, and noon is noon even in a mirror. "Oh my God, it can't be noon already, can it?" His mirror image fails to reply, perhaps because John with his shirts is already zooming across the hall into his bedroom.

For cardiological purposes, John has to swim half a mile Mondays, Wednesdays and Fridays, and lunchtime is when his indoor pool is open to the public for a peaceful hour, between student classes mornings and afternoons. Ah, but is it really Wednesday? Muddle sloshes fearfully through John's mind. Yes, it has to be Wednesday, because last night he watched that one-man show on TV, where the credits at the end listed dozens of people. "So, you see," he says aloud, "if I put my mind to it, I *can* remember things. But I must hurry, or I won't be able to do all my laps." Perhaps Theresa-Angela is right. It really is pleasant to hear his own voice resounding in an otherwise empty apartment, a kind of reassurance he's still alive. But in his mind's ear, he hears the whistle that he's sometimes late enough to hear blown a quarter of an hour before the next batch of youngsters sixty years younger than himself enter the pool. On those occasions he can hear them, all screaming for some reason, while he dabs deodorant into his armpits in the lonely locker room. That's around the time he sometimes remembers he forgot to shave before going there. Well, today, at least, he has already shaved, although he has to check to make sure, and not with toothpaste, although—who knows?—maybe with.

He frantically crams changes of underwear and socks into what he calls his "beach bag," in memorium for the good old days he did not have to worry about skin cancer, remembers to lick stamps onto his morning's batch of letters, and, for the sake of exercise, rather than take the elevator he trundles down the twelve stories to empty his letterbox, crammed full with not only letters and subscribed to publications but the usual flyers about pizza deliveries and cut-price sales. It takes some juggling to keep his received mail separate from the mail he intends to post, as he trundles farther down to the second sub-basement where his car is parked. Remember, he orders himself in complete silence, the left hand is the In-Box, the right hand is the Out-Box, because he is only too painfully aware he is capable of putting the wrong handful into the mailbox four corners down his street.

And of course, wouldn't you know? He drives right past the mailbox, having forgotten he intended to stop there. So now he has to lose even more time by going two blocks out of his way to the local Post Office, where he relievedly makes sure he is inserting the right batch of goods into the slots. Phew, at least that's done!

In the swimming pool's parking lot, he reaches for his beach bag, and it isn't there. It isn't there? But of course it *has* to be there! Where else could it be? And how can he swim now, without his bathing suit, his goggles, his towel, his own special soap in a plastic box in the pouch to the right whereas his wallet is in the pouch to the left— "My God!" he exclaims aloud, for he recalls his driver's license, credit cards, pool subscription with photograph, money (and so on) are all in his wallet inside the missing beach bag.

He manages to recall he kept his eye on his car while he posted his letters, so no one could have stolen it from beside the driver's seat. Could he have absentmindedly taken the bag out with him, at the post-office, and set it down while he inserted his letters into their slots, then left it? He drives back there, but sees no beach bag beneath the slots. Could he have set it down in the garage before setting off, while he first put his car key into its door? After all, he was then having a hard enough time keeping his two batches of incoming and outgong mail straight. Or even have set the bag onto the car's roof while he fumbled with his keys, only to have it sail off with its contents into the street somewhere along the way? Panic squishes its hysterical fingers around his throat.

Nowhere in the streets back to his building does he see a beach bag, nor, damn it all to hell, anywhere on the two-way ramp or on the oil-splotched floor of his garage. Well, at least he knows what he has to do next, which isn't always the case. He has to zoom upstairs (with the elevator, for he never walks up the stairwell, which would be more exercise than his poor heart would allow him to survive) and immediately telephone the credit card people, a start to all the boring motions he shall now have to go through to set things straight. Guilt is the next reaction, for he feels it is a serious misdemeanor to have driven both ways without a license on him. "Damn, damn, damn!" he says aloud, alone in the elevator, thereby recognizing most convincingly the value of talking out loud to himself. "Hey, it really does relieve," he sees his mirrored image announce to him.

The elevator doors unguillotine themselves and a pair of young louts try to enter before John can exit. The he of the pair is wearing more gold rings in his earlobes and one nostril than the she, and of course neighbors no longer say "Good morning" to one another. In front of the front door John takes to be his own, he has to wonder in silence (for who can tell who's listening?) why now, of all times, does his key not work? "Who's there?" comes a woman's strident voice from behind the door. The possibility of his house-cleaner's having come a day early is still sloshing around on his inner television screen when he sees a name that is not his own behind a transparent plastic oblong, and he hears himself already proclaiming to the woman as to himself, "Whoops! I guess I'm on the wrong floor. Sorry." And of course when he wheels around he sees "10" as plain as day on the wall opposite the elevator's door. Surely it wasn't there when he exited the elevator. Well, two flights he can go, and does, up the stairs two at a time.

Confirming this is now indeed his own door, John could scream, because his key still does not work. Can he be losing his mind? Is this really and truly the onset of Alzheimer's,

Leslie Schenk

despite his extravagant tests? No, because the key he has been diddling with is the wrong one, the key to his storeroom, same brand, Yale. The correct key slides into the lock like a finger into peanut brittle, no, peanut *butter*, you fool. He swings open the door, and there, there on the chair beside the entry and exit from his apartment, depending, there sits his beachbag. "How can this be?" Has he spoken aloud? He's afraid so. Already a new habit?

Shame and relief flush through him alternatively, like suds and rinse in a dishwasher. His safety-valve of a scream never having happened, he has to talk with somebody, anybody. Cancelling his phone-the-credit-card-people preprogramming, John phones up Theresa-Angela instead, prepared to blast his excess steam into the wireless mouthpiece and thereby into one of her ears.

"Is that you, phoning me at lunchtime?" she crackles at him. "Haven't I begged you a dozen times not to phone me at lunchtime?'

John cannot recollect. "Have you? Why would you do that?"

"Do you never listen? Do you never register what I say? Because this bag of old bones can't eat when she's upset, that's why, and you always upset me. You upset me because you don't hear a word I aim at you. You don't listen."

"Theresa-Angela, I do listen, really I do. Only I can't retain."

"You're incontinent already?"

"Not that kind of retaining. Don't *you* ever listen? Don't you hear what I tell you? I don't know how many times I've told you my memory and I are going our separate ways, to the extent that I inflicted upon myself a brain-scan to see if Alzheimer's was starting (cost me a fortune, too), and they couldn't find any trace. They told me it's normal for people my age to become so preoccupied they get sidetracked, remember?"

"John, old squirt, I'm eight years older then you, and *I* don't get sidetracked."

"Oh, really? Do you remember what you ate for lunch yesterday?"

A long silence that does not really nudge itself along with ticks and tocks, but John feels it does. Finally, "Touchée," Theresa-Angela says, audibly distressed.

"And don't you think a bit of cocoa and sympathy, no, commiseration's the word, rather than bawling me out for something I can't help is called for—" But Theresa-Angela has hung up. Which means she too is facing up to the fact she is on the slippery slope. It isn't any comfort, to the contrary, to know that now they both know they are slithering down it, at their respective speeds, toward The End. Here it is, one P.M., and John has no appetite, none. Growing old, he figures, is the one thing you can do only alone, all by yourself, involuntarily, a one-man show, unassisted, unaccompanied. Ah, there is one other, dying, he recalls with a gulp.

"Well," he addresses himself in a statesmanlike voice, satisfyingly aware he sees himself in no mirror, "One of these days I'm going to put two slices of bread into the coffee machine and pour water into the toaster, which will blow up the whole place, me with it, and that will be that."

Dear Wonder Woman

Please protect my sister
through the trials
sent her way—
cancer,
operation,
radiation.

Do what I cannot—
place your body
in front of hers,
snap on those silver bracelets,
raise your wrists
to deflect the bullets

so that she
can have
some rest.

simply doc

old doc
hard-faced railroad engineer
tie slave
fixer of motor things
hammer underdog pouring a couple
on the table
reminiscing for the best of times

wife cheats
and a fair-haired boy is born
you learn
life has no honor
in a sardine city
where everyone is a mackerel or
a jellyfish in the
downtown downstream
they tease and flirt
but you remain clean
behind your huge untrimmed shrubs
perhaps your small defiance
in this homogenized block of well-kept row houses

if they knew
if they could only understand

you were found in your lounge chair
under the pear tree you planted
after dolores was born
your head obscenely tilted
toward your envious tomatoes

it was during supper when the news
seeped like barbecue smoke through our screen door
i was the only one to finish eating

i was the only one who ate your tomatoes
when your wife offered them to the neighbors
in that late summer
i was the one she paid to uproot
your shrubs and pear tree
two days after a shovel firmly patted earth down upon you

True North

—For John

Touch the ground, little monkey—Red, yellow, gold, Mediterranean
blue ribbons stream across my canvas and find hope.
There is no meaning in this. Words are words and images with prayer.
Like a deep breath on a cold morning, before I take off my jacket
and jump in with the others, swimming to an iceberg.
Leaving bear-footed prints on the snowy shore,
ten times the size of who I thought I was.
The brisk water bounces about me and cradles my body.
For the moment, I am satisfied and can think of nothing to want.
Then I remember. I can hear the sound
of my heart pounding so loud that it hurts my ears.
Solve the puzzle, find my soul. Find the fire in my belly.
Find the wisdom of the ages. Find the truth about my lisp.
Fill in the blanks with my genealogy family tree—dot-com or no.
I have roots, some withered—some strong—some dead and burned,
but I still feel like an orphan.
Each day a tight-walk rope ride—clumsy words—wrong turns—
Cross-eyed looks. Lopsided snarls and pleads.
I communicate like a stone.
Like cold, hard steel.
Like a lost lamb.
Like a snowflake.
Like a fly on the wall.
I was meant for more than this.
I have risen like a phoenix in spite of family shame.
Tip dancing across the smoldering embers of pain and grief
collecting a new history.
I walk the earth in peace. While the others cast tidal waves of
hate and doom.
I want feet on the ground, mother earth welcoming me every day.
Safe harbor. True North. Good teeth. Less poison. More Grace.
I have a story. It started with hate. And I believed that for a while.
The blood, the bruises, the scars, the screams, the hiding, the escape.
But the hate turned into love. And that is what's real. Today.
Because of you.

keeping a distance

I was trying to write about L.A. and realized I have
no
eloquent
thoughts
about a place that
has held me for
twenty-eight years—At which point my computer broke
allthewordsclungtoeachother,
the space bar became a moot point.

Desperate for metaphors
I—was—forced—to—use—dashes
which stilted my rhythms
and made L.A. worse.

This just after my electric car window refused to close.
Space being forced open.
Protection taken away.

In between my anger and frustration, I searched for
meaning
in words unable to keep a distance—I am as remote
as L.A.
which made the anger bigger,
for this town is sprawling with space,
although one tries desperately not to label L.A. as spacey,
but as leading the pace,
politics in every crevice.
This land juiced by appearance.

All I can say is that I know no one in L.A.
Everyone I was fourteen with
has left.
The girls married, the boys drifted out to sea.
I've lost in-kind donations of time and faith.
So many people don't know that I've been hipped and hearted here,
educated and operated on.
Maybe that's why I write,
or is that why I'm *un*known?

Every night, my laptop and I retreat
to the café with passable coffee and beautiful strangers who nod
in the incandescence.
Seeing a handsome entrance I wonder if something like love could happen
but handsomeness is often followed by a smiling girl
or a fine solo specimen buying eclairs for two.

I know no one in L.A.
so do I talk about earthquakes, the riots, movie stars too famous to mention?
I am not famous nor particularly boobious
yet my network debut featured my cleavage.
It framed a card trick.
The rest of my body has yet to appear.

If I can't write about L.A., what kind of poet am I?
L.A. is the desert ocean,
the place without tornadoes or ice,
full of the midwesterners that had to go left
and hipless women, those thin-browed gals
who have short brown women take care of them
and their manicured babies.
Fake-boobed beauties who buy hothouse tomatoes for $5.99 at Whole Foods
and drive to yoga in tanks.

Trying to write about L.A. makes me hostile.
It's not the land's fault,
the land is hope and knowing. It erupts over stress
and grows roots from exotic visitors.
It's the city that sells every spice.

L.A. feels like a city only when I'm above it,
coming in for a landing.
Twinkling lights in tidy grids
red and white veins,
as if the place was organized, indexed
and waiting for me.

My favorite place—the canals—
picture book of bloom and calm.
Romance of bridges, ducks and rich gardens.
Quack, wing, flutter, rosemary, and honeysuckle.
Reflection of bloom on the water, orange bougainvillea, rose thickets
thick with peace.

L.A., my longest residence—
in two minutes it'll be three decades.
Los Angeles, the place I don't leave.

Terrie Silverman

White Kitchen

(toward a line by Laurel Ann Bogen)

Your taste was never that princely.
It had origins in some border town.
How did so many fish heads end up down there?
The Rio Grande is supposed to be dry, man.
Bad weather & bad tuna.
It seems funny now
after 30 years.
I knew I was breathing too hard
in that huge white kitchen
at that yellow table
when you resisted
the temptation to plunge
a steak knife into my chest.
When I'm honest with myself
I admit it was one of those times
when being speechless
would have helped.

Never silent,
the white kitchen
a riot of sound.
Amidst tomatoes
and other perfect fruit,
we painted it.
There were other rooms
to hide in.

So, we broke a few plates
in that white kitchen.
It's true.
We were crazy,
crazy with hope.

Ode to My Nipple

I thought you too small
perched on the tip of my grapefruit breast
like a button
with barely any areola to surround you
I thought you immature,
unlike the lush, overgrown nipples
nestled in their pools of red or purple,
of other women
I hid you away, thinking you were caught
between girlhood and womanhood;
until, one day,
after giving birth,
my breasts rounded with incoming milk,
you, my button nipple, still barely making a statement,
I sought help from a nurse in the hospital ward
to place my baby's mouth just right.
Oh, she said, *you have the perfect breasts for nursing,*
good nipples!
Well! What do you know?
Not for me, the sore and battered
nipple too lush for its own good,
you, my friend,
were a clear target
prefect in size
for a tiny mouth.
You would introduce me painlessly
to the delicious slow burn of letdown,
met by the grateful hunger of
a baby whose body still needed mine.
And as I would hold him,
his languid eyes gazing up at me,
his mouth closing and opening rhythmically
upon you, my little button nipple,
I know, I would never
speak ill of you
again.

Yours

Beloved, take over my life.
Infiltrate every nook and cranny of my existence.
Guide me, show me, command me, give me orders.
Make me surrender to you no matter how I feel
or how you act.
With your love, pin me to this good earth,
trap me in God's net and don't let me go.
Teach me the ancient secret between predator and prey.
Kill me, rip me apart, eat me.
Show me the wisdom of being Food.
I don't care how you do it, just please, I beg you
do not leave me to wander the earth,
do not leave me intact and uneaten.
Please, please do not let me get lost
in the madness of my self-sufficiency.
Don't let me suffer an uncomplicated life.
Redeem me of all politeness.
Please ruin my favorite dress.
Cover me with love bruises.
Please let me know the ache of being had by you.
Chain me to your heart, ignore my protests.
Shut me up, slap me, bind me, tie me to the edge of infinity.
Lock your hand around my wrists,
encircle my ankles in your grip
and don't let my cries stop you from your mission.
Reject all my pleas.
Be deaf to the horrible names I will call you.
With your will and with your courage,
penetrate my lies, burn through my masks,
liberate my one and only true face.
Do not stop at anything
until I have submitted to the palm of your hand,
until I am bright and radiant,
shining softly in the arms of my captor,
completely relaxed in the afterglow of death.

Thrill

There's a woman stealing
a shoe on
the second floor of the Salvation
Army, downtown Detroit
I watched her, as the blown-out speakers
of the stereo department pumped
Bachman Turner Overdrive.
She casually stuffs the shoe in
her purse, others sift through
racks
she's middle-aged, well-dressed
probably on lunch from an office
desk job
I hear the speakers still straining . . . churn
    You ain't seen nothin' yet
     b b b baby you ain't seen nothin' yet . . .
and she sees me
her eyes hit mine
she smiles a half-hearted smile,
collects herself
down the stairs, my eyes follow her
she'll be back tomorrow for the other shoe
it's an affair we carry on
just enough of a thrill to turn me on.

Nikita K. in Kuba

My father's friends called him *El Puerco Ruso*,
the Russian pig, and they'd laugh, laugh hard
while they smoked their cigars on our porch.

My mother worried that such talk might get
my father in trouble, get him arrested, and it did,
dos veces. Twice we spent sleepless nights

because my father had been arrested for counter-
revolutionary activities, so they said, and I didn't
mind because I got to stay at a next-door neighbor's

house, slept in the same room with their daughter,
five years older than me, on a cot next to hers,
and at night while she held my hand, I smelled

the gardenias beyond her window and I slept
like the baby I was, and I dreamt of coming
back each night, to hear her quickened heartbeat

on my pillow. The next morning off to school
I went, from the classroom wall hung Nikita K's
picture, jowly, pig white, and I would laugh,

laugh so hard the teacher would have to stop class
and ask me what the problem was, and I would
simply drop on my hands and knees and *oink*,

oink! my way up and down the aisle, kids kicking
my sides, taunting me to lick their boots, shoes,
lick up all the slop in their lives, ours, mine.

Last I Saw Her

She was munching
on a taco or two,
had mild sauce, I think,
and spoke quietly
saying it wouldn't work.

Can't help but think if
we'd gone to McDonald's
she would still be here,
for I have never known
any woman to leave
after a Happy Meal.

Release

Today I have not woken up.
I saw the maid come in
with a pile of clean white
towels and go stiff, her body
leaning back, drop them onto
the floor and run out.
I tried to imagine how I
looked, my mouth half
open, my head off the side
of the bed, my hand hanging
palm up, scooping the air.
I gazed at the world upside
down. A woman on the tv
screen mouthed words im-
passively, the picture showing
dead bodies in the icy field
behind my invisible house.

It was so relieving to be
far from the madness—deaf
in a peaceful hotel, waiting
for the maid to come back
with a manager, which she did,
stood above me close enough
for me to see up her alabaster
legs and let my head crawl
between them, her fingers
trying in vain to straighten
her skirt, while the picture
on the screen bounced, apcs
too, going through the empty
streets, the smoke running
into the sky down, a cow
holding onto the ground
ceiling, and all that damn
business of containing life.

She lifted my head gently
onto the pillow, her palms
cold and sandy, my eyes
almost touching her nipples,
two protruding buds ready
to explode in the lidded light,
and for a moment only I caught
my face in the mirror, a smile
of release on my milky lips.

The Treasure

Every day, I ate the middle
of each slice of bread,
and removed the crust
to be saved for another day.
I placed these delicate rations
in a yellow sack.
I wanted to devour them,
one crust at a time,
but saved them instead, chanting—
  I won't be hungry
  I'll have my treasure.

During an air-raid,
forced out on the snow
I left the bread behind.
Cold air stabbed at my nose
as we walked to the bunker,
as we lowered ourselves into the dark,
waiting for the bombs to stop falling.

Back in the barrack,
the empty yellow sack—
as if the wind had blown inside it.
The crusts of bread were gone.
Even the crumbs nowhere to be found.
They stole my bread—
the other prisoners
eating the scraps of my existence.
I didn't ask,
didn't inquire
of the starved faces around me.
I just ate the crusts
one piece at a time.
A treasure to be consumed.
Nothing to be saved.

First Kiss

Sitting on the steps outside
she held a bag of cherries.
They were spitting the seeds out
as if
in a race.
Whoever spits the farthest wins!
The prize . . .
a kiss.
He won,
but it didn't really matter.
They sat there
kissing in the afternoon sun,
lips stained red,
and their mouths flavored with cherry.

Picture-in-Picture: A Schizophrenic Odyssey

From burning darkness into light, a resurrection,
end of a grave journey. Swallow pills, and wall of
bodies, shadow–Nazis, sliced wrists.
Instead, tropical vistas where blossoms and parakeets
dip in the sun. *Normal function*—a term of bliss
and a way across the fields of fire.

Still, he was wary of the TV, clicking worlds in flux,
picture-in-picture unreality. When snake-filled
flames rose again, his father, the King of Spades,
urged him to press his palms to their heat
and call them illusion, turn fire to bougainvillea.
But unlike Father, he was a no-count deuce,
and a wilderness of monkeys was eating his brain.
Instead of college, he'd stay, sell shoes.

So, more meds until chimps behind his eyes were
caged and he became poster boy for schizophrenia.
There was a law degree. Book contract. Movie option.
An apartment in the Palisades. A pregnant fiancé.
Pills, though, tamped brightness, choked his words,
and his father, king of gaudy flowers, was dead.

Once, the schizophrenic talked of *tikkun olam*,
how one man could heal the world
and of his mission—to redeem pariahs,
prove the damaged could serve. But flames began to
peel his soles, turn flowers to ash, hatch snakes,
and the monkeys, uncaged again, forked up
his brains. Then, blood, blood everywhere,
and a fiancé who would never be a mother or a bride.

Flintstones Juice Glasses

I feel like a pickled egg. I drank too much Petite Shirah last night with my friends at dinner. There is nothing petite about it now. *Que Shirah!*

I must feel like my mother felt every day of my childhood. Well, she probably never felt like a pickled egg because she kept drinking the pickling juice. She drank Hill and Hill Whiskey. She hid her fifth of whiskey on the top shelf of the tall corner kitchen cabinet. She would take swigs at all hours. Sometimes I followed her to the kitchen. She was too out of it to notice that I was shadowing her. On her tiptoes, she would pull the fifth down from its place of shame and take a gulp right from the bottle.

When she was being ladylike about her tippling, she would drink from my Flintstones juice glasses. She used the Flintstones glasses as shot glasses. Fred and Wilma somehow made boozing innocent.

I begged to get the Welsh's grape jelly. The jelly container was actually a Flintstones juice glass. The problem was that I hated grape jelly. But I coveted those glasses, and I ate the jelly despite the fact I despised it. Soon I was a proud seven-year-old with a collection of six Flintstones juice glasses. I loved those glasses. I earned those glasses. Each one was a different Flintstones cartoon and color. Yellow Dino, orange Bam Bam, aqua Pebbles, white Fred. I was so proud of them. I was so proud of me and my resolve for grape jelly. Grape jelly became my favorite. I was a collector.

I remember when she broke the first Flintstones juice glass. When she took her snort of Hill and Hill, the jolt of her poison relaxed her grip and down plummeted my beloved glass. My heart shattered too as the glass hit the hard linoleum. How could she break my Flintstones glass? I had worked so hard to earn it. Hill and Hill was more important than me.

I remember when she broke the second Flintstones juice glass. It was then when I anticipated the end. I foresaw the day when I would have no collection of Flintstones juice glasses.

I remember when she broke the third glass. And the fourth.

I remember the last two. I would try to hide them behind the other taller glasses.

I remember when she broke the fifth one.

I remember when she broke the sixth one.

Then there were none.

I didn't cry. I didn't pout. I just stopped feeling. A part of me gave up. A part of me closed off, never to be disillusioned again. My remaining feelings were swept into the trash with the last few shards of glass.

Welsh's had stopped making the juice glasses. I could no longer be a collector of Flintstones juice glasses. She broke the glasses. She broke me. Welcome to the end of my childhood.

Displayed on my antique Irish spice hutch in my dining room, I have a beautiful art deco bowl and some cobalt blue glasses and plates with a matching pitcher. Among the latte cups, pictures, and candles lay my prizes. Yellow Dino, orange Bam Bam, aqua Pebbles, white Fred. Find the right antique store and pay $20 a pop, and you can try to make up for your childhood.

Touch from Beyond

I reach out to him. To touch him. Palm facing out with my fingers spread. My finger tips feel the air: questing, sensing, testing. I stretch my arm out as an antenna. Seeking. I search the air with my eyes. They blur and no longer focus. Then I see him standing there. Just to the right of me, facing me. He stands motionless, looking at me. His smile almost not there on his lips. His silver hair brushed back off his forehead. His six-foot presence filling the air. I hear the music that's playing, surrounding this space. I turn toward him. I take a step forward and raise my arms to circle them 'round his neck. I stand on my tiptoes and lean forward into him.

Our energies blend. His large-boned arms wrap around me. Encircle me. Touch. Blend. My body sighs. I relax. I drink him in. Soothing, mellow, fluid. I smell him into me. Rich, lush, calming. Touch. We step, slow drinking step after slow calming step, moving with the music, moving with each other, moving beyond time. I open my eyes to half-slits to know this is real. They fill with yearning tears.

Warmth, his warmth. Tasting his essence. Strong, centered, protective. I bury my face into the side of his neck and forget what is now. Touch. Warmth. I want the moment to last. And last. How wet hunger rolls down my cheeks.

I bathe in his comfort, I soak in his touch. Sucking it in, feeling it in, burying it in, imprinting the memory deeper in my cells. We float, in comfort, suspended in a void. No veil cloaks his world of beyond where one lives after death from the one I live in now, alone. We can touch for this moment.

I see his chest skin beneath the "V" of his blue shirt. The scattered chest hairs lying there looking back at me. I sense his heart beat. I sense his breath that moves the hair on the top of my head. He makes no sound and speaks no words. Touch. Bonded. United. We move in our symphony together. Warm. One. Soul touching soul.

The music, its beat; I sob, my mouth, my chest. I jerk back to the line between worlds. A howl; my arms, my hands, my sides, my body. I thud. Land. He's gone. Emptiness. Air touches me now. My skin screams. Calls. Ache. How crazy am I? Tears. My body. Touch. His skin against mine. Cocoon of his body. Nestled in. Drink in. To touch. Touch. Ache for his touch, yearn for his touch. Cry for his touch. Salt, my mouth; wet, my chin. Where? Here. Now. I am left with the touch of air, left with the touch of sound. I will never feel his touch again. Never feel his breath. Never feel his sound. Never feel his taste. Never feel his look. Never feel the salt, the skin, the air, the sound. Never feel his physical touch again.

Chopin Prelude #14

Rushing shadow torrents move quick
spilling forth within the night
Deep voices rumble,
erupting,
crowding in my head
spewing forth worlds that lie between word spaces
where the multitudes of diverse dimensions speak out
in fractured diamond cuts
Chasing my faith
Rattling my being
Chilling my fears
I look over my shoulder
hide my face in anguish
and cry tortured tears

At the Foster Home

They are not unkind, the family
that took me in. I even
have my own room—curtains
fluttering in the breeze.

In the mother and father's
bathroom, I smear my lips
with her red lipstick. Then
he comes in. Huddled behind
the sticky, plastic shower
curtain, I hear his breath quicken.

The mother sleeps with a gun
under her pillow, a little flinty thing
with pearlized handles. He shows
it to me when she is gone.

At night the perfect daughter
materializes from the hot breathing of my
longing. Outlined against the wall,
target practice flat body. In some
alternate universe, I am her. Starched,
yellow dress tied with a bow in back,
white socks ruffled at the edges,
T-trapped Mary Janes.

I reach into her shadowy chest
through the smallest, center circle
where the heart should be. *Daddy*, she
whispers, *stop that. It tickles.*

Sinner Man Sings the Unending Blues

The fat woman in overalls
Draws a magic circle around her home
With finger-filtered marigold seeds
That keeps the pigeons, him, away

He's hungry and the Cool Springs
Trailer Park has been good to him
Yesterday, a raspberry pie cooling
On 4B's sagging wooden porch

He's a real sight dozing that tree
Out front, a fellow with gooseflesh-
Colored skin, a tucked sleeve
Where his right arm once hung

In the far-off purple of horizon
The storm clouds convulse and churn
Like a weather-witch gone crazy
And every bolt of lightning's got his name

The Stint

And I don't make those mistakes anymore
because I'm not allowed to sing
Anymore

And I haven't held the child
in what seems like ages
because we don't touch
Not here, we don't
lose ourselves to
innocence.

And sometimes
when the night has fallen and we're
suffocated
by the cold
whispered screams,
The paved walls smile
and they tell jokes
But I don't laugh anymore

because I'm not that girl
anymore

Nadia van de Walle

brooklyn, three stops out

Shadows raced along the pink wall, streaking right to left in long
rectangular slits of muddy brown. This was the way we watched trucks pass by
on the freeway, tracing their shadow-tails with our fingertips. When we were
done we'd shut the blinds and lie on the floor, salsa music spilling in from the
Mexican restaurant downstairs, the jalapeño smell tickling our noses. We'd shut
our eyes and pretend that we were holed up in a shack somewhere in Havana, or
on the hills above Caracas, pretend that we didn't smell the exhaust fumes, the
burning of rubber on tar. You'd pretend your eyes didn't hurt, weren't glassy,
and I'd play along as if I hadn't read your diaries, all the entries about Her and
how she was still flicking in and out of your life like a tongue in your ear.

Sunday Morning Blasphemy

When I pass Morning Star M.B. Church today
you are not in the car beside me,
your hand inching along my thigh,
then up my red skirt,
while I suck
the boiled peanuts
too hot
for my timid tongue.

No, this morning is different with my hangover headache.
As rain falls lightly, I conquer the road
traveled before
on impulse,
push past with requisite sadness,
remember the late night, the longing.

As we drove away that night,
I threw back my head and wished
on that white wooden star
over the doors
for the church to be Baptist,
so that my sin would be sweeter.

You, being from Mormon country,
couldn't understand this misplaced Catholic girl.

Stuck in Traffic

Who are they talking to anyway in the dark of their cars? Leather interior, clipped in, hooked up, microphone at their lips, talking to no one I can see. I count them on my way home stuck in traffic. Fifty at least. Total potential car wreck. Too many people not paying any attention, and I'm so not getting noticed. I'm a tight little ball like a skein of yarn at the hobby store waiting for some elderly lonely lady to come upon it and feel her heart light up and know: *Oh, for once, I won't be alone, I have my yarn.* Her face is old and creased and a bit of jam from that morning's breakfast of toast and lukewarm tea stains her strip of dry lip. She stands with a stoop bowed by disappointment and too much sitting and not enough doing and I am afraid that's me standing there. I expected so much more, but all I got were two can pans and too many baskets of dirty laundry . . . *don't you know?. . .* I'm a fan-fucking-tastic housewife. I never burn the toast, no sir, I keep the floors clean, cook like a pro, wrestle dust bunnies to their deaths. My blow jobs are A-Number-One, but the second I want to write, the words fall off the table and onto the floor and somebody has to sweep them up. I feel like my knees are broken. The teacher said *stay in your seat* and I've been here ever since. Waiting, clean, pressed, presentable. Legs in black wool tights—I am such a good girl. I think *if I stop brushing my hair I'll be okay* it will be my rebellion, my little revenge on the people who think I'm here to be seen and not heard. But that doesn't change anything because babies can still come when I'm not prepared, and my body will break, will burst, will hurt and I won't see who I am. I get lost so easy. Floating away on biology. Inventing nothing new, but conforming to something ancient, primordial, and programmed like leaves falling in autumn and baby birds hatching in spring. I didn't ask to be part of any cycle. No monthly period / no birth and death / no love and hate. I just wanted to have a good time, get laid, whatever, maybe sign a few autographs. All this other rigamaroll, this psycho-babble, this poor-me/no-one-understands-me crap is just a come-on. Every girl needs an angle.

Fick Says Fuck

A good night,
I'd call it,
a solid
if unspectacular
night for the backup
first baseman—
errorless
with two walks
in four trips
and best of all
he ran up
the pitch count
on our 97 M.P.H.
fastballer,
22 in 3 ABS,
Fick's finest
in the 7th inning,
when Schmidt
threw him 9,
only one fewer
than needed earlier
to strike out the side.
True, Fick
eventually
grounded to second,
but Schmidt
with his iffy elbow
was gone
after the 8th.

So Fick did good
yet still said fuck,
not in shame
(after all
they tied it up
against our closer),
no, it was awe
at the guy
who ended things
in 10, first pitch
off the rookie
Trey Hedges
hello bleachers
a little right
of straightaway

center, #39
on the season,
652 career,
his second
lights out
extra-inning
walkoff jack
in 3 games,
except the first
went to dead
right, over
the wall,
the walkway—
Sploosh!—
SF Bay.

To be exact,
the *Chronicle* reported
Fick said, *I hope*
I don't ever see
f—— Barry
Bonds again
because I don't give
a s—— what
anyone says,
he's the f——
best. Magnanimous
under the circumstances,
a gothic tribute
from a minor hero
and baseball may be
better than ever;
however, *fuck*,
the word,
ain't what
it used
to be.

The Day after Saint Patrick's Day

I hate when this happens—
when I forget a family birthday,
especially when the person is dead.
The least I can do is remember
even if the person was a loser like Dad.
He became my step-dad
because Mam could not decide between
John and Dan—the men after her hand.

Which one would you like as a father? she asked.

John had already wooed me,
given me the most expensive skates
in town and at seven, I was
the roller-princess of my street
so of course I said *John.*

When I think of John, it's this
that comes to mind—not the pipe smoke
and alcohol he boozed into the house
each night, not Mam's wailing
about unpaid bills that seeped through
the papered bedroom wall—so the least
I can do is remember his birthday
(especially with St. Patrick nudging)
stop what I'm doing, look at
his cunning smile in the cracked wedding photo,
think of the roller skates
(which cost all of five shillings)
and smile back.

Bunny Berrigan Loses His Chops

horn's haig and haig
or four roses soliloquy

a blow plays
blood
the busted lip on "i can't get started"

maybe concrete hair
or trombone solos
cut short
or remain timeless
chipped off till the end

old boys
like pops
suck juice
the numbness spreading
like prairie fire

black and white prints
to hold
your tongue
frozen
so dry
so gone
from yesterday's bell

Pink Lust

Does it really matter
not having a girl?
And why is it shameful
to want one?
I am lucky to have
two children;
two fabulous boys who I love
beyond measure.
But the longing for a girl
isn't going away.

Is it the pink clothes
I want to dress her in?
Shallow, I know.
Or that I'll want to shop with her
like I did with my mother?
Of course, my mother has always
hated shopping.
I might never be
the 'mother of the bride.'
No daughter to chat with
on the telephone.

I am not interested in worms.
I don't want to be an honorary boy
I am proud to be a girly girl.
I grew up thinking women rocked.
Maybe I needed to discover
the joys
of men.

Three children?
A bit mad.
Two already push me to my edge.
Another boy?
A lot of testosterone.

Is this pink longing
just one more thing
I must let go of,
one more loss
I must accept
in order to more fully embrace
what I already have?

I do adore
my men.
I like being loved
by them.
Maybe my boys will like the telephone.
Perhaps I should take myself shopping,
shroud myself
head to toe
in pink.
Perhaps I will be a woman
who loves men,
who raises wonderful men,
who is loved gloriously in return,
by men.

Victorious

I remember how good it felt the first time I was victorious. I was eleven years old. "If you believe it will land, then it will land," said my father stretching out his finger toward a nearby butterfly. He struck a pose implying I was to follow suit. Out of loyalty, I did. He was shirtless. He had no chest hair. I was embarrassed at how tight his shorts were and that they still smelled that new polyester smell. Sears, I think. My father's seriousness about this lesson made me respect what I perceived as the poet, the philosopher, in him. I didn't know then that he and I would share the same shaped forehead, one that promised intelligence yet wrinkled too young.

It was much too hot outside to stand barefoot. The air already smelled scorched and unhealthy in that L.A. kind of way, like a fire was ready to ignite somewhere and threaten us on this jut of cement levitating somewhere above Los Angeles at the end of a long treacherous driveway, a driveway my father navigated too many times while inebriated. I could smell my long straight hair baking in the heat. My arm was already tired but I was determined not to buckle. Convinced I would be occupied for some time, my father escaped again to the company of his twin brother. Dean and Don. Frick and Frack.

Keeping still made me dizzy. My eyes were so fixed on that butterfly I could almost anticipate its next move, as if it were connecting invisible dots in the air of some image that would later reveal itself. The sun splintered through the trees, playing with my depth perception, making them shrink in comparison to this immense insect. I could hear my father's dry-whiskey laugh behind me. I would not know until later it had been meant for me. I stood there long enough for my father to knock back four more tall boys, for the light to change from cadmium yellow to burnt orange, for another dreaded day to be closer to an end, and long enough for the butterfly to land.

I made some minuscule motion for my father to come over. I could feel the heat of pride expanding in my chest but I still stood fixed to keep the magic going. My father made his way over to me. His eyes were glassy and he swayed in his drunkenness. Even with six tall boys in him he looked small to me. I brought my finger down into his frame of focus. His visibility was impaired. He collected himself just long enough to exhume, "Well, I'll be damned." In that moment I knew he never expected that butterfly to land; he'd only been mocking me.

I felt the freedom of being beyond his grasp. I pulled the butterfly close to me. From a distance it had been beauty and grace but up close it was grotesque—not at all what I had expected. I looked past the butterfly at my father in triumph and let the butterfly go.

Anniversary

Mother is a stranger
dressed to go out.
In the oval mirror above
her glass-topped dressing table
which I am barely tall enough to see
I watch her comb her hair,
take out gold earrings from a case,
apply makeup (eyebrows first,
then lips, ruby red.)
Her black evening coat
lies on the flowered bedspread.
The click of her high heels
on the hardwood floor announces
a special occasion, awash in Chanel,

all more mysterious because
I've never seen her dust and dab
powder and perfume. She stares
at the mirror so long and sadly
that I put my hand in her lap.
Downstairs, I hear my father yell,
"For Chrissake, Arlene,
get a move on it!"
A hasty kiss, then she's up and gone
while I stare at the mirror
trying to see
what made her sad.

To My Sister

When we lived in Fresno
thirty years ago
we buried you there.

But we didn't stay.
We scattered like straw in wind
to different directions.

None of us has been back
to see how the earth
healed over you like a scar.

I wonder if passersby
note that this grave

seldom has flowers,
or how the wind parches the earth,
how sparse the grass.

At the foot of this site,
a cedar (like the ones you loved)
lifts its head, as though searching.

I had to come back
to touch your stone again—
and to remember
how the dry, raw wind
screamed goodbye.

Anne Wilson

From Mourning to Morning

Pulvis et umbra sumus

The path sick sorrow takes passes through this place.
I was the night man, told to dress crow-formal
to greet somberly, to point dismally, to look potentially sad

or vaguely pious. No smiling and—like the airport—
no jokes. In the break room, above the veneered dresser
where the shoe polish and pornography were kept,
a laminated poster gave the rules in black magic marker:

If you wear white socks with your suit, you will be fired.
If you have overnight guests, you will be fired.
If a casket is missing, you will be fired.
If you leave before being relieved, you will be fired.
If you fail to answer the phone, you will be fired.
If you tamper with the crematorium, you will be fired.

After nine o'clock, after I'd taken the widowed
and the un-consoled gently out by the elbow,
I was free to change or study or watch t.v.
or sleep or try to until morning.
Or stare at the bodies.
I held my breath to imagine their breathing.

Once I dreamed that a giant came and silently
pulled the roof off the funeral home, and
the giant could not tell the difference between
the pointy, pale head-heavy corpses
under their sheets on their metal carts
naked as Mung bean sprouts,
fresh from the examiner's perscrutations
and me.

With my first check I bought a cell phone,
kept it hidden like a pistol.
With call forwarding, the world was my funeral home.
I'd take the Cadillac hearse out on the interstate and open it up.
It rode like water off a stone.
I'd drive to Hardee's, drive down to the coal piers,
hear the river swell and breathe, the laughing gulls.

I quit before they fired me.

Bathe me in red

Wrap me in its seductive robe
and watch me dance
on the clouds at sunset,
a harem girl before her sultan.

Bathe me in red,
kiss me with parted lips
and send me pulsating
through your veins
slithering on your thoughts.

Bathe me in red,
give me a name, a cause.
Make of me a revolution.

Come closer.
Here I am.
Take your time.

Look It Up

"Focky," my dad said. "Focky this, focky that. Focky. Focky. Focky."

"So?" I said.

"What is this word meaning?" my father asked. He had spent twelve years in America, but still struggled with his command of the English Language. "Always focky. Everywhere people telling me this. Look it up, Aggie, and tell me what it says."

I complied and opened my unabridged OED, a gift my parents had bestowed on me for my fifth birthday. They'd instructed me to master the language so I could guide them through America, reading billboards and advertisements for them. I flipped through volume 'F'. I said, "Not in there. You sure it's spelled F-O-C-K-Y?"

"I'm not sure about anything," my dad replied. He pounded our no-assembly-required table. "Ah, what use are you? You skip a grade. Straight from first to third and what do you know? You are not understanding simple words."

I cursed my father for consenting to take me out of second grade when I'd demonstrated my practical drawing skills and large vocabulary. This put me at a distinct disadvantage in the seventh grade. Everyone else had undergone puberty and nipple hair while I waited for a growth spurt. My parents had annointed me as their great hope, the one who would live out the American Dream while they lived out the immigrants' tale, but sometimes I didn't even understand what they were talking about.

"How'd I get my name?" I asked my dad, my Baba.

"It's a famous name. Agamemnon. I can hardly say it. My professor in Hong Kong greatly admired this Agamemnon. A famous and great man. Agamemnon, I mean. A hero. And it's the longest first name ever. So we chose it for you."

Agamemnon Beethoven Chin. That's me. Shortened to Aggie, or Eggy, as some schoolyard bullies prefer. Those geniuses invented other derivatives like Egghead and Agah-agah. Given a choice in the matter, I'd have christened myself Superman Chin or Flaming Fireball Chin. I asked my dad, "Can I change it when I'm of legal age?"

"How can you ask such a thing?" my father said. He looked wounded, as if he had invested a great deal in my initials. "It is part of you. We named you and you have grown into your name."

"It sounds funny," I said. "It doesn't even sound American."

"The name is classic," my father said. "Wait a while and they will become popular again. You wait and see."

At least my English name was better than my Chinese moniker: Chin Hwa Pee.

Some of the first words I learned turned out to be fake: woo foo, chinky, ching-a-ling.

"What," I asked my mother, "does 'ding dong' mean?"

"Where did you hear that?"

"Some kids. They say it's Chinese and I should understand it." Hardly a day went by when I didn't hear a new word on the school bus. I sat in the front seat, but still heard taunts from the back. They called out to me, shouting at me.

"Say again?" My mother leaned forward, up to her elbows in yeast. She made Chinese dumplings every Friday, using her thumb to create small dents in the dough.

"Ding dong!" I said.

"Maybe it's Mandarin Chinese. It sounds like 'understand' to me," my mother said. She laughed and patted my head. "Your Chinese pronunciation is so bad. I will teach you someday."

My Chinese didn't improve much beyond those elementary fake words. My parents scolded me in their native tongue and they swore in Chinese, yelling at each other. Chinese characters looked too complex, violent and intimidating to study. The scrawls and strokes pointed in different directions and ended in sharp edges as if they could cut you.

I found comfort in English words, looking them up and memorizing their spellings and etymologies. Thumbing through the crisp pages of the dictionary made me feel powerful and in control. I could find any desired word in three flips max.

Despite my large vocabulary, I never spoke in public. This perplexed teachers, who described me as "talented," "diligent," and "intellectually curious" on my report cards. They tried to encourage me to speak, but I kept silent.

People suspected I had a speech impediment or had lost my tongue. When called upon, I mumbled and sputtered, failing to enunciate. I knew all these words, knew how to use them in sentences, but I couldn't voice them. I felt like a fraud speaking English, reinforced by the fact that most people didn't expect me to understand them.

When I went out with my parents, shop clerks shouted their questions slowly as if we were all imbeciles. "Paaappper or plaaassstic?" the pimpled girl asked with a sympathetic stare, snapping her gum.

That's why I learned to stay mute.

Our school bus dropped me off a block from home. Every morning I had to wait for the yellow vehicle with boys who had developed an extreme hatred for me. They were usually sedate in the morning and showed up at the last second, their lunch bags flailing. But after school, they took out their frustrations on me.

I jumped off the bus. A group of thugs approached me. They had chased me up the fort and stuffed me into the hollow rubber tire during recess. When I saw them outside school, there was an awkward beat, as if they weren't sure how to treat me in public. But then they assumed their swagger and started calling me names. They said, "Egghead! How do Chinese people choose their names? They drop a bunch of spoons! Ching-chong-bing-bong."

I'd heard all the jokes before and kept my head down. They trailed behind me. I turned red, as Mrs. Hoover overheard my humiliation. She told the boys, "Now. Now. Everybody behave and get along. Hello, Aggie. Study hard."

They stifled their laughs. I knew Mrs. Hoover's attempts at pacification would only instigate further assaults. As we rounded a corner, they said, "Chinese girls have sideways slits."

I quickened my pace when one of them popped up in front of me. They pushed me to the ground and said, "Fuck you, wimp."

Sprawled on the ground, I peered up their nostrils. The setting sun outlined their blond hair, giving them faint halos. They prodded me with their feet. Tears welled up in my eyes. I'd be incoherent in a minute, a total loss for words. I knew it was now or never. "Fuck you, too," I said, summoning all my strength. "Focky, focky, focky."

Carson H. Wu

回归（一） / The Return

不要睡去，不要
亲爱的，路还很
不要　　森林的
不要失掉希望

请用凉凉　　水
把　　　在　上
或　　着我的肩
度过朦胧的晨光

　　　的暴风
我们就　到达家
一片圆形的绿地
铺　　塔　房

我将　
守护你疲惫的梦
赶开一群群黑夜
只留下

...don't go
Dear, the road...long
...too near
the forest's enticement

...dress
...n snowmelt on your...
...or lean on my shoulder
...he hazy m...
...ifting the transparent...

...green disk of land
around...pagoda
...re I will guard
your weary dreams
and drive off the flock...
...aving only bron...
...round the pagoda...
...tiny wa...s quietly
...crawl...p the beach
and draw ba...trembl...

Translations

Overleaf:
Gu Cheng's "The Return," translated by Aaron Crippen
@Archipelago, www.archipelago.org

YEHUDA AMICHAI

Yehuda Amichai is one of the leading contemporary Hebrew poets. He brought novel innovations to the Hebrew language. Amichai invented Hebrew expressions and helped transform a classical Biblical language into a rich, modern vernacular. His poetic subjects ranged from descriptions of Jerusalem to vivid depictions of emotions including grief, mockery, love, and loss. He also integrated contemporary issues and addressed questions about war and nationalism. Amichai was born in Wurzburg, Germany, but his family emigrated to Jerusalem in 1936. His first volume of poetry, *Now and in Other Days*, was published in 1955. The work was well-received by critics and respected by readers. In 1963, Amichai published a book of collected poems, and a selected works volume was printed in 1981. Again, the poetry was highly regarded, and Amichai was awarded the prestigious Israeli Prize in 1982. A bilingual edition of his poems, entitled *Poems of Jerusalem,* was published in 1987. Until his death in 2000, Amichai had published eleven volumes of poetry, two novels, a book of short stories, children's literature, radio sketches, and a number of plays. Today he is the most widely translated Hebrew poet.

Translated by Cynthia Glucksman

A Pity, We Were Such a Good Invention

They amputated
your thighs from my hips.
As far as I'm concerned—
Doctors. All of Them.

They dismantled us
Each from each other.
As far as I'm concerned—
Engineers. All of them.

A pity. We were such a good invention
and loving: An airplane made from man and wife.
Wings and everything:
We ascended a little from the earth.
We flew a little.

Like the Inner Wall of a House

Like the inner wall of house
That has been made into an outer wall after war and destruction,
I found myself suddenly,
And early enough in life, I nearly forgot
What it means to be inside. Already no pain.
Already no love. And near and far,
Are both at a great distance from me—and equal.

What happens to colors, I cannot imagine.
Their fate is the fate of man:
Faint indigo still slumbers
In the memory of navy and night. Paleness sighs
Within a scarlet dream. A wind brings smells
From far away, but itself has no scent. The Hatzav leaves
Die long before their white flower,
Which never knows
About the greenness in spring and dark love.

I lift my eyes to the mountains. Now I understand
What it means to lift eyes, what a heavy weight
It is. But the hard longings,
The pain-never-again-to-be-inside—
forever.

Once, a Boundless Love

Once, a boundless love cut my life in two.
And the first portion continues to twitch
at another place, like a severed snake.
The years that passed have calmed me
and have brought healing to my heart and rest to my eyes.

And I'm like a man who stands in the Judean desert
opposite a sign, the "Elevation of the Sea."
And he will not see the sea, but he knows.
Thus I remember your face in every place
at the "Elevation of your Face."

All the Generations before Me

All the generations before me donated me,
Little by little, so I would be erected here in Jerusalem
All at once, like a synagogue or charitable institution.
This binds. My name is my donor's name.
It binds.

I'm approaching the age of my father's death.
My final will is patched with many patches,
I need to alter my life and death
daily, in order to sustain all the prophecies
that were prophesied to me. That they are not lies.
This binds.

I have passed my fortieth year.
There are jobs I am not given
on account of this. Were I in Auschwitz,
they would not have sent me to work,
they would have burned me immediately.
It binds.

GU CHENG

Gu Cheng (1956–1993) was a figurehead of the Obscure or "Misty" school of Chinese poetry. Associated with Bei Dao and Shu Ting at the underground *Today* magazine, he burst onto the Beijing literary scene during the Democracy Wall movement of 1979 and gained popularity until by 1986 he was literally being mobbed by fans at his readings. In 1998 a film based on his life, *The Poet*, was released in Hong Kong.

Translated by Aaron Crippen

Zoo Snake

smoothly you slide out of stones
and leave yourself there
you have forgotten yourself

a ring of warm lamplight
sand, water, filthy glass
air hot under tungsten filament
sand, water, a stick on the glass

the tungsten subtly swells like a wound
a glassed-in, smooth-worn stick
sand strewn around the wound
sand, water, light spread around the wound

light gathers around the wound
clogged, the wound subtly swells
a dried stick like a leaf
a little coil of warm hurt

the distant foam keeps on roaring
a child's hand sucks at the glass
the days and nights will take him away

The Coming

Please open the window. Caress the fall wind.
Like tea leaves settling the summer day clears.
The nightmare's over, the twisted shades gone.
My breathing is clouds. My wish is a song.

Please open the window, and then I will come
set your black hair flying against the clear sky
over humming rooftops, soft flags and people
walking minutely, raising no dust.

I have come. Put an end to this waiting.
Just close your eyes and find my lips.
Once a boat drifted from a beach toward cliffs
while the sun, like its oars, slanted into cool dreams.

Oh there's no king of kings, no soul of souls.
You are my lover, my inextinguishable life.
I want to be in your blood, telling distant stories.
The city's a tomb, laid over the voice of memory.

I Am Still Picking at that Golden Tobacco

I am still picking at that golden tobacco.
You take my hand, saying *no*,
the vein on your calm arm climbing to a peak.
They've carried you into the cemetery.
Now you push through the white stones and flowers.

Saying *no*, with your smoky gold eyebrows,
you tell me a posthumous noontime story
of a village on a green riverbank in wavering waterlight,
where on peacock-proud bushes a bather's wrinkled clothes
are covered with hornets;

students whittle pencils and spit from the bridge,
threatening each other with poplar switches;
the wine seller drives his brown pony;
and a pair of red mothers carrying coconuts—children—
linger until the dapper border guard approaches.

Iron wire strung around a backwater place.
A hand rising from the water. History at rest in the fields.
A crying river kissing his lips. Mist descending into the gorge.
Redbirds hunting for food among roots.
And you say: *Air, the coolest fresh air.*

KRZYSZTOF KARASEK

Krzysztof Karasek, b. 1937, published over a dozen volumes of poetry, plus a few novels and books of essays; he edited the anthology *Contemporary Polish Poets: Polish Poetry since 1956* (Warsaw, 1997). In English, his poetry appeared in the anthology *Humps and Wings: Polish Poetry Since '68* (San Francisco, 1982), *Periphery,* and other magazines.

*Translated by **Dobi Zalewska** & **Janusz Zalewski***

Vision of Extinction

—For Juan Rulfo (1918–1986)
con todo il afecto y la amistad

My skeleton is cleaning down to the snow of the bones,
lovely ants, why have your jaws
dragged me to the humid home,
where certainly an impatient future waits,
full of roots, glow-worms and moles,
to hide me in its eyes, like in a spatial
underground, before a deluge—in vain—
for me to be able to say to these ants: No!

So I am free. What does that mean now,
when mushrooms took me over, mosses, ferns,
and for a lodging rented sands
whitened castle, property of my skull
ample, in which the wind runs wild?
I am a Viking. I sail in my life boat,
floated by the stream, drowning through the waves,
joining Orpheus and company,
somebody waits for me out there, who integrates by word
a subject nothingness. Who
will tell these ants, what clouds do not.

The Raskolnikovs

Raskolnikov enters the room
old woman is still breathing
He leans over her
kisses her
twice
with an axe
in mouth (first time
lovely, second time
deadly),

---

he steps
through blue stairs
down.
Axe and body
bread and wine (vine)
Raskolnikov is still breathing

water floods his mouth
Red Sea pours out from behind his jacket's collar

—When the high tide comes—
he says
pointing with his finger to the shapeless fish of air—

the ship is sick of the sea.

Mouth of Man Ray

Through darkness of the day
as through flower of an unknown name
a light stream flows;
where a voice remained,
since mouth of the speaker moves
on a live screen of extinct memory

I hear voices of humans
and voices of animals,
buzzing of a bee in a torrid afternoon,
and whisper of a bark-worm
gnawing into the walls of a Doric town; I hear
march of a river through the landscape
And the most beautiful of all, singing of
Warsaw song

Voices from the air, voices from the earth
in a vibrating atmosphere of August—
are born
fade away; above them
big, trembling abyss of speech
And somebody's mouth
moving as in soundless dream

BOGDAN LOEBL

Bogdan Loebl, b. 1932, published 10 volumes of poetry, lyrics, several novels, and collections of stories; his poems appeared in German, *Das geballte Faust der Rose* (Halle, 1992); and in English, *A Non-genuine Pole* (Warsaw, 2000).

*Translated by **Dobi Zalewska** & **Janusz Zalewski***

Clenched Fist of Rose

—For Krystyna and Jaceck Jankowski

My element is hatred
I seldom leave it and it rarely goes away
apparently smears my skin around with venom
but in fact contains a full set of vitamins

love requires constant nursing
alimenting with tender words and gestures
it develops and blossoms
only in positive temperatures

hatred lives on hatred
grows abundantly in tropics and on poles

the wiser the wings love fastens to us
the higher the altitude we fall down from

hatred teaches us walking on earth
not stepping on fragile herbs of exaltation
teaches concretes such as axe knife or gun
recommends breathing not sighing

my element is hatred
it contains vitamins and animal proteins
contains everything what lets me live on
in the conviction that there is in man
something so pure
as a clenched fist of rose

A Tree

In my dream a tree grows up
it has bare branches
like hooks for hanging stretches of beef
grass around a tree or maybe hemp
wind crushes it like a skilled hand of a ropemaker

in my dream hands grow up
toward bare neck
they take me under arms take my shirt off
grass under foot is rough or maybe hemp
branches bleached like a bone in an anthill

in my dream a tree grows up
its branches reach
the waking where my bare neck is shining
and I do not know where I will float to
    through a dream more and more shallow
whether an axe will fly in on time for rescue

JERZY PLUTOWICZ

Jerzy Plutowicz, b. 1947, published 10 volumes of poetry; translates from Russian and
Byelorussian; his English debut was in *Stroker* in 1999.

Translated by Dobi Zalewska & Janusz Zalewski

the will of francois villon

this case to allocate space
for a situation testifying just one thing
everybody was born to utilize four boards
in times when counting errors are easy to make

and linen onto the face to cover the wound
possibly to shout down silence
and not to clog the throat saving on air
of the one whose kingdom is the size of soil under feet

viva la muerte

it's not true that time is a kaleidoscope with replaceable mirrors
crayons tubes of paint heads of plaster
when the deck escapes from your feet do not think about storm
flower-people garden-towns
wagon-society pushed away to dead-end rails

salty taste of wind
mouths are looking for luck in the air land and water
while it is hiding under an eyelid
jealous of the liberator demanding admiration
in the memory theater actors are wearing masks

fishing boats only boats
a woman with flower in her mouth only woman
flower will replace biography
sky-blue prince in silver gallery
and blood
more red than blood of a bull in which the great toreador washed his face

red sun red snow
red smile

door to the world
white door without handle

the machine of paul klee

do not desire do not remember and do not ask questions
the death guard is veiling pupils with a wing
and ignites repulsion as a tutelary spirit
goose bumps appear after first night

gulp of cold water mirror crushed with a heel
pail full of haven water flooded a cellar
to go through a hallway white as fear to go constantly forward
the one who looks back through his left arm knows he'll not return

blind nestling of dawn ripens here
inside a house dark as hatred
or a swarm of bees entangled in the brain
when an eye flows out as a drop of lead

behind the seventh gate of dream behind the knife naked as love
to build a precise mechanism for chirping
time pinches an eyelid as a grain of sand
rests in the shadow of light

ROMAN ŚLIWONIK

Roman Ś liwonik, b. 1930, published over a dozen books of poetry and some stories; he was co-founder of a prestigious Polish magazine, *Wspõtczenosc* (1956). He was published in English as early as in 1967, in *Steppenwolf,* and in the anthology *Four Contemporary Polish Poets* (Madison, WI, 1967, translated by Victor Contoski).

Translated by Dobi Zalewska & Janusz Zalewski

Poland

I

Arrives the Pope And around
it becomes white And holy
even blue
at the same time Faces of people
become clean
flows away to the fields
smell of naphtaline from clothes
in opened cabinets

Arrives the Nobelist
and people
begin to speak verse
and cry with Tears of a poet

Departs the Pope and the Nobelist
and even grass
seeing bare Battered as soil dullness
doesn't want to grow here

II

And They found origins here
and to them thirsty return
Maybe only in dreams
Lord elevated them
above the raised
empty hands of a crowd
and never
could it be more sadly
than at the moment when I cannot tell
why And what is this pretense

Both a Pole and a Man

To unknot a Pole To open
this fist Clot
of tendons Veins and muscles
Close Obscure Shrunk of evil
Bleached of wrath Stunning envy
pulsates Like hammers in temples
muddying envy Scorched Flooding with web eye

to unknot a Pole To straighten
let the blood freely flow
and eyes
from procession Holiday eyes Blue
and words from prayers forcing At least
to move the lips
let them become a miracle An idea
let them softly recall the content
not difficult Accessible Spoken
at weddings Baptisms And funerals
Let space send the light down
at white Sweaty brows

Captivities Starvations Plans from sand
of war
like hells whirl in memory
if one must live with all that
this means
that this is the rhythm of a planet
that the universe lives on that
or
that's carelessness of vanity

Therefore
Open yourself Straighten
squeezed with ignorance Cosmos
can only be tamed with pride
all this is short And sad
and very little knowledge is needed
remember only the words
from weddings Baptisms And from funerals

TÁHIRIH

The poems of the nineteenth-century Iranian mystic poet Táhirih (Arabic: pure) have seldom been translated into English. Also known as Qurratu'l-'Ayn (solace of the eyes), she was the first woman of Iran in modern times to achieve a public presence through her poetry. Writing in traditional, rhyming forms—often ghazals—she wrote mystic love poems with deep religious significance. Becoming a prominent follower of the Babi movement (later the Baha'i Faith) in 1844, she advocated the complete reformulation of Muslim law to meet the needs of a New Age. She is best known for deliberately entering a gathering of religious men without a veil as a symbolic act of defiance. She was imprisoned and eventually executed as a heretic in 1852. The following sampling of poems are from *Táhirih: A Portrait in Poetry: Selected Poems of Qurratu'l-'Ayn* (Los Angeles: Kalimat, 2004).

Translated by Anthony A. Lee & Amin Banani

Point by Point

If I meet you face to face, I
will retell—erase!—my heartbreak,
pain by pain,
word by word,
point by point.

In search of you—just your face!—I
roam through the streets lost in disgrace,
house to house,
place to place,
door to door.

My heart hopeless—broken, crushed!—I
heard it pound, till blood gushed from me,
fountain by fountain,
river by river,
sea by sea.

The garden of your lips—your cheeks!—
your perfumed hair, I wander there,
bloom to bloom,
rose to rose,
scent to scent.

Your eyebrow—your eye!—and the mole
on your face, somehow they tie me,
trait to trait,
passion to passion,
love to love.

While I grieve, with love—your love!—I
will reweave the fabric of my soul,
thread by thread,
warp by warp,
woof by woof.

Last, I searched my heart—page by page!—I
looked line by line. What did I find?
You and you,
you and you,
you and you.

Start Shouting!

Angels! Saints! All you holy ones above!
My true lover just walked in. Start shouting!

Night turned to day, dark into light. He's here
without a veil to hide his face. Start singing!

The Sun is up, it's rising in the West.
You armies of God's ecstasy! Start moving!

Iran set aflame, and Tehran burning,
pure spirit rises from his place. Start dancing!

At daybreak nightingales don't sing. The cock
struts out and birds of Glory start praising.

When my lover asks, *Am I not your Lord?*
even the gods reply in awe, *Thou art.*

His mighty river overflows, and floods
a thousand desert Karbalas[1]—to start.

The arches of his eyes will make the feuds
of warring faiths and creeds to disappear.

Moses and Jesus in heaven are stunned,
and all the holy ones are lost down here.

Two thousand Muhammads hear thunderbolts,
they wrap themselves in cloaks, tremble in fear.

The sea storms—it casts up its shining pearls.
To give way to the sun, the dawn makes haste.

Men melt, mountains quake before his beauty.
His majesty lays whole kingdoms to waste.

[1]   The place of the martyrdom of the Imam Husayn, and so a holy place for Shiite Muslims.
Christians might substitute the word "Calvary" to have an idea of the significance of the
location.

And me, destroyed by two strands of his hair.
The moon of his face drives me to despair.

Beloved, when will I see you up there,
see the light of your face, the shine of your hair?

The moon now has me mad with restless love
in the agony of my separation.

Just Let the Wind . . .

Just let the wind untie my perfumed hair,
my net would capture every wild gazelle.

Just let me paint my flashing eyes with black,
and that dark flag would make the world rebel.

Yearning, each dawn, to see my dazzling face,
the heaven lifts its golden looking-glass.

If I should pass a church by chance today,
Christ's own virgins would rush to my gospel.

Proclamation

Now hear me!

Since I proclaim what's manifest and true.
I speak the word of victory to you.

Strip off your rags of law and pious fashion.
Leap naked into the sea of compassion!

And how long in this wicked world of war
will you stray from your homeland, and how far?

Say: Be! and it will seem both clear and plain:
What comes from God returns to God again.

Running after You

So many will die of grief in their chains,
trembling with desire, running after you.

Although my true love comes to ravish me,
I'll stand before his sword, and gladly too.

My cruel lover invades my bed at dawn,
and I see beauty—the sunrise breaks through.

No pagan in China has such roguish eyes.
No musk compares to his hair wet with dew.

You ride past God and common folk careless—
just women, horse and saddle in your view.

You scorn this wine, you curse who pours it,
to follow hollow penance. What can I do?

I'll walk the beggar's path—though bad—it's mine.
It's Alexander's road that you pursue.

Ride past my camp, on your road to nowhere.
May you have all you wish, for it's your due.

While imprisoned (under house arrest) in Tehran some time before her execution, Táhirih was
summoned to the presence of the Shah, who was curious to see this now-famous woman. Apparently, he
liked her looks and proposed to make her one of his wives if she would abandon her new religion.
"Running after You" is supposed to have been her reply.

REVIEWS

Reviews

Overleaf:
Photos by Melanie Daye

On/Off the Beaten Path

R.D. Armstrong

The Lummox Press, 2001
P.O. Box 5301, San Pedro, California 90733
http://members.tripod.com/~Raindog/
50 pages, $6.00
ISBN: 1-929878-27-3

In R.D. Armstrong's *On/Off the Beaten Path*, the poet attempts to engage the shamanic/archetypal through a sequence of events, feelings, fears, confrontations in an automobile on a journey from L. A. to Albuquerque. Experientially, it is the journey to connect with mentors. It is written in language that evokes heart that exists in the now but also is beating pained with the past. It's like a Morse Code of the poet's special dialectic, evoking places, names, landscapes which will take the poet back to a landscape of pain, of youth & excess, of mortality.

Jim Harrison once wrote, "The poet is only a sorcerer bored with magic who has turned his attention elsewhere." Armstrong has turned his poetic attention to the open road:

> Perhaps it's the way the desert
> camouflages its constant state of movement
> hidden from our casual glimpses out
> across the seemingly endless nothing
> that sets us up for the next surprise . . .
> a land devoid of definition
> a blur of shapes
> of dirty
> washed-out colors . . .

The beaten path is the poet's love/hate relationship with an ageless landscape as well as his own interior one that for every mile, every small town, every butte, every railroad track crossed, is connecting him to his past. The "accursed shadow" that dogs his every move.

The beaten path is the long (I don't mean epic) poem as travelogue, something akin to Blaise Cendrars's *Prose of the Trans Siberian*—a confessional, a stream-of-consciousness piece, a journal entry. It is as if the desert Southwest is drawing the demons out of the poet at an alarming rate & placing them in his peripheral vision, sometimes, just out of reach of his language. It is what gives this poem its tension, its verisimilitude. Once he lands in Albuquerque at the home of a fellow poet, the sustenance of talk & camaraderie diminishes the shadow, but only for awhile. The Shadow is potent, it is the Trickster of Southwest Native American lore that scours the arroyos, stands of cholla & city streets for souls like the poet's. All Armstrong had to do was take the trip, air it out

with language, attempt to make sense of it. In New Mexico, they're all here: the arche-
types, the shamans, the whackos, the Humpbacked Flute Player, Raven, Trickster
Coyote, the curandera, the bruja. If what Everson says is true, & I paraphrase, that for
the poet the main way to evoke the shaman in oneself is to engage the demonic,
Armstrong certainly has done this. But I don't like to throw around the word shaman
too much. It's overused. Not every poet is one any more than every poet is an outlaw,
but in both cases you can tell in a New Mexican minute who isn't.

On/Off the Beaten Path is an engaging work. You read as Armstrong sometimes
struggles with his language against the landscape; but when both merge at times into
that magic whole, it is powerful: you feel his *duende*; you can sense his vulnerability &
you know he'll be back to stalk the Shadow—that's why he's a poet.

Reviewed by John Macker

Mules of Love
Ellen Bass

BOA Editions, 2002
260 East Ave., Rochester, NY 14604
http://www.boaeditions.org
89 pages. $13.95
ISBN 1-929918-22-4

The title of this book says it all, and many of the poems support
the meaning: the lucky ones are Mules of Love, not just of erotic
love, but of the details and particulars of a "dirty" house, the sand a child carries into
the room, or the mold on refrigerated bread. And what are those things "mules" of? We
can only ask—and make our metaphors, which are part of the Eros of perception itself.
Nothing eludes the care of such written emotion, naked and attentive. The opening
poem in this collection states: "Everything on the Menu." That includes "the hard
nugget of [her lover's] pain," which the narrator of the poem "Basket of Figs" would lift
". . . tenderly, as a great animal might / carry a small one in the private / cave of the
mouth." These are libratory poems about the struggle that accompanies the develop-
ment of personality over a lifetime. Learned, inherited, or thrust upon us: worry,
disconnection, and dread are existential elements in our human personalities. In her
poem "The Thing Is," Bass writes of such a confrontational instant when you must

> hold life like a face,
> between your palms, a plain face
> no charming smile, no violet eyes,
> and you say, yes I will take you
> I will love you, again.

There's ecstasy and humor in this book, but it's the Mule idea, and I think it is an important one—the steady bearing of the inevitable weight of circumstance—that carries these narrative lyrics to the watery trough.

Reviewed by Doren Robbins

One Hand on the Wheel
Dan Bellm

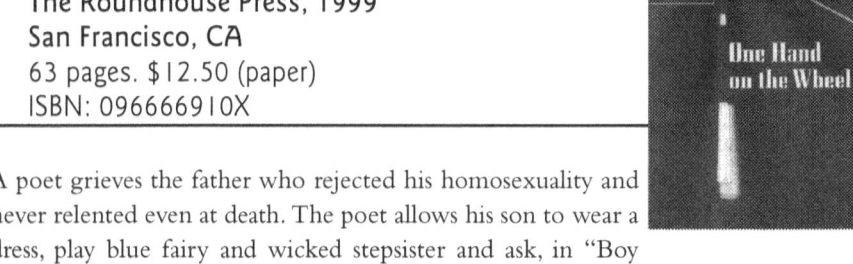

The Roundhouse Press, 1999
San Francisco, CA
63 pages. $12.50 (paper)
ISBN: 096666910X

A poet grieves the father who rejected his homosexuality and never relented even at death. The poet allows his son to wear a dress, play blue fairy and wicked stepsister and ask, in "Boy Wearing a Dress," "If we cut off our / penises then we'd be girls, wouldn't we, Dad?" The son likes to play the girl parts of stories; he likes their speeches and their dresses and their shoes. "Am I beautiful, Dad," the son asks the poet, who associated his own father with "work shirts, the smell of an Army uniform." Clearly Bellm was not allowed to play girl games. This is a poetry which breaks a cycle of abuse and rejection, which forgives, which changes history. It is necessary poetry.

It is also beautifully and subtly crafted. "Lament" puts forth an aesthetics of loss.

There should be more empty space on the paper
. . .There should be more silence for him
the one taught to ask less
told to wait without hope
left to comfort himself
who decided to tell no one
. . . There should be a blinding darkness
. . . A terrible
soundless
whirlwind
erasing.

The poet appreciates and is saddened by the working-class culture which rendered his father strong, silent, comfortless. The poet knew his father by hands "scarred over nicely, the tip sawed away . . . handshakes that hurt," words that hurt. "Don't you be homosexual, too," the father calls to his second son as he throws both out of his house.

Bellm's was not an easy reconciliation. In "Damage" he seems to be talking with a teacher at a poetry workshop. "There's a kind of a beautiful damage," the teacher says, apparently admonishing him to write his truth. "I wouldn't call the damage a

---

gift / . . . If I could make him pay, I wouldn't," he says of his father. Bellm questions revenge and recovery as impulses to poetry. "Admire the fury in a banished soul / brought up right. When I hear order, I obey."

Perhaps we are to understand that his father's discipline underlies Bellm's exquisitely chiselled stanzas, his stripped-down yet musical lines. The father expected "the Catholic heaven, the resurrection of the body," yet is made immortal by the son who seems to reject everything: machismo, intolerance, the hard work of hands. Unless, of course one perceives poetry as making, as carpentry, as the hard work of hands. Does the son reject his father's Catholic heaven? There are veiled allusions here of conversion to Judaism, a *midrash*, a blessing, some Hebrew. Perhaps Bellm will be more explicit in his next book.

One Hand on the Wheel is the first offering of the new California Poetry Series, designed to celebrate diversity of poets whose work is identified with the state of California. A fine beginning, I look forward to more.

Reviewed by Nancy Shiffrin

The Carrington Monologues

Terri Brown-Davidson

Lit Pot Press, 2002
3909 Reche Rd. Ste #132
Fallbrook, CA 92028
http://www.litpotpress.com
113 pp. $11.95

But I knew I wasn't just a virgin
but frigid as a field in January—
painting'd claimed that emotion and made it spiritual.

"The Genesis of Carrington's Relationship with Gertler: The Slade Academy Years"

Its cover glossy, luminescent, strikingly black and white, Terri Brown-Davidson's *The Carrington Monologues* intrigues with its brashness, boldness: a gorgeous blonde, nude, her back to the viewer. Vibrant shadows, softened highlights draw the eye everywhere the photographer desires us to look. This is a cover that beckons us to peek, so we take a little glimpse. Then another. Open to read and find ourselves submerging quickly. That's when we realize the cover art is no accident, for within this volume of poetry breathes a life drawn so convincingly—a shadowplay culminating in brilliant bursts of light or a surging darkness—that one wonders if the poet's truly been there, back to the early 1900s, if she's stumbled onto a secret time-doorway and accepted an invitation into the mind of Dora Carrington.

The Carrington poems explore the inner and outer life of artist Dora Carrington, whose all-consuming love for the Bloomsbury group writer Lytton Strachey, a homosexual, leads her to abandon serious dreams of an art career—as well as an incredible (though raw) talent—and instead devote her life to the pursuit of an unattainable craving. Frigid in her younger years, Dora's creativity is in inverse proportion to her sexuality, decreasing as she expands her experiences with an array of men. What Brown-Davidson accomplishes is not a benediction of Carrington, nor is it a condemnation.

In *The Carrington Monologues,* Brown-Davidson successfully envisions—and shares that vision—human nature at its most poignant and painful. A woman living on the razor's edge: from an emotionally abandoned child, precocious artist, intensely strong-willed girl to an all-grown-up sexual toy, her creative light dimming. Lytton's constant companion, but yearning to be more.

Brown-Davidson's created an incredibly believable fictionalized world, a powerfully lush version of Carrington's actual life that transcends the physical here-and-now, seducing us with the deft precision of a camera's lens, the irreverent madness of the artistic genius's eye.

Reviewed by Season Harper

Driven into the Shade
Brandon Cesmat

Poetic Matrix Press, 2003
P.O. Box 1223 Madera, CA 93639
http://www.poeticmatrix.com
93 pages. $12.00
ISBN: 0-9714003-3-4

Driven into the Shade is not "dark," it's chiaroscuro. At a poetry festival headlining the blissful Billy Collins, Brandon Cesmat read "Where Was Fidel When I Needed Him?"—a poem about electrifying a father's genitals and admiring Castro—to a San Diego crowd of about 400 K–12 students and their parents. That Cesmat's protest poem received some of the loudest applause of the day says as much about the complexities of American families as it does about *Driven into the Shade*'s aesthetic for articulating the liabilities of the light and attributes of the dark.

The 'Fidel' poem could serve as an emblem for *Driven into the Shade*, which unapologetically insists that the domestic and the political, the private and the public, the profane and divine are intimately connected. Occasionally in contemporary poetry, these connections get severed and the dichotomies become either piles of I'm-okay/you're-okay mush or distant planets of smug transgression and literary isolation. Using fine distinctions, Cesmat travels the antipodes with a rebellious clarity that seems to say the contemporary stakes—especially in his California—are too high to be left to anything less the narrative poem imbued with the diaphanous imagery of metaphor punctuated by music.

When Cesmat writes in "Gracias, Sabás," "Today I look at flour tortillas as topographical maps / brown and black hills in the white desert / where *masa harina* rose into the palms that made them," he moves from the mundane to the humane to the divine quickly and clearly, as if he were revealing a new trinity, a new communion for America's sin of historical amnesia.

Perhaps more interesting than Cesmat's milieu of the United States as a part of Latin America is his less-than-innocent view of family. Poems such as "Shadow Around the Ring" portray children unromantically, describing a love of dedication and gumption that is probably more honest than many families would like to admit. Cesmat celebrates such love in "Ice Drum," where a father and son throw ice and rocks onto a frozen pond they swam in the summer before:

Surfaces change and we say nothing
as my stones ping and crack
and his ice hums and sizzles
on this morning when only my first born and I hear this music
back through the seasons
and down to the bottom.

Since the book seems to track a voice from boyhood to fatherhood, idealizing neither time, thus giving the collection a relentlessly honest arc. Imagine Blake born in L.A.'s rumbling sprawl instead of London: *Songs of Experience* sung in a bluesy voice.

Families, rather than being the vessel of survival, become the crisis to be survived. In the title poem, the narrator tries to keep his mother and father from divorcing, and in doing so destroys himself. If that narrator is also the father of the haunting poem "Sons," then family becomes something of a Promethean Fire. Perhaps most frightening is the contemporary sonnet "Between Covers":

On this planet all lines intersect if we follow
them far enough. Our poor mother bets all on her children,
believing us more faithful than lovers though we abandon
her a day at a time. She is an egg we split and leave hollow.

Rather than leaving the reader hollow, *Driven into the Shade* fills one up, as if feeling hollow is a failure to acknowledge that the dark is full with its own atmosphere.

Reviewed by Mark Steinbeck

Ice Drum
Brandon Cesmat

Gaernarvon Press, 2003
4665 Mississippi Street, #1, San Diego, CA 92116
14 pages. $8.00
ISBN: 0-9716383-0-6

The chapbook *Ice Drum* by Brandon Cesmat is a tease, a snack, an appetizer. In the book Cesmat writes about an icy pond "where / the sun falls only eight inches deep" and beneath the warm water is a multi-dimensional world that is deep blue, dark green, and black—that is far away from "remembered light," and that contains a kind of proof at the bottom. Cesmat's chapbook, like all chapbooks, is a tease because the reader only becomes acquainted with the top of the pond, the tip of the iceberg, the promise of a fine writer. Rich in themes, the chapbook chronicles the demise of southern California. In the poem "Californiatown," Cesmat admonishes the reader: "This is how to taste California, the developing rot like wine going bad, / dry orchards and planned communities confirming the future tense." Like a flower pressed between pages, he tries to capture the vanishing beauty of southern California in poems like "Pomegranates." "In the windbreak along the avocado grove, / pomegranates brush against the coyote's fur. . . Don't deny the juice and leave the / pomegranates on the branches for crows." Another theme in the chapbook is fathers and sons. One of my favorite poems is "Where Was Fidel When I Needed Him?" Though Cesmat was afraid to follow in his father's footsteps and botch the job of raising children, he is not afraid to begin a poem with "The son I didn't want waits until I sit on the bank / before running downhill and jumping on by back." He's not afraid because one of the proofs at the bottom of this book is his fathomless love for his sons. As with all good chapbooks, the reader will close this one hungry for more of the author's work.

Reviewed by Susan Luzzaro

Shelter
Lisa Glatt

Pearl Editions, 2000
3030 E. Second St, Long Beach, CA 90803
http://www.pearlmag.com
64 pages. $10.95
ISBN: 1-888219-13-0

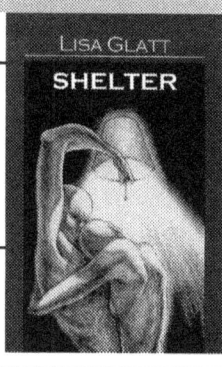

In her most recent collection of poetry, *Shelter,* Lisa Glatt adeptly maneuvers a road of personal pain, healing, and self-discovery, while embodying a collective voice of modern women and speaking to the affects of human emotion with resonance, wit, and heart-wrenching candor. The themes throughout the work—pleasure teamed with angst, bravery marching alongside fear, and the indistinguishable parallels between love and lust—characterize a generation of young women whose sweeping attempts at autonomy have perhaps unfairly classified them as immature and unintelligible misfits. Glatt's poetry responsibility deflects those myths by combining pathos and humor to focus on issues common to the art of contemporary female living, ultimately demonstrating that self-reliance can be achieved in the face of real tragedy.

Although many of the poems characterize unusual circumstances, her accessible language and unpretentious poetic delivery fully engage the reader. In "If You Have Sex with a Married Man," Glatt's candor refrains from indulging in over-the-top sentimentality. In short, she calls the spade a spade:

> . . . be suspicious when he says, *I hate to go*
> *home—I'd rather stay a month with you.*

> . . . consider that if that were so
> *you'd* be his wife—and what would you be
> then, but the deceived woman in furry slippers,
> standing in the driveway, blowing kisses?

Glatt is fluent in the art of frank dialect and maintains the integrity of the work without alienating her reader, clearly demonstrating that hers is a voice of maturity and experience.

In "The Body Is in Charge," Glatt describes a terminally ill mother's deft talent for making dresses, but more specifically, illuminates the narrator's own reverence for her mother's capacity to live so completely while staring down death's door, the irony being her mother's ability to create something for her body, while simultaneously suffering the betrayal of her body:

> Tonight, my mother stands in the hallway, pulling a bright red
> number over her bald head, working the stretchy fabric over her
> shoulders. And she is beautiful, at the edge of everything,
> standing on that cliff in our hallway, working the vivid dress
> over her still-sexy thighs.

Glatt shares feelings of impending loss without self-indulgence, allowing the reader to see the work with total separation from the author—an essential attribute for any poet whose objective is to move beyond self-beneficial therapy. Women identify with the scene because it speaks to female vulnerability in relation to outward appearance; moreover, Glatt's transformation of language into viable human emotion enables the reader to benefit from her wisdom.

Glatt's poetry brings comfort to her contemporary female readers, specifically those whose personal struggles read like an excerpt from *Shelter*. She deserves a seat alongside the likes of Sharon Olds and Dorianne Laux as a poet whose voice will continue to speak the language of the female condition and sympathize with women struggling to emerge from dysfunction intact.

Reviewed by Rebecca Jane Benitez

Flares on Water
Nicholas Kolumban

Black Swan / Széphalom, 2001
1068 Budapest, Városligeti fasor 38 Hungary
http://www.inaplo.hu/sz/index.html
142 pages. $8.50
ISBN: 1-877969-18-8

It certainly takes courage or unusual life experiences to write a book in two languages. No, *Flares on Water* is not a bilingual book where American poems are neatly translated into a major or a minor tongue. *Flares on Water* contains, bravely and astutely, 74 American and 32 Hungarian poems. The author, now an American citizen, was raised in Budapest, Hungary and came to the U.S. as a teenager during the devastating battle against the Soviet army in 1956. Still, after 40 years, the author takes up the mantle of an outsider in his poems. In "Recalling Resumés" he remembers that his personal life could only be defined by the data left out of his resumé such as his lovers, his personal friends and his blooming backyard. In "Nicholas Kolumban in 1999" and "Metamorphosis," he seems to know that, if anything, he became two people, thus completing the process of acculturation. He is both an American and a Hungarian, just like the artist Escher's creation—the geese—are of two forms and are "tearing loose from one flesh, / soaring into life as opposites / but feeding from a single core."

Kolumban has numerous poems about his friends and animals. He coins touching eulogies for a dead friend:

You're the Redon soul-flower of my porch,
my conscience dressed in black.
Do you feel the dusk?
Do you darken?
Where is your luminous soul?

He shows off Princeton, New Jersey—"a piece of Americana"—to a European friend or visits affectionately a fellow poet in Michigan "where nature is spacious, / where people speak as vividly as birds." In the case of a Hungarian childhood friend, he laments the fact that he (the friend) had been unable to return to his birthplace for 33 years because he had fought during the Hungarian Revolution and was condemned to death in absentia.

Indeed, Kolumban's intimacy with animals such as white rats, dogs, and cats brings to mind Neruda's open, life-affirming familiarity with swans, mongoose and orang-utans. Kolumban lets the white rats out of their cage and encourages them to use his body "as a connecting road." He only muses about the probability that "love must keep captives." He believes that his dog Maddie has been "elevated by love." In a poem about aging, he maintains that "he always loved animals back." It appears that love is a central theme of Kolumban's book of poems. To accept and to be accepted with open arms is a necessity for him, he who became by a quirk of fate a captive of a new continent.

Reviewed by Tom Ruschak

The Science of In-Between

An Anthology of Nineteen Contemporary Hungarian Poets

Nicolas Kolumban, Translator

Box Turtle Press, 1999
184 Franklin St, New York, NY 10013
254 pages.
ISBN: 1-893654-01-X

We can never have enough anthologies, filled with bad poems as well as good, the mediocre hobnobbing with and receiving reflected glory from the "immortals," everyone equal in the community of paper.

But, sometimes, an anthology brings us back to a sense of poetry as a "fiesta," a celebration of voices, a carnival where the sublime and the three-headed chicken are shown in their true light, as each being, in however small a way, mirrors reflecting the qualities of the other.

With the publication of *The Science of In-Between*, Nicolas Kolumban has put together a book whose variety of sensibilities and styles is never ponderous, never snobbish.

If this anthology of contemporary Hungarian poets had been compiled by an earnest, noteworthy American poet, it may have concentrated on the usual "dark" tones of exile and repression, on the "Hungarian" poet as Eastern European stepchild to Franz Kafka. Thanks largely to Mr. Kolumban's ability to translate, as well as his own sense of gentleness and humor, we have poems as frankly comic, joyful, and deceptively plain spoken as Katalin Mezey's "The Confession of a Newly-wed:"

> In high school, the girl sitting next to me
> told me once
> that her parents got a divorce.
> I asked her why and she reluctantly admitted:

"Mother always made watery gravy."
Since then, I make gravy with stock,
carefully testing its thickness.
I want to make certain that my husband will find
another reason for divorcing me.

Note how casually Mezey turns an otherwise standard "eager to please" new wife story on its head, making the last few lines a wonderfully cynical and comic statement on the idea of "pleasing" anyone. "The Confessions of a Newly-wed" reminds me of the best Hal Sirowitz "mother said" poems. But in "This Is No Secret," "The Old Policeman" and "Albatross," Mezey ups the stakes, using her knack for gently surrealist and wry imagery to skewer accurately and painfully the oppressive pall of Hungary under the Soviet regime.

Mezey is a poet I've never read before and now look forward to reading more of. That is one of the prime achievements of a good anthology. The anthologist takes you by the hand and points out choice sites, places of wonder you may just want to investigate in a fuller, more leisurely way.

Tibor Zalán is another poet with whom I was not familiar, and with whom I am now enamored. His playful, wounded, hyperbolic love poems remind me of Apollanaire's, only they are even more staked to the comic possibilities involved in addressing the "beloved." Like may Eastern European poets, Zalán is adept at what I'll call "natural surrealism," the strange images and leaps that grow out of the soil of absurdist governments, the sort of surrealism that is embedded into the brains of the oppressed and the exiled. This sort of absurdity is never contrived, never done for the sake of confusing the issue. Rather, it aids and abets the sharpness and wit with which one combats the banality of evil. All that aside, note the sheer exuberance of these lines from Zalán's poem, "When It's Not Fashionable to Write about Silence, I'll Portray Your Silence":

. . . If I'd portray your silence, I'd write about your
unearthly authority
I'd recount your sobs among dented pots.
I'd write about your perennial anguish
In my sleep, jazz musicians go on strike, wearing
my shirts.
They occupy stages that collapse into blue light.

Sándor Csoóri is the most famous poet in the group of nineteen, and, at least by the evidence of this anthology, not necessarily the best; and that is good news indeed for the reader, for Csoóri is certainly no unwanted guest at this banquet. His poem, "In the Root Cellar" is especially poignant:

This where you've ended.
You speak eloquently, although age-spotted, bent leaves
rustle in front of your words
and drop, with you, into the nothingness of autumn.

Perhaps Csoóri's lyricism is more congenial to American tastes. He seems far less surreal, far more in the tradition of normative free verse, and his poems announce their importance, have a gravitas, at least in translation, that makes them seem somehow officially good. They are good; but, American poets, with their somewhat knee-jerk disdain for exorbitance, would do well to learn from the other Hungarian acrobats represented in this anthology, all of whom seem able to defy gravity itself. Consider the genuine terror and originality of these lines from Ottó Tolnai:

> I'm skinning a rabbit on the porch
> Houses like toy blocks I'm daydreaming
> a gun shot The rabbit jumps up
> this is not death yet
> Between my legs a road with trees
> We hug each other on the razor-sharp hook
> This rabbit is a true athlete:
> small ass, wide shoulders
> His tongue a dirty rose petal
> in my mouth

The Science of In-Between is essential reading for any intelligent poet who wants to know some of the better work by Hungarian writers both in Hungary and in the "greater Hungary" of exile. Kolumban should be embraced for his clear, concise translations. This is a truly well-wrought book of poems.

Reviewed by Joe Weil

Fingerpainting on the Moon
Writing and Creativity as a Path to Freedom

Peter Levitt

Harmony Books / Random House, 2003
New York.
226 pages. $21.00
ISBN: 0-609-61048-1

Early in his long-awaited book on creative process, *Fingerpainting on the Moon*, Peter Levitt says, "I have written this book to help readers become the happy geniuses of their households," deriving his image from William Carlos Williams's poem, "Danse Russe." He weaves storytelling, personal disclosure, and discoveries from sages in many spiritual paths, including Islam, Judaism, Christianity, Buddhism, and Hinduism, with poetry, exercises, and commentary derived from his own discovered wisdom to help readers nourish their imaginations in joyful and surprising ways.

Peter Levitt

Levitt has fashioned a book that functions as part practicum and part spiritual guide on how to enter the world of creativity in one's own medium, whether that medium be writing or the visual or performing arts. His exercises are precise in their practicality and his commentary is expansive across the range of what Leibniz called the "philosophia perennis," the perennial philosophy that recognizes and explores the divine in all elements of the universe.

Levitt's work calls all the world into play—"play" is an important concept here—to explore topics constellated around creativity, which include the nature of risk, resistance, fear, imagination, desire, and self-knowledge; what gives us joy; what helps us complete ourselves and, in so doing, repair the world. The resulting chorus of voices reveals and expands Levitt's themes, encouraging readers to explore the interconnectedness of every aspect of the universe, a concept Levitt returns to again and again.

"Please" is an operative word in *Fingerpainting on the Moon*. "Please," here a gentle exhortation and an extension of respect from writer to practitioner, invites the reader to participate in each suggested exercise. Who can resist this kind of invitation? By building his exercises as gently and as organically as possible out of the discussion in each chapter, Levitt models what he wants us to practice. See, he says, you can do this. Here is a way you can build a life based on practices that allow you to accomplish your dreams, as an artist and as a human being.

The reader learns to trust Levitt's voice because the intimacy he creates with his reader models the intimacy he would like each reader to cultivate with him/herself and the creative work that reader would like to accomplish. This intimacy is one of the more remarkable aspects of Levitt's book. It is based on a conscious myth-making and a self-understanding that suggests those special moments of insight that we call into being or cultivate through exercises or rituals can become, through consistent practice, organizing principles of our lives, moving out of "specialness" into the ordinary. When they are no longer special, but have become part of our everyday way, then, Levitt tells us, our creative lives can assume their full power.

There is often a danger in this kind of book that when an author reveals himself, when he injects into his discourse personal information, the work may unravel quickly into ego. Levitt avoids this trap by deftly offering just enough of the right story at the right time, by interspersing his own stories without those of others. His literate, lyric prose reveals the depth and breadth of his years of study and teaching. He offers us his understanding of human nature and realizes our need for a teacher who will show us respect and compassion. He shows us how each reader can call forth her own creative powers and leads us to understand that "Everything is permitted in the imagination."

As I read this book, I learned the best way for me to use the exercises: I made a date with each chapter. I suggest readers who want to integrate Levitt's exercises with their own creative process set aside uninterrupted time for work. This kind of careful consideration gives room to decide which exercises to practice. As Levitt tells us, "What matters in all of your writing is the quality of attention, of presence, that you bring to yourself and the world."

Peter Levitt's *Fingerpainting on the Moon* is meant to be a holy and joyful, precise and elegant guide to creativity for all of us who feel we are in some way dying or have never completely awakened to the possibilities in our lives. It is about the making of art, and more important, the making of our lives. "Yes!" and "Now!"

Reviewed by Ann Colburn

Livelihood
Phoebe MacAdams

Cahuenga Press, 2003
1256 N Mariposa, Los Angeles, CA 90029
96 Pages. $12.00
ISBN: 0-9715519-1-X

Livelihood

Phoebe MacAdams

Phoebe MacAdams begins her new collection, *Livelihood*, with a poem that is more question than invocation. "What is teaching, anyway?" she asks. She understands that there is no answer, only many responses, and honors the question instead. Throughout this book, notable for its quiet power, she explores what it means to be a teacher, to live daily with the young and disenfranchised, to share their frequent despair and rare, but profound, hope. These poems are homage, to the creative spirit, to the natural world, to friends and family, and especially to the high school students who inspired the book's title.

Livelihood is divided into three sections. The first, Poems 1986–2002, explores the connectedness of all things encountered in daily life. The opening poem evokes "Hathor, goddess of schools,/ her loving embrace" and ends with the "Old English *tocen*, / token, a mark, a sign: here!" For if she is here, we are too, called in to witness the transformative power of language over the mundane. If we are lost "in the complicated halls" it is poetry that leads us home, that brings us together. It is this sense that informs one of the finest poems in the book, "Connectedness: My Students, My Husband":

I teach the roundness of things, which
starts with my wedding ring, the circle
of teaching, of notebooks, of writing.

By the end, the poem opens to enfold not just husband and students, but the reader also: "and all of us go round / full of sky, like stars."

Like stars, too, are poems that radiate light even when relating unspeakable sorrow. Life in an inner-city school, such as the one where MacAdams teaches, is rife with the kind of tragic circumstance that would be unacceptable anywhere else. We learn, in "Hard Season," that

> This month
> four students have been killed:
> Steve and Frank shot by random bullets,
> Mercy killed by a hit and run driver
> and last night, talking to Jeffrey
> and his family at back-to-school night,
> I heard about his best friend, Mario,
> shot last week.

By this time we have read about Steve and Frank and Diana, and we learn about Jeffrey and Lydia, their often bitterly painful lives and their triumphs over random death. "This," MacAdams writes, "is a hard season for my students, / who grow anyway." And she gives them what cannot assuage their grief, but only mark its presence: the gift of poetry. The poem ends with the acceptance that this is all she can offer: "This is for them."

There is much that the students, and the act of writing, give MacAdams in return. It is often said that the best teachers are those most open to learning, and *Livelihood* is as much about learning as it is about teaching. In "That's About It," after a discussion with students, the poet reflects on ancestors, on death and its inevitable approach. She mourns leaving:

> It has taken me fifty years to love this life,
> our house, this beautiful summer, our food.
> My husband is in the next room
> making happy noises with his computer.
> . . . we pay attention.

It is this exacting attention to the everyday, to the people who surround her, that make the poems in this section so memorable.

Also rewarding are the three longer poems that make up the middle section. Here, the poet connects her past, "I remember Christmas parties at Aunt Mary Peltz's," with the present and the deeply troubled school district where she labors. Her students understand the trouble. They've been there. They reassure her: "It's a matter of survival." MacAdams juxtaposes the simple acts the students perform with so much faith to the deception by the school district officials that led to the 1989 teachers strike. "How," she asks, "do you lose $200,000,000?" Always with unflinching details, she documents the personal turmoil that leads her to conclude there is no other solution but to "lock the door to my classroom / and strike."

Many years pass between "Teacher Strike: 1989" and the poems in the last section, which cover a year of teaching from July 2001 to April 2002. These final poems again acknowledge that often the question is more important than the answer. "What is truth?" the poet asks the students. Then: "I don't try to answer these questions. I just ask, / then I sit back quietly and smile." One feels throughout this work the resonance of these questions, even after the horror of watching, with students, "thousands die" on

September 11 and knowing that despite all the urgent directives from school district officials to teachers, there is absolutely nothing adequate to say.

MacAdams tells us in the introduction that "the Buddhist idea of Right Livelihood" means "a profession that is honorable and does not bring harm to others." That the poet can reflect on a year of teaching with its endless struggles and frequent disappointments and say, "There is a joy in all of this," demonstrates that she has, indeed, chosen a right livelihood. How fortunate her students must be, and how lucky we are, to have this poetry that not only does not "bring harm" but provides such pleasure.

Reviewed by Kathleen Tyler

Reunions
Harry E. Northup

Cahuenga Press, 2001
1256 N Mariposa, Los Angeles, CA 90029
256 Pages. $15.00
ISBN: 0-9649240-9-9

How often have you visited the Poetry section fervently hoping for something new only to find yet another translation of Dante or a typical university press issue?

In the 2001 harvest season, a handsome, cobalt blue cover beckoned, depicting an atelier with beaming lamp and the illuminated, considerate face of an author. When you open *Reunions* by Harry E. Northup you begin one of the finest volumes of poetry ever published in Southern California. Northup's seventh book is even stronger, braver, more clearly written and realized than its excellent predecessor, *The Ragged Vertical*.

For those unfamiliar with Northup, think William Carlos Williams born mid-century in Nebraska and moved to Hollywood. He writes from his core out. You find he is a devoted husband and father, deeply dedicated to acting. Through all, the soul of a poet rises, falls and rises again. He dreams, remembers, sings, and gives thanks and praises. In no time you know his heart, his mind, his wife and son, his home, his neighborhood, and his jobs.

The scenes of *Reunions* course all over the illustrious, variegated L.A. timespace: the unemployment office on Venice Blvd. to a Picasso-laden room in the County Museum of Art; the 99-cent store on Normandie to an inn on Pismo Beach; the basin's Silver Spoon diner to a ranch atop Beachwood Canyon; the heyday of the Sunset Strip to the desert mountains of Idyllwild.

There's raw reporting: sensitive and frank, embarrassed by nothing, afraid of no truth. Northup crafts brief but thorough narratives with pictures, inner and outer dialogs, and the specific, precious details of life that both ground and vitalize poetry. This is a rare poetic with which anyone can identify.

Northup gives all and asks for nothing back from the reader. He is utterly without literary pretension or device. For this alone he's a most important writer in his community and in the American language at large.

Because Northup does not shrink at all from comprehensively expressing his hopes, fears, and realities in love, work, aging, or his family's well being, the reader is transported dreamlike by the kinetic tableau of urban life—not unlike that depicted in the six Martin Scorsese films, including *Taxi Driver* and *Mean Streets*, in which Northup performed—without graphic violence as dramatic crutch.

Instead, Northup honors all things peaceful and tender. He writes of heartfelt encounters with the children of his deceased teacher Ann Stanford; the tension of baseball games as his beloved Dodgers face playoff elimination; empathetic run-ins with brother artists on the streets of East Hollywood; signal experiences reading HD, John Donne, Basil Bunting, and Hart Crane; the sweet high jinks of his cats; and the "vicissitudes of professional acting" about which Robert Peters says no one has ever written more movingly.

Northup evinces the holiest regard for his family, friends, city, and arts but his surest passion is his wife Holly Prado. Anyone who's attempted a Valentine's Day sonnet knows the wrenching mission it is, yet Northup writes shining accounts of his love for Holly on a weekly, sometimes daily basis—as the faithful dating of each composition in *Reunion*'s six sections, covering 1995–2000, reveals.

We're in a new millennium, a new year, a new world order—new everything by so many measures. Poets and poetry aficionados must soberly assess the state of the art. These are lean times for publishing and fine arts and there are very few practitioners delivering any news anyway. We lose far more masters than we herald.

Harry Northup, with the gift of *Reunions*, presents one of the definitive poetic chronicles of the physical and emotional scope of Californian and American life in the last thirty years or more.

Reviewed by John Feins

Nightwalking
Joel B. Peckham

Pecan Grove Press
64 pages, $12.00
ISBN: 1877603732

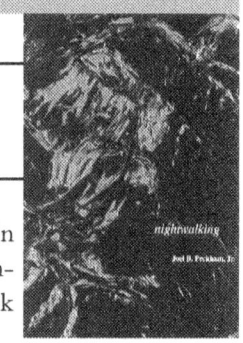

Joel B. Peckham's first book of poems, *Nightwalking*, unfolds in an urgent, manic, wild desire to communicate something essential, even elemental, to the reader: line by crafted line this book less comforts in its relentless pacing than offers us the tumult of life, its atavistic dreams and desires, its violent cadences, its shocking and tender diminuendos.

Ambitious and muscular, these poems do not apologize for their raw edges but still contain within them a large tenderness of heart for the people and places they evoke. "'O' Street, Lincoln, NE," for example, is a place

> where no-one
> lives but everyone works, where every breath is wind-blown,
> and like paper driven past the stoplights over the rise
> in the hill to the blackened windows of a 'gentlemen's club'
> where a neon woman, her mouth open, whispers her lie—we want
> you here, anything can be bought.

Like the haunted consciousness that speaks in these poems, Peckham is a night-walker who is out stalking a darkness that both mirrors his own insomnia and something eating away at the culture itself.

Equal part narrative and lyric, these mini-stories become part of a larger context: most of the poems center around working class men and women—ghosts really—whose stories are rarely told and less often heard ("I hear them in the whine that resonates in old metal," from "South Side Aneurysm—6:10 A.M.") and whose haunted lives are captured in Peckham's granite images, of a man bent over a steel press, a woman snapping laundry from a clothesline. His attempts are always for the gut reaction of where these people live at the dream-nadir of their lives and gestures, often past the breaking point; he is an astute, albeit indirect poet of social conscience, of those a society either leaves behind or fails to notice in the first place, lending his characters a threadbare dignity in the face of crushing forces.

This volume speaks from a consciousness that tries to break out into democratic song, to claim the song and story of many, not just the privileged (or academic) few. Crows, grackles, prairie falcons, wounded deer, hitchhikers, ghosts, immigrants, and idiot savants populate these poems, a bestiary that swirls in the process of living and dying and being reborn in Peckham's imagination, a reach that often succeeds and sometimes fails, but which is unremitting in its hunger to feel and to embrace. "And now this—," he writes in the collection's most powerful poem, "Cage Cry," "something wild, bleeding and caught in the wrong world." The same can be said for the sensibility behind these poems, one shot through with a driving but nameless remorse, by turns dramatic, soaring, and almost giddingly intense; Rilke's epigram that "beauty is nothing but the beginning of terror" finds deep resonance in a first book like *Nightwalking*, only here the terror cleanses even as it cleaves, redeems even as it pulls asunder.

Reviewed by Robert Vivian

Beyond Rhyme and Reason

Annie Reiner

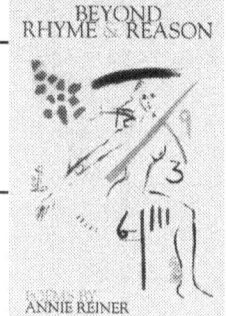

Red Dancefloor Press, 2002
PO Box 4974, Lancaster, CA 93539-4974
64 pages, $14.95
ISBN: 1-88168-15-8

Every real lover is a genius.
Genius is madness
without fear,
while knowing
there is much to fear.

Delve, twist, gyre in the nimble whirl of our deepest human fibers. *Beyond Rhyme and Reason* is a door through which to enter sweet in-betweenness, a twilight, the heart's intuition. It is here Ms. Reiner moves as a curious child in shadow asking, "What's that?" for the very first time.

Have you ever tried to write a poem in silence? I have a fat drawer of failed attempts. But Ms. Reiner writes:

My first language is

[Silence]

It's a complex music
like rain on the roof . . .
Every drop a poem.

later the words:

My first language is silence
in which I hear these breezes speak

She understands, treasures and communicates with grace the shape that has no shape; she hears what too few of us do. The cover, a painting by Ms. Reiner, is alive with the same silence and space she knows.

"I try to be sensitive to these faint signals of inner life as they emerge to speak to and color our worlds," she writes in the Afterword. (The "Afterword" alone is worth buying the book.) I wish I knew whether to credit painter Annie, poet Annie, playwright Annie, short story Annie, or psychotherapist Annie for her agility on the page in capturing the shadows we have felt but seldom name, but the Foreword suggests it's a combination of them all. She knows epiphany, and the poems are full of these moments:

. . . the choice moment, the moment of choice in
which the soul knows itself. The world stops.

Reiner writes without armor. There are no jaded personae or sarcasm or grinding axes to protect her. It is straightforward, and when she asks the first question we ever asked ourselves—*Who am I?*—we feel it. Then, she questions questions with a plethora of queries, and I can't stop myself from mulling over this one, "Does our lust for an answer molest the question?"

Like many of us, she admits:

I don't know what a poem is
but I write them,
I don't know what I am
but I certainly keep busy
with thoughts and love and other stuff.

I know what a poem is and I know our world and lives are enlarged when we return to the existential and renew the search for what is true "in a world where the world is the world / and not an illusion of paradise." Time and time again Reiner lights a premise, then playfully explodes it as a contradiction.

When we tell the truth
we have glass bodies
and can see all the way through
to our birthdays—
the candles
and the blood.

Ms. Reiner offers the reader the distilled salt of life's briny moments. She confesses and admits catastrophe, but there are no plates of half-eaten meals, no shadows of silverware to ponder; she prefers a larger palette: Time, Silence, Love, Wonder, The Universe, and God. Her childlike awe refreshes these concepts and my own re-asking of basic questions long ago shelved.

No book is good without a good reader (Ms. Reiner might insert the word "dancer," from "Humpty Dumpty Had a Great Fall"). If readers bring Awareness, and a lively whole consciousness that values and thinks of things as large as the universe—then I am confident they will find the garden of words and silences of *Beyond Rhyme and Reason* lush, unique and provocative. It is a rewarding journey: part soul, part sky, part mystery, part love, part play. Again Reiner succinctly says it best:

I'm a crazy singing bird
that does not know its way,
but when it's really cold,
how—I don't know—
I always end up in Capistrano.

Reviewed by Richard Weekley

Annie Reiner

Ghost Diary

Lee Rossi

Terrapin Press, 2003
520 Washington Blvd., #417,
Marina del Rey, CA 90292
92 pages. $14.95
ISBN: 0-9719122-1-1

Ghost Diary
Lee Rossi

Let's make one thing clear: this is thinking man's Viagra. In an age when men and women torment one another for the amusement of television audiences (think *The Bachelor*, think *Temptation Island*), a work like this devoted to the thrills and pitfalls of seduction is a welcome change of pace. Once upon a time we had a word for the ritualized looks and hints, conversations and delays which formed the substance of romance; we called it courtship. Now what we get is two or more people sniffing one another like dogs then going off to the bushes to copulate, usually with the wrong person. Courtship, of course, even an extended one, is no guarantee that two people will be right for one another. We wouldn't have Jane Austen if it were. But courtship engages the imagination and the spirit, not just the glands.

On the evidence of this book, its author has been around quite a few blocks, but is most at home at the intersection of Body Street and Spirit Avenue. Even the poems which focus on the author's time in the Roman Catholic seminary wrestle with the angels of earthly love. One of my favorites, a *louche* and blasphemous piece entitled "Fat Tuesday," has for its speaker a young seminarian plotting to escape the confines of his own and his Church's inhibitions. "Already," he tells us seated at dinner in the refectory,

> I can hear King Neptune's
> call, conch to his lips, his giant
> pitchfork lifted to the heavens,
> I can almost touch
> the nymphs and Nereids,
> swarming sole and grouper
> swimming the murky streets.

Delicious, that pitchfork, that conch, King Neptune filling in for the Devil and Queen Venus both! And how about those souls and groupies?

Later in the same poem, he tells us that he'll need no special garb to join the festivities. In his cassock and Roman collar, he's already in disguise:

> Just another reveler
> in my black cape and cassock and mask, blithe emblem of betrayal,
>   God-mocker

the Defrocked, wearing my dress
so fetchingly, who can resist
the play of hands on silk,
the quick, biting kiss?

Not all the poems in this collection are so happily criminal. More typical is the title poem, which examines the complexities of philandering with another man's wife. "Love can kill," he declares, "but who can live without love?" The poem is a series of rueful one-liners that leave us laughing and gasping in the same breath.

The best thing you could say about the hotel was
it was cheap.

We lay there sweating into the sheets.
I watched the cracks in the ceiling
to see if they'd stop moving.

The refrigerator under the sink whistled and laughed
like a comedian who keeps telling the same joke.

I thought of her husband somewhere out there
in the vast suburbs
and wondered if I'd rather be him,
cool and furious, my anger totally justified.

Most of the poems in this book have a strong narrative thread, but there's more to their artistry than a series of sore-throated reminiscences. Allusions, echoes, and imitations of other writers abound, John Betjeman and Mary Ruefle co-habiting with Vicente Huidobro and William Wordsworth. It's a rich and heady soup. Sonnets, ballads, and free verse are all well-managed. Especially noteworthy are two stunning prospect odes, "Paseo Miramar" and "Mount Desert," which anchor the termini for this poet's spiritual journey from unable-to-love to no-longer-able-not-to-love. While hearkening back to "Tintern Abbey," both de-form and re-form Wordsworth's cool Romanticism into an impassioned cry of hurt and triumph. At the end of "Paseo Miramar" he avers, "It has taken so much / time scouring that huge stone, / my heart, to hold the girl beside me, / giving thanks for all I've lost."

These poems are hopeful in the midst of loss, heartfelt even at their most cynical. Lee Rossi is a poet unafraid of taking risks, either in his life or his poetry. By turns ingratiating and callous, callow and worldly wise, he dares to reveal all sides of the lover he has been. So when he enters the pulpit and preaches his own syncretic gospel, as he does in "California Orange Light Sutra," we recognize it as teaching borne of experience and self-examination. He admonishes us, if you

love something:
Love it so deep
the fist un-makes itself
as flower, and spring
forgets it was ever born

Love it all the way back to when
there weren't no lovers
and no love, cuz baby
if you want to plant
your pelvis in this mud
be ready for the Lord
to use your backbone
for a stake

Many times throughout this book I thought about how poor Faust was saved by his love for a good woman, and I remembered what Goethe said at the end of his epic examination of pride and love: "The Eternal Feminine pulls us upward." Married three times, Lee Rossi is the kind of guy who'd engrave the words "The Eternal Feminine" inside at least one of his wedding bands.

Reviewed by P.C. Spectre

This Rare Earth & Other Flights

Tom Sheehan

Lit Pot Press, 2003
3909 Reche Rd. #96, Fallbrook, CA 92028
http://www.litpotpress.com
231 pages. $16.00

There is style here, on the surface, in the cracks, at the core: an elegant, understated, demanding, powerful style. It is the study and style brimming a life. Its complications, nuances and the overtly outright bring joy and sadness, bright days and dark, as distinct as the Lanthanides of its title, intricate as an organism . . . singular, cellular, human. Tom Sheehan is experienced with the style of life. From before he was even born, his deliberate attention to people was in the genes, as solid as his bedrock Irish soul, the touchstone, the sacred cairn found in the fog, beside where you will settle for sound comfort. Makes you smile, contemplate, or cry when you land on his word-rock. You think not? Here is some of it:

Somehow hands carry off
hard memories of handshakes.

They find solitude in pockets
and dark burials of lint.

Often they surprise thighs
surprising them with muscles.

Late afternoons, at brick labor,
they're apt to sneak home for rest.

Shovel handles give them polish;
pick handles, proud rind of callus.

They remember pine resin, horseshoes,
how crowbars throw selves backward.

Left hand has intimate recall
of fastball's inside threat;

right hand for a first stick shift
on a '46 black Ford convertible,

moments, it seems, after war was gone.
They lock magic behind another's back.

Hands give the sleight of messages
hanging passive as window weights.

They promote scabs and resolute scars,
toss knuckles out of position,

meet acquaintances abruptly;
flesh of lovers is a longer row.

When they fold finally, one on top,
nothing else is left for chance.

You didn't remember you knew that much about your own hands, had to read it to be remembered! This tactile sense, tickling, running them up and down a body, the warmth and throb of a pulse, the impress of years before, are still felt today. Especially the impress of friends and family, and the hands of the finishing fold. What was learned from and taught by those hands. What instruments, those gentle hands.

This Rare Earth & Other Flights is a simple collection of poems, general and personal life stations: universal, social, intimate, confrontational. It is a collection of moments, some mundane, some simple and sweet, others shaking, such as those moments when the catch in the throat gasps with memory. We've all experienced it, yet here is someone who speaks of it, praises it, encourages it because it is life . . . images that ache, a heart skip, a smirk, a knowing swelling, a real smile, and yes, as I read, I see that he knows me just as I recognize myself in him. Tom Sheehan and his cosmological view from Saugus, Massachusetts, will draw you close with memory and experience, people and places, in a recall of life and lives, a touchdown with the touchstone.

Reviewed by Tom Weddle

Let Those Who Appear

Kazuko Shiraishi

New Directions, 2002
80 Eighth Avenue, NY 10010
49 pages. $12.95
ISBN: 0-8112-1510-5

For Kazuko Shiraishi, as it was with Walt Whitman and his direct pantheistic connection to the world and the cosmos, compassion is implicit to mystical thinking. This is clearly evidenced in her recent poems "The Afternoon of the Sheep" and "The Wild Pigs of Kalimantan" from her new collection *Let Those Who Appear.* This compassion is present in the later poem especially when, after recounting the terror of the wild pigs caught in a forest fire caused by humans, she feels the helpless tragedy of their experience:

> The wild pigs are walking this way crashing through
> My notebook plunging their burnt
> Black hooves of grains into my heart.

And surely "The Cuckoo Sings," the poem that concludes *Let Those Who Appear,* is a mystical elegy for our time. It appears that the singing is dramatic and tragic because Shiraishi's cuckoo does not know the ozone-protecting layer is ripped apart; it does not know the seasons are out of whack:

> Nevertheless whether it does not know it or does know it
> A single voice with a beautiful melody of premonition
> Perching on one second of a hundred million years the cuckoo sings.

I cannot speak for the originals in Japanese; however, Samuel Grolmes and Yumiko Tsumura have adapted Shiraishi's poetry into English with a precision and immediacy that helps to extend her reputation as an outstanding poet.

Reviewed by Doren Robbins

The Wren Notebook

Rick Smith

Illustrations by Judith Beaver
Lummox Press, 2000
PO Box 5301, San Pedro, CA 90733-5301
70 pages. $10.00
ISBN: 1-929878-16-8

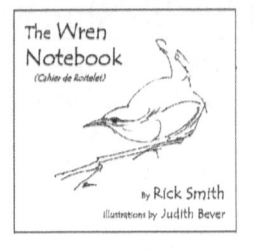

Rick Smith's spare yet dense poetry is reminiscent of Basho, the Japanese haiku master, and displays much of the same restraint and discipline. But Smith's poetry is not limited by any specific form, other than the sound and feel of the language itself, to which he pays particularly close attention.

The dominant factors here are voice and imagery. These aren't just more hum-drum tales of domestic realism posing as poetry, nor are they "nature poems" as such. The figure of the wren is the continuous metaphorical thread that runs through this compact, elegant book, appearing and reappearing in various guises and incarnations; as nest builder, as potential prey, or as chimerical shadow flitting through the clouds, creating a sort of palimpsest of mythical manifestations in settings as diverse as Madagascar, Dakota, Lisbon and the Flatiron Building in New York City. In some poems we're seeing the world from the point of view of the omniscient observer, giving the poems an added dimension of self-reflexive introspection. The world as wren, wren as the world.

Rick Smith's poetry is eloquent, lyrical, and highly evocative of the sense of nature that us wingless creatures don't normally have access to (or have lost touch with), addressing the reader with a flutter of wings, a flash of thought, or a swoop through boundless skies. Judith Bever's pen-and-ink drawings complement the poems in a thoughtful way, amplifying the already unified feeling of this collection.

Reviewed by Mark Terrill

Feeding the Animal

John Thomas

The Lummox Press, 2001
P.O. Box 5301, San Pedro, CA 90733-5301
48 pages. $5.00
ISBN: 1-929878-32-X

Poetry By John Thomas
Cover by Claudia Parentela

Two personae struggle in these 26 poems: one moodily returning to questions of conscience; the other doggedly searching for a pure/real poetic statement. It is not ironic that both succeed, the first phantasmagoric: a sodden body is exhumed,

> I look away through the thin veil of rain . . .
> The page on which I write: it has become
> enormous
big as a church-wall, crudely painted white.
The letters of the words are far too large to read,
and the rain streams down across them.

In several Poe-esque poems, Thomas's festering persona, "Sinks and dies / in the cold hour before dawn. / Had this not been darkest night / we should not have seen it at all" ("The Art of Assemblage"). Yet as in Poe's "Ulalume" and "Usher," persona and reader willingly suspend disbelief for these nightmare journeys, and

sink
right out of sight between two lines.
These are very ancient matters.
Magical. Ghosts edge closer
to the snapping coals.

Good chills, but as immemorially, of course, 'magic' is a thin veil beyond which loom distress, horror and self-torment. The other persona observes reality steadily ("hitchhiking in the '60s"):

Christ, all the hours, waiting for a ride,
memorizing the dirt at my feet. . .
I could have written
a pretty fine book: *The Tragic and Marvelous*
Roadside Debris of Central
and Southern California . . .

To be nothing, and feel the wind
of the big trucks passing.
Debris: even the word
is beautiful.

In another poem, he astutely watches the dismantling of a neighborhood sundeck, but actually writes a fine eulogy for a Mrs. Nigel—"cruelly hanged there"—and for universal mortality, the poem "a tiny cry, at best, in the earth's thundering / peristalsis." Morose poetry, but a gloom artfully, persistently, controlled—and worth a read.

Reviewed by Tim Scannell

Late

Cecilia Woloch

BOA Editions, 2003
260 East Ave, Rochester NY 14604
80 pages. $13.95
ISBN: 1-929918-42-9

Cecilia Woloch's third book, *Late*, is not only full of tender, sensual poems, but it is also imbued with realistic inspiration in facing deep losses. This is a book of mature modern-day love poems, love of family and place, friends and lovers, with a knowing eye on the price of such loving, paying the price, and moving on, loving again. What is most compelling is that throughout these poems Woloch never concedes to being overshadowed by lovers or for that matter her own sorrows, and therefore the poems pay close lyrical attention to the beautiful in life, even in dark moments, and to living bravely.

In the title poem that also concludes the book, we are given, in the form of ana-phora, a condensed progression through young love, conflicts of the heart, failed marriage, and a widow-like disposition. When newfound love comes, the soul nevertheless leaps to the occasion. The poem is a miniature of the book's structure.

With the line, "Or had I met you in the early wind of my solitude, I might have snapped," one is reminded of Mexico's celebrated feminist poet Rosario Castellanos, who often portrays damaging passion in a male-dominated Catholic world. Castellanos is attracted to self-annihilation as in "Warning to Whoever Comes":

> . . . all I wanted to do was sleep
> long and deep the way
> a happy woman sleeps.

But unlike Castellanos, who often sees death as cleansing, Woloch is willing to rise from the ashes:

> Instead, you came late, you came after I'd made myself into harbor and chalice and wick. More like the ashes than any warm hearth. More like a widow than wanton, beloved. And you lifted me over the wall of the garden and carried me back to my life.

Among the central themes is Woloch's love for her father and the inevitable grappling with his death. She finds inspiration again through reading Rukeyser at the father's bedside. In fact, a number of exceptional woman poets are quoted or invoked to become Woloch's guiding spirits. Rukeyser's words come as if from a ghost.

When I'm dead, even then . . . I will wait for you in these poems. Who was speaking then, and to whom? I'm still listening to you.

In "Here's to You, Jesus Robinson," Woloch recounts through her own imaginings the childhood story of a German friend who was sent off to the countryside for the duration of the second world war, and how an African-American soldier, in a moment that resembled Communion, had given him chocolate wrapped as a gold coin. The experience is visionary: the first black man he had ever encountered is both beautiful and generous:

How sunlight fell into his hands; how darkness melted on his tongue. How a man named Jesus Robinson stopped the war inside him once.

Woloch's lyrical voice resonates naturally through a range of poetic forms. Her prose poems are often as incantatory as her pantoums, but always with a relaxed, accessible diction. Woloch's method is not only a heightened attention to rhetorical structure but also to the multiple senses of words themselves, as in "Dzien Dobry."

Dzien, I called out
to the bright empty room—
having meant to say
thank you, dziekuje,
and said only *dzien*, only
day, for *dzien dobry*,
good day—when I woke
to the grace of *eat that*
which is offered, knew,
in that light where to turn.

"Dzien Dobry" is set in the lower Carpathians, just one location in a book that travels from childhood Kentucky to L. A. to Paris, whose filth Woloch exuberantly honors as honest and liberating: "Paris is beautiful like this; it's the beauty of love of the body of love."

Woloch accepts that happiness is forever endangered, an understanding reinforced through recurring images of the ephemeral, birds and ashes, but above all, particularly in a time full of anger and hate, she knows when to open the curtains, when to celebrate life through her generously humane poetry.

Reviewed by Jeffrey Greene

The Adventures of Dwayne

Dwayne Wylie

Self-published, 2001
24 pages, out of print

Some chapbooks defy description, defy a traditional review. Such is this limited edition chapbook by Dwayne Wylie, a raw and blunt exposé of the author's adventures across the United States. The combination of lyric gesture and quirky diction keep the reader riveted to every line. What's going to happen to Dwayne next? The characters he meets on the road function as both parody and comment on the Kerouac roster of street people and poets. At times it's hard to tell whether certain linguistic effects were intended or just come naturally from the voice of Dwayne. Is Dwayne the author, Dwayne Wylie (spelled like the poet Eleanor Wylie, he comments in one poem), an alter-ego, or a completely fictional creation? It's not unlike the pilgrim named Dante in Dante's *Commedia*. Where does one Dante end and the other begin? One asks the same question here. The writing exists outside the bounds of correct poetic diction, and outside the bounds of purposeful literary manipulation of voice to seem outside the bounds of correct poetic diction. It forces the reader to confront the nature of language and voice, and what makes a piece of writing compelling. There's no substitute for authenticity, and when that authenticity is compelling, it sometimes becomes difficult to say exactly why. Imagine in the days of Caruso a Tom Waits or a Joe Cocker cutting a record. Or a Jackson Pollock showing one of his paintings alongside Giotto. I think if I were to crawl into one of the caves of Altamira, I'd find *The Adventures of Dwayne* equally at home with the painting of the bison, both beyond artistic criticism.

Reviewed by Todd Parker

BIO

GRAPHICS

Good Times

Years

Biographies

Michael Andrews, co-founder/publisher with Jack Grapes of Bombshelter Press and *ONTHEBUS*, lives with Flo in L.A. He has published ten books of poetry, including *Coffin Lumber* and *The Poet from the City of the Angels*, and has produced three unusual portfolios of photographic prints and letterpress poetry. He has recently finished two books of poetry; his first book of philosophy, *The Gnomes Of Uncertainty*; five screenplays; two un-publishable novels; and is currently creating photographic and poetry montages as digital images while stumbling along on a massive novel about Vietnam and the boomer generation. To support these disgusting habits he works as a computer programmer/analyst, pays outrageous taxes, and suffers the usual atrocities of free market predation.

Phil Asaph received his M.F.A. from New York University, won a grant for poetry from the Vogelstein Foundation, published works in *Poetry,* and is now completing a novel-in-verse, *Nick's Bar & Grill,* a sexual-spiritual comedy set on the north shore of his beloved Long Island.

Herman Asarnow's poems, essays, and translations have appeared or will soon appear in such places as the *Seattle Review, Beloit Poetry Journal, Southern Humanities Review, Marlboro Review, Clackamas Literary Review, South Dakota Review, North Dakota Quarterly, High Plains Literary Review, Rattle, Poet Lore, The Chariton Review,* and many other journals. He lives in Portland, Oregon, where he serves on the English faculty at the University of Portland.

Cynthia Atkins's poems have appeared or are forthcoming in *American Letters & Commentary, Bomb, Bloomsbury Review, Chelsea, Rivendell, Seneca Review, Tar River Poetry,* and *Verse,* among others. She was a recipient of a 2002 Creative Arts Fellowship from the Virginia Center for the Creative Arts. Currently, she is a Visiting Assistant Professor of English at Sweetbriar College, and artistic director of Writers@Jordan House Center for the Creative Arts. She lives in Rockbridge County, Virginia with her husband, Phillip, and their son, Eli.

Anne Babson won the Columbia Journal Prize for 2003, and was nominated for a 2001 Pushcart for work appearing in *The Haight Ashbury Literary Journal.* She has had work appear in *Rio Grande Review, New Song,* and *The Penwood Review,* among others. She is the author of four chapbooks and was the winner of the 2000 Working People's Poetry Prize. Her poetry has been featured on both regional and national radio programs. She sits on the board of Women's Studio Center and on the Literary Committee of the National Arts Club.

Amin Banani is Professor Emeritus of Persian and Middle Eastern History at the University of California, Los Angeles. He is co-translator (with Jascha Kessler) of *Bride of the Acacias,* a volume of the poems of the modern Iranian poet Forugh Farrokhzad.

Lisa Becker was born and raised in Northern California. She earned her Marketing degree from San Diego State University. She has written two chapbooks and currently works as a production supervisor on feature films. She lives in Encino with her husband Josh, their daughter Scout, and stepchildren Ethan and Kendall.

Paul Beckman has been published in *Playboy, The Connecticut Review, Other Voices, The Writer's Voice, Northeast Magazine, Parting Gifts, Verve, Next Phase, The Artful Mind, Tributary, Alacran, Web Del Sol,* and *Sugar Mule.* He has been nominated for a Pushcart Prize four times. In 1995 a collection of his stories, *Come! Meet My Family and Other Stories,* was published. He received his M.F.A. from Bennington.

Rebecca Jane Benitez is a new writer currently employed full-time as a police officer in L. A. County.

Alan Berman (design editor) has taught Web, desktop publishing, creative writing, and guitar courses in high school and community college. He has designed award-winning books and literary magazines for Bombshelter Press, Tebot Bach, and other Los Angeles presses. Berman has written or edited for *Literary Magazine Review, High-Power Rocketry, Guitar Review,* Toyota USA, and PowerPoint Live.

Michelle Bitting was born in Santa Monica, California in 1964. She received her B.A. in Dramatic Art from U.C. Berkeley, and has enjoyed careers as a modern dancer and a chef before becoming a mother, poet, and devoted outreach worker. She has just begun to seek publication and her work appears in *Mudfish*.

Stacey K. Black is a writer/painter living the dream in Southern California. She's currently working on a novel.

Daniel Bourne's first book, *The Household Gods*, came out in the Cleveland State University Poetry Series in 1995. His poems have appeared or are forthcoming in *American Poetry Review*, *Ploughshares*, *Field*, *Shenandoah*, *Prairie Schooner*, *Many Mountains Moving*, and *Marlboro Review*. He has been the recipient of several Ohio Arts Council poetry fellowships and has published translations of Polish poets. He teaches at The College of Wooster, where he edits *Artful Dodge*.

Eve Brandstein has been a major studio executive, a producer, a director, writer/creator, and casting director. She is an educator and workshop facilitator who has led writing and performance groups. Her poetry appears in various publications and she is one of the organizers of Poetry in Motion, and publishers of *The Hollywood Review*, an anthology of L.A. poets. Born in Czechoslovakia, raised in the Bronx, N.Y., she presently lives in Los Angeles with her son.

Dorothy Duncan Burris is a 16-year veteran of the *Kalliope* collective and poetry editor of *Kalliope* Volume 15, No. 2. Burris has published poems in *Negative Capability*, *The Sow's Ear*, *West Branch*, and *The Cape Rock*, among others, and short stories in *The Coe Review*, *Habersham Review*, *The MacGuffin*, *Kalliope*, *Rhino*, and *Women's Words*. She was born in Cleveland, Ohio, but has lived in Florida for forty years, where, having raised three children, she now tends two dooryard citrus trees, and jogs and rollerblades.

Elena Karina Byrne's first book, *The Flammable Bird*, is available from Zoo Press: www.zoopress.org. She is completing another, *Masque*, and a collection of essays entitled *Poetry and Insignificance*. She served as poetry consultant to the Getty Research Institute and runs the poetry reading series at the Getty Center. She is also poetry consultant and moderator for the L.A. Times Festival of Books. Recent and forthcoming publications include *The Yale Review*, *Poetry*, *Verse*, *American Poetry Review*, *Paris Review*, *Painted Bride Quarterly*, *Colorado Review*, *Prairie Schooner*, and *Ploughshares*, among others.

Diane Carr was born in Dallas, Texas and has lived in Memphis, St. Louis and Chicago. She received her B.F.A. in Acting from the Webster Conservatory of Theatre Arts and studied screenwriting at Northwestern University. Diane worked as an actress in the off-loop theater scene in Chicago before co-founding Edgar Road Theatre Company where she co-wrote, produced and appeared in *Triad*. Since moving to Los Angeles, Diane has been working as a grant writer for The Sundance Institute and Independent Feature Project/West. She has completed a screenplay, *Do a Girl a Favor*, and is currently working on her first novel.

Crysta Casey has been published in *The Monthly Review*, *The Seattle Review*, *Fine Madness*, *Pontoon*, and others. Her first book is *Heart Clinic* (Bellowing Ark Press, 1993).

Brandon Cesmat performs as the poet-vocalist in the art ensemble Drought Buoy. He also serves as area coordinator for California Poets in the Schools (CPITS) in San Diego. He earned his M.F.A. from San Diego State University and currently teaches literature and film studies at a number of Southern California colleges. His chapbook, *Ice Drum*, won the 2000 San Diego Book Award for poetry.

Kevin Clark's poems have appeared in numerous magazines and collections, including *The Black Warrior Review*, *The Antioch Review*, *The Denver Quarterly*, and *The Georgia Review*. The Academy of American Poets selected his book *In the Evening, No Warning* for a grant from The Greenwall Fund. He's also published three chapbooks: *One of Us* (Mille Grazie Press), *Granting the Wolf* (State Street Press), and *Window Under a New Moon* (Owl Creek Press). His literary criticism has appeared in numerous magazines, journals, and books. Presently, he's a full professor of American Literature at California Polytechnic State University in San Luis Obispo, California.

Bill Clawson is a retired gentleman, philosopher, poet, and walker who lives in Santa Monica.

Ann Colburn taught English, journalism and creative writing at Crossroads School in Santa Monica for more than 20 years. She currently works with One Voice, a social service agency that helps inner-city high school students realize their dreams to attend college. She is a poet and practitioner of Zen meditation.

Michael Coldwell's three novels, *Fast Break* (1995), *Camp All-Star* (1996) and *Nothing But Net* (1997) were published by James Lorimer & Company (Toronto, Canada). His poetry has been published by *AIM: America's Intercultural Magazine*.

Carrie St. George Comer's recent publications include *Conduit*, *The Hollins Critic*, *Pleiades*, and *Black Warrior Review*. Her manuscript was chosen for the 2000 Joseph Langland Prize, sponsored by The Academy of American Poets.

Aaron Crippen is the recipient of the 2001 American Translators Association Student Award and the 2001 PEN Texas Literary Award for Poetry. His edition of *Nameless Flowers: Selected Poems of Gu Gheng* will be published by George Braziller in Spring 2005.

Diana Darby's second CD, *Fantasia Ball*, was released this summer on Delmore Records. Web: www.dianadarby.com

Eric K. Delehoy is the founding editor of *Gertrude: A Journal of Voice and Vision*. He has had poetry and fiction published in *Upstairs at Duroc*, *The Rockford Review*, *Seedhouse*, *Weird Sisters*, *Emerging Voices*, and *Tenth Street Miscellany*.

Christine DeSimone was born in Los Angeles in 1977. A fourth-generation Californian, she received a law degree from U.C. Hastings. Her poems have appeared or are forthdcoming in *Hawai'i Pacific Review*, *Concho River Review*, *Bellowing Ark*, *Bllue Collar Review*, *Eclipse* and *Brevities*. She currently practices law in the San Francisco Bay Area.

Evelyn Duboff was born in Montreal, Quebec, and lives in Brentwood, California. Her work has appeared in *Penstrokes*. Her short fiction, "Daring & Other Stories," was presented as a theatrical reading by The New Short Fiction Series in July 2000 and was a *Los Angeles Times* "Pick." Staged readings of her short fiction have been performed at the NoHo Theatre Arts Festival 2000, 2001, and 2002. She has written one chapbook.

Gary Every's most recent book is a fantasy adventure, *Inca Butterflies*. His previous books include the collection of desert essays *Cat Canyon Secrets* and *Barrio Libre Poems*. He has had poems appear in *Lynx Eye*, *First Class*, *Chiron Review*, *Nerve Cowboy*, and many others.

David Fedo is a native of Duluth, Minnesota, and has published poems over the past 30 years in *Poetry East*, *Commonweal*, *Chelsea*, *Many Mountains Moving*, *The Dalhousie Review*, and *Voices International*, among others. He is currently academic dean and professor of English at Curry College in Milton, Massachusetts.

John Feins is a Los Angeles-based writer.

Lisa Feintech was born in L.A. She is a mother, wife, artist, writer, and physician.

Jennilyn Fisher is currently living in Upland, California while pursuing her climbing and writing ambitions.

Michael C. Ford is the author of several volumes of poetry, prose, plays and spoken word recordings (one of which earned a Grammy nomination). His most recent volume of work, *Emergency Exits: The Selected Poems 1970–1995* was honored with a 1998 nomination for the Pulitzer Prize.

Marianne Franco was born in Boston, MA, in the middle of five brothers and sisters. She went to Emerson College to study writing for film and television. She now lives in Los Angeles.

Robert Fritz obtained his B.A. at Northwestern University where he studied writing under Beth Nugent, among others. He's been writing for nearly 12 years. *Slowbook No.1* is his first chapbook.

Scott Gallaway is an instructor at Bowling Green State University. His poetry has appeared in *Cumberland Poetry Review, Crucible, Permafrost, Half Tones to Jubilee, The Hiram Poetry Review, The New Delta Review, Touchstone, Illuminations, Evansville Review, Midwest Quarterly*, and others.

Peggy Geisler is a graduate of the University of California, Los Angeles, and holds a Master of Arts Degree in Marriage and Family Therapy from the California Graduate Institute in Westwood. She is also a licensed psychotherapist. She was born in Santa Fe, New Mexico, and in 1978 moved to Los Angeles, where she currently lives with her husband.

Cynthia Glucksman studies literature and drama at the University of California at Santa Cruz. She is fluent in Hebrew and is pursuing a focus in Jewish literature. Cynthia has published a number of poems and translations in various campus publications. Her one-act play, *Doorman*, was the centerpiece production in the Chautauqua Theater Festival in May 2003.

Teri Goldman is a social worker and writer living in Santa Monica, California. She is the author of the chapbook *Indigo Days*.

Jeffrey Greene is the author of two collections of poetry, *To the Left of the Worshipper* and *American Spirituals*, as well as the memoir, *French Spirits*. He lives in Paris and in Burgundy.

Barbara Griest-Devora teaches literature and writing at Northwest Vista College and lives with her husband and two children near downtown San Antonio, Texas. Poems have been published in journals such as *The Chattahoochee Review, Spoon River Poetry Review, Borderlands, The Wisconsin Review*, and several others. Poems are also forthcoming in *Potpourri* and *The Texas Observer*. "Getting It" appeared in the Winter/Spring 2001 *Sycamore Review*.

Donald Gutierrez is a retired college English teacher who taught at Notre Dame and Western New Mexico University. He has written six books of literary criticism and scholarship and over 100 essays, papers, and reviews, as well as two memoirs of Berkeley and Kenneth Rexroth's San Francisco in the 1950s. Much of his work has focussed on D. H. Lawrence and, more recently, on Rexroth (whom he regards as still the most underrated major American poet of the 20th century). Gutierrez's main concern since retiring in 1994 has been with human rights violations and the global domination of American mega-corporations.

Jennifer Haft is an actress who performs pieces based on her poetry.

Katharine Harer's poems have appeared in numerous magazines including *ZYZZYVA* and *Five Fingers Review*. Her books include *Spring Cycle (Encanto, 1980), In These Bodies* (Moving Parts, 1982) and *The Border* (Bombshelter, 1984). She just won the Slipstream Award for her chapbook *Hubba Hubba*.

Season Harper holds the M.A. in English/Creative Writing from the University of Nebraska-Lincoln. She has published poetry in *Cream City Review, Rocky Mountain Review of Modern Language and Literature, Santa Clara Review,* and other journals.

Natasha Harris is a recent graduate of Emerson's M.F.A. program in Writing, Literature and Publishing. This is her first publication.

E. Kelly Harrison was born and raised in Atlanta, Georgia. She received a B.A. in English Composition and graduated from the University of Kentucky. She now resides in Los Angeles, California with her four dogs and horse where she works for a developer. She is a member of the Los Angeles Poets & Writers Collective and continues to write prose and poetry.

Kaylin Haught has published in *ONTHEBUS* and other literary journals, including the Library of Congress *Poetry 180* project on the internet, edited by former Poet Laureate Billy Collins, and in the anthology including selected poems from the site, *Poetry 180: A Turning Back to Poetry*, (Random House), edited by Collins. Forthcoming poems in *MS. Magazine* and in a new anthology by Bloodaxe Publishers of England. She lives in Seabrook, Texas.

Alice Hayward spent her childhood in Kalispell, Montana where her father hunted and traded for what their family didn't raise. During the winters she and her mother were often snowbound. These isolated periods led to Alice's love of literature and art. Alice's Montanan childhood, Irish/Catholic background, and Los Angeles residency are reflected in her work. She currently lives, writes, and paints in Los Angeles.

Michael Hemmingson's work has recently been in *Fiction International*, *The Aux Arc Review*, etc. His latest books are *My Dream Date (Rape)* with Kathy Acker (Eraserhead Press), and *Expelled from Eden: A William T. Vollmann Reader* (Thunder's Mouth Press).

Patricia Hill is a freelance writer and editor with an M.A. in literature. She has had work published in *Peregrine*, *The Massachusetts Review*, and *Southern Poetry Review*.

Beth Hirsch is a singer-songwriter living in Los Angeles. She released two albums in 2004. (See www.bethhirsch.com & www.pale3.com for further details.)

Nika Hoffman has taught creative writing, film, and English in Los Angeles for the past fifteen years. She has written several dozen critical essays for *Magill's Literary Annual* (Salem Press). Her short fiction has appeared in several national small presses and has won numerous awards.

Karen Holden is a poet, teacher, book artist and painter. A native of Los Angeles, she holds a B.A. From Scripps College and did doctoral work in Psychology at the University of Illinois. In 1985 her artist's book *Behind My Own Disguise* was exhibited at the Metropolitan Museum of Art. She has also had several one-woman shows of her paintings. She was the recipient of four California Arts Council teaching grants. In 1998 her volume of poems *Book of Changes* was published by North Atlantic Books. From 1991 to 2000 she served on the faculty at the Frank Lloyd Wright School of Architecture, where her work extended into the realm of integrating writing, literature and design. Most recently she was poet-in-residence at the Long Beach Museum of Art.

Mary Holmes graduated from Hollywood High School. Her background includes visual and performing arts as well as an 11-year private practice in clinical hypnotherapy. While all three of the preceding have been nationally published and/or televised, this is her first published poem. Contact her at maryholmes@aol.com.

Michele Hugus was born and raised in Southwestern Pennsylvania. She moved to Santa Monica, California 23 years ago where she currently works as a Registered Nurse. This is her first published work.

Ran Huntsberry has poems published or forthcoming in over 55 literary magazines, including *Ascent*, *Many Mountains Moving*, *New Letters*, *Midwest Poetry Review*, *Nimrod*, *Pennsylvania English*, *Piedmont Literary Review*, *Poet Lore*, *The Small Pond Magazine*, and *Wisconsin Review*. He is also anthologized in *Idaho's Poetry: A Centennial Anthology*, edited by Ronald E. McFarland and William Studebaker.

Thea Iberall has had poetry and short fiction published in *Rattle*, *Spillway*, *Common Lives/Lesbian Lives*, *Peregrine XVI*, *Next . . . Magazine*, and the *Lesbian News*. Thea has given numerous poetry and fiction readings in Southern California and New England, and has three chapbooks. She represented Los Angeles at the 1998 National Poetry Slam Competition in Austin, Texas, where the team made it to the final four out of 45 cities. She is working on her first novel and is currently enrolled in the Masters of Professional Writing Program at USC.

Rachel Iverson lives with her husband, son and daughter in Los Angeles. She earned a B.A. in English Literature and journalism from Valparaiso University and a J.D. from the University of Minnesota. Her poems and prose have in appeared in journals including *The Philosophical Mother*, *Illume* and *Books and Babies*. She also serves as a monthly columnist and poetry editor for *Literary Mama*: www.literarymama.com.

Jayson Iwen is a creative writing Ph.D. student at UW-Milwaukee. Poems have been published in *Poetry Motel, Sheepshead Revue,* and *The Blue Canary* and are forthcoming in *New American Writing* and *The Southern Indiana Review,* in addition to a number of interviews and experimental book reviews in *The Cream City*'s 25th-anniversary issue.

Allison Johnson was born in Santa Monica, California, raised in Tarzana, and graduated from UCLA with a B.A. in French, studying theater arts along the way. She is the author of *The Way Home,* a novel rife with family conflict, and co-authored *Your Self-Confident Baby.* Her essays have appeared in *The Los Angeles Times,* and her short stories performed at L.A.'s New Short Fiction Series. Johnson lives in Aliso Viejo, and is currently at work on *The Running Girl,* a coming-of-age novel set in Los Angeles.

Richard Jones is the author of numerous collections of poetry and several limited editions, the most recent being *The Blessing: New and Selected Poems,* published by Copper Canyon Press. He serves as the editor of the distinguished literary journal *Poetry East,* which he founded in 1980, and is the director of the Creative Writing Program at DePaul University.

Stephen Graham Jones has stories in *Alaska Quarterly Review, Beloit Fiction Journal, Black Warrior Review, Cutbank, Gulf Coast, Oconoclast, Meridian, Open City, Pleiades, Quarterly West, South Dakota Quarterly, Sundog, Vincent Brothers Review,* and more, including anthologies and the 6th edition of *Writing Fiction.* He's been nominated for a Pushcart a few times too. His first novel, *The Fast Red Road: A Plainsong,* was published by FC2 in 2000; it was a finalist for the Texas Institute of Letters Award and won an Independent Publisher Award; he is also the author of *All the Beautiful Sinners* (Rugged Land, 2000) and has two more novels forthcoming.

Jean Katz, born in Iowa, now lives in Los Angeles, California. She works as a consultant with school districts and non-profit organizations, facilitating organizational planning. Her poetry and essays have been published in *ONTHEBUS, Spillway, Rattle, Writing for Your Life, The American Rabbi, The Journal of Learning Disabilities, The Journal of Career Educators, Inflections,* and *FutureSearching.* Recently Bombshelter Press published her first book, *Chaos and Dancing Stars.* In 1979 she co-founded the Los Angeles Very Special Arts Festival at the Music Center, celebrating the performing and visual arts skills of children and adults with disabilities.

Judi Kaufman is a long-time community activist, published poet, and entrepreneur. She has been active in the AJC (American Jewish Committee) for many years. She is also a member of the UCLA Board of Visitors. Judi was diagnosed with a malignant brain tumor in 1997. In 1999, Dr. Timothy Cloughesy and Judi co-founded Art of the Brain, an annual event that has raised over $700,000 for UCLA Neuro-Oncology Program's brain cancer research. She is the author of several chapbooks; her first full-length book of poems, *Passion and Shadow,* was published in 2000. Judi lives in Los Angeles with her husband Roy; they have two daughters, Jennifer and Suzy.

Jarret Keene teaches at Florida State University, where he also serves as editor of *Sundog: The Southeast Review.* His Pushcart-nominated stories, essays, and verse have appeared in recent issues of *ACM, Chelsea, The Connecticut Review, The Laurel Review, The South Carolina Review, The Texas Review,* and *River City.* His most recent book is *Meat Out of the Eater* (Superstition Street Press, 2000).

Jesse Lee Kercheval is the author of a poetry collection, *World as Dictionary* (Carnegie Mellon UP, 1999); and *Space* (Penguin, 1999), a memoir about growing up in Florida during the moon race. Her work appears in *Ploughshares, TriQuarterly,* and *Prairie Schooner.* She teaches creative writing at the University of Wisconsin, where she directs the Wisconsin Institute for Creative Writing.

Kulwant Khalsa lives in Los Angeles with her husband. She grew up in Chicago, and attended Beloit College where she got a B.A. in Psychology and Sociology. Her graduate education was at the University of Massachusetts in Amherst where she received a M.Ed. In Humanistic Education. Her short story, "Last Thursday," appeared in the fall 2003 issue of *Aquarian Times.*

Carol Kivo lives and works in Southern California. Her work has appeared in *Rattle* and *Rivertalk.*

Jillisa Hope Knutson is a native of southern California. She graduated from Christopher Newport University with a bachelor's degree in English, and she now works in Virginia as a technical editor for NASA. Her poetry has appeared in *The Researcher.*

Stephen Kopel has work in *Skylark, Haight Ashbury Journal, Plainsongs, The Lyric, Troubadour, Sensations Magazine, Icon,* and *Comstock Review;* his work was nomined for Pushcart Prize XXV.

Alexandra Kostoulas has a B.A. in literature from the College of Creative Studies at UC Santa Barbara. Currently she lives in Santa Barbara and teaches English as a Second Language. She writes poetry and prose. She has published her work in *Into The Teeth of The Wind, Catalyst, Fire Magazine,* and *Poetry Greece.* She has also published seven chapbooks of poetry with Wild Guppy Press.

Steve Kowit was born in Brooklyn and schooled on Manhattan's Lower East Side. He is the author of several collections of poetry including *The Dumbbell Nebula* (Roundhouse Press), and *In the Palm of Your Hand: The Poet's Portable Workshop.*He also edited the *Maverick Poets* anthology. The recipient of an NEA Fellowship and other awards, Steve teaches at Southwestern College in Chula Vista, CA.

Judy Kronenfeld's poems have appeared in *Poetry International, Passages North, The Manhattan Poetry Review, Pearl, Potpourri* and others. She is the author of a book of poems, *Shadow of Wings* (Bellflower Press, 1991) and a chapbook, *Disappeared Down Dark Wells, and Still Falling* (The Inevitable Press, 2000). She teaches in the Creative Writing Department at the University of California, Riverside.

Charles Kruger is a writer, actor, and teacher living in Northern California.

Carol LaForet is a writer from Bucks County, Pennsylvania. Her first book, *Take Home the Sea,* a volume of seaside poetry, was published by Days of Yore in February, 2001. In recent years she has had more than 100 poems appear in over 50 literary journals and magazines.

Susan Laguna grew up in Aptos, California, then moved to San Francisco, where her son and daughter were born. She has twenty years of involvement as a classical guitarist and was apprenticed as a hand bookbinder throughout her twenties in the San Franciso Bay area. Susan holds an M.A. degree in Clinical Psychology and currently resides in Ocean Park, Santa Monica with her family, Nicholas Dylan and Marina Blanche. This is Susan's first published piece.

Maxine Landis lives in Ventura County and is a member of the Ventura County Writer's Club poetry group. She taught poetry and creative writing and worked as a California Poet in the Schools. She has a B.A. from Antioch and has done graduate work at California State University, Long Beach. Her work has been published in *ONTHEBUS, Spillway, Blood Pudding, Satori, News From Inside, Solo,* (online), *Earthbound, Cpits, Sure, Struggle, Voices, San Fernando Poetry Journal, Volno, Earthwords, Retooling for the Renaissance,* and others.

Pamela Lane is a television writer and producer and member of PEN. She currently divides her creative energy between *Meet My Folks* and *Who Wants to Marry My Dad* for NBC and her original poetry and prose. After completing her first novel, *Defying Gravity,* Ms. Lane is starting on a non-fiction romp entitled *What Women Really Want, Secrets of a Professional Gigolo.* She can be reached at one_smart_girl@yahoo.com.

Anthony A. Lee teaches African American history at West Los Angeles College. His poems have appeared in *ONTHEBUS, The Homestead Review, Warpland, Arts Dialogue,* and other journals. He was awarded the 2003 Nat Turner Poetry Prize from Cross Keys Press. His first book of poems is published by White Cloud Press (2004).

Stellasue Lee's work is published in numerous literary journals as well as four volumes: *Crossing the Double Yellow Line* (2000); *After I Fall,* a collection of four Los Angeles poets; *Over to You,* an exchange of poems with David Widup; and *13 Los Angeles Poets,* the ONTHEBUS Poets Series Number One (Bombshelter Press). She received her Ph.D. from Honolulu University. Poetry Editor for the literary journal *Rattle,* she hosted the *Rattle* Reading Series at the Skirball Cultural Center in 2001.

Linda Lerner's work has appeared in hundreds of journals, among them *The New York Quarterly, Chelsea, Bouillabaisse, Ragged Lion Anthology,* and *Slipstream*. Seven collections of her poetry have been published; the most recent is *Greatest Hits (1989–2002)* (Pudding House Publications). Her interview with Hayden Carruth appeared in the 50th issue of *The New York Quarterly*.

Lyn Levine is a therapist, wife, mother, and grandmother. She lives in Los Angeles.

Roz Levine was born and raised in New York City. She received her B.A. from Queens College and her M.S. from City College. She has spent the last 30 years living in Los Angeles where she worked and raised two daughters. Roz has been published previously in *ONTHEBUS* and *The Sun*.

Namoi Lieberman is a psychotherapist and photographer who lives in Santa Monica.

Lyn Lifshin's most recent prizewinning book (Paterson Poetry Award), *Before It's Light*, was published winter 2000 by Black Sparrow Press, following their publication of *Cold Comfort* in 1997. *Another Woman Who Looks Like Me* will be published by Black Sparrow Books at David R. Godine. Also, just published is *A New Film by a Woman in Love with the Dead* (March Street Press). She has published more than 100 books of poetry, including *Marilyn Monroe* and *Blue Tattoo*, won awards for her nonfiction, and edited four anthologies of women's writing, including *Tangled Vines, Ariadne's Thread,* and *Lips Unsealed*. Her poems have appeared in most literary and poetry magazines and she is the subject of an award-winning documentary film, *Lyn Lifshin: Not Made of Glass*, available from Women Make Movies. Her poem, "No More Apologizing," has been called "among the most impressive documents of the women's poetry movement." Her web site is www.lynlifshin.com.

Mona Locke's poetry appears or is forthcoming in *South Dakota Review, MidAmerica Poetry Review, ONTHEBUS, Negative Capability* (among others) and many anthologies including *The New Poets of Los Angeles*. She wrote a supplemental college text for West Publishing Company, has 150+ fiction, non-fiction, and photography credits in newspapers and periodicals such as *The Los Angeles Times, The Oakland Tribune,* and *Emphasis* magazine, and is on the editorial board of *California Quarterly (CQ)*.

Susan Luzzaro teaches English at Southwestern College, and lives in Chula Vista, California with her family. She has been awarded the Los Angeles Arts Council Award, an AWP Intro Award, a Breadloaf Scholarship, and first place in the Santa Cruz National Writers Union Contest for her poetry. Her poetry has twice been nominated for a Pushcart. Trask House books published her chapbook of poems entitled *Complicity* and West End Press published her book entitled *Fresh Envelope*.

Laurie MacDiarmid's poetry has appeared in such venues as *Pennsylvania Review, Antioch, Iowa Woman, Carolina Quarterly, Louisiana Literature, Flint Hills Review, Karamu* and *Cottonwood*. She is Writer-in-Residence at St. Norbert College in De Pere, Wisconsin.

Sarah Maclay's poems have appeared in *Hotel Amerika, ZYZZYVA, Solo, Poetry International, Cider Press Review, Poetry Bay, lyric,* and other publications. Her third chapbook, *Ice From the Belly*, was released in 2001 by Farstarfire Press. She has been a Poet-in-Residence at Beyond Baroque, where she also co-edited the anthology *Echo 6 8 1*. Born in Montana, she earned a B.A. at Oberlin College and an M.F.A. at Vermont College, where she twice received nominations for the AWP Intro Award. A semi-finalist for the Tupelo Press First Book Award, she currently teaches writing in Los Angeles, and she's the new book review editor for *Poetry International*.

Richard Manners has both a Bachelor's and Master's degree in Music Composition and has run his own jingle production company for 30 years. His compositions run the gamut from a violin concerto commissioned by the Chicago Symphony to Ronald McDonald TV music tracks. He lives in Woodland Hills, California, with his wife, Mimi. "Privacy" is his first published literary work.

Vilma Martinez was born and raised in San Salvador, the capital of El Salvador. At age 20, she left her country to pursue her dreams and to get away from a restrictive environment. She settled in Los Angeles, married, raised a family, acquired an education and became a licensed Marriage and Family Therapist. Her work has been published in *Spillway, Reflections of Love, a Poetry Journal* and *ONTHEBUS*. She has published two chapbooks and has another one on the way. She has read her poetry at the Sedona Library in Arizona.

Kathleen Matson was born in Ohio and studied great American writers at George Washington University in Washington, D.C. She is a member of the Los Angeles Poets and Writers Collective. She has written five chapbooks, produced and directed a short film on makeup entitled *Ritual 93*, published interviews with film director Henry Jaglom and actor Viveca Lindfors, and acted in Jaglom's *Venice/Venice* and *Shopping*. Kathleen lives in Brentwood, California.

Michael P. McManus was a 2001 and 2000 Pushcart Prize nominee and was selected by the Louisiana State Arts Council as a recipient of an Artist Fellowship award. His poems have appeared or are forthcoming in numerous publications including *Cold Mountain Review, The Louisiana Review, Poet Lore, Rattle,* and *Spillway*. His first novel is currently represented by Cambridge Literary Associates.

Erika Mikkalo received the Tobias Wolff Award for short fiction from *The Bellingham Review* (1998). Her voice was recognized in the finals of the Poetry Center of Chicago's Seventh Annual Juried Reading, and received the Millenium Poetry Award from the Writers' Publishing Cooperative (2001). Other work is forthcoming in *Nimrod International Journal, The Hawaii Review, BOGG* and *The Beloit Poetry Journal*. She holds a M.F.A. in fiction writing from Columbia College, Chicago. One-half a book of poems is available under the title *Other Stations* at www.essentialbooks.com.

Michael Milburn has published a book of poems with the University of Alabama Press, and has a book of essays forthcoming from Mid-List Press. He teaches high school English in New Haven, Connecticut, and nonfiction writing at Yale University.

Bill Mohr was born in Norfolk, Virginia, and grew up there and in other Navy Port towns. After moving to Los Angeles, he published and edited *Momentum* magazine for five years, and founded Momentum Press. He published almost two dozen books between 1975 and 1988, including two anthologies: *The Streets Inside* (1978) and *Poetry Loves Poetry* (1985). Mohr has been a visiting scholar at the Getty Research Institute in Los Angeles, as well as an Andrew W. Mellon Fellow at the Huntington Library in San Marino. A chapter from his work-in-progress on West Coast poetry during the Cold War was included in *The Sons and Daughters of Los: Culture and Community in L.A.* (Temple University Press). He has taught creative writing and literature at the University of California at San Diego, Beyond Baroque Literary/Arts Center, Idyllwild Arts, and Otis Art Institute. His poems have appeared in several dozen magazines, including *Antioch Review, Blue Mesa Review, Sonora Review, Santa Monica Review, Ribot,* and *Zyzzyva*, as well as many anthologies and spoken-word compilations. A few copies of *Hidden Proofs*, his first full-length collection of poetry, are still available from Bombshelter Press. His most recent collection of poems was published by Cahuenga Press in 2003.

Lisa Marguerite Mora grew up in Venice, California, attended UCLA where she received a bachelor's degree in English, and now works at the Bodhi Tree Bookstore. She has been published in *ONTHEBUS, Rattle, CQ* (California Quarterly) and *The New Moon Review*.

Robert Nazarene's poetry appears or is forthcoming in *The Beloit Poetry Journal, Boulevard, Green Mountains Review, Ploughshares, Prosodia,* and *RATTLE*. He is a graduate of the Georgetown University School of Business Administration.

Harry Northup has had eight books of poetry published: *Amarillo Born; the jon voight poems* (Mt. Alverno Press); *Enough the Great Running Chapel* (Momentum Press); *the images we possess kill the capturing* (the jessee press); *The Ragged Vertical* (Cahuenga Press); *Reunions* (Cahuenga Press); and *Greatest Hits, 1966–2001* (Pudding House Press). Northup has made a living as an actor for 28 years, acting in 37 films, including Scorsese's first six films, and in 42 television shows, including *E.R.* New Alliance Records has released his *Personal Crime* (new and selected poems 1966–1991) on CD and cassette audio recording, and *Homes* on CD. He lives in Los Angeles with his wife, Holly Prado Northup.

Gordon T. Osing's poems have appeared in *The Southern Review, The New Yorker, Plainsong, North Dakota Quarterly, New Letters* and many others. He teaches in the Creative Writing Program of the University of Memphis, where he founded the River City Writers Series, now in its 21st season and under student direction.

Mia Pardo is a graduate of The New School for Social Research's Graduate Writing Program, and a winner of an Academy of American Poets college prize in poetry.

Todd Parker reviews books for journals and magazines. He is the author of a book of poetry, *Lampshade Twister* (Roanoke Press), and a novel, *Crushing Defeats* (Cottage Books). He lives in Europe and Sweden, and travels throughout the world.

Joel B. Peckham, Jr. lives in Western Michigan with his wife, the poet and nonfiction writer Susan Atefat Peckham, and their two sons, Cyrus and Darius. His poetry and scholarship have been published in numerous journals throughout the United States, Great Britain, and Canada, including *American Literature*, *The Black Warrior Review*, *The Malahat Review*, *ONTHEBUS*, *Prairie Schooner*, *The Southern Review*, and *Yankee Magazine*. With Susan he is also co-founding editor of the online literary journal, *Milkwood Review* <www.geocities.com/milkwoodreview>. His first full-length book of poems, *nightwalking*, is published by Pecan Grove Press.

Charlie Reilly teaches English at Mongomery County Community College in Pennsylvania. His interviews with writers like Amiri Baraka, John Barth, E.L. Doctorow, Nikki Giovanni, Joseph Heller, Alison Lurie, Arthur Miller, John Updike, Kurt Vonnegut, and Tom Wolfe have been published in a number of journals and, to date, have been collected into fourteen books.

Alice Rene was born in Vienna, raised in Portland, Oregon, and has a Masters degree in Social Welfare. She lives in Woodland Hills, California where she writes poetry, short stories, and has recently completed a memoir.

Tom Rich moved to Montana having retired as a social worker in Nashville, Tennessee. His poems can be seen in *The Rockford Review, Poetry Motel, Medicinal Purposes,* and *Ibetson Street Press,* among others.

Christopher Robbins lives in Atlantic City, New Jersey with his wife and two kids. This is his first published poem.

Doren Robbins's poetry has appeared in over fifty literary journals, including *The American Poetry Review*, *North Dakota Quarterly*, *Cimarron Review*, *Indiana Review*, *International Poetry*, *Hawaii Review*, *Paterson Library Review*, *Sulfur*, *New Letters*, *5AM*, *Exquisite Corpse*, *Willow Springs* and *Hayden's Ferry Review*. His most recent collection *Driving Face Down*, won The Blue Lynx Prize, Lynx House Press, 2001. Currently, he is professor of Creative Writing/Literature at Foothill College where he is coordinator for The Foothill Writers' Conference.

John Rodriguez is a Bronx poet studying for his Ph.D. in English at the CUNY Graduate Center.

Bertha Rogers's poems appear in journals and anthologies and in several collections. Her translation of *Beowulf*, was published in 2000, as was her poetry chapbook *A House of Corners*, winner of the Maryland State Poetry Competition. In 2001 she was a featured poet at the International Poetry Festival in Quebec. In 2002 her poem "Rhomboid" was selected by Alfred Corn as winner of the Lyric Recovery Poetry Competition. She has been awarded fellowships at the MacDowell, Millay, and Hedgebrook artists' colonies and at the Hawthornden International Writers Retreat in Scotland.

Leda Rogers was born in Brooklyn and moved to Los Angeles when she was ten years old. She won several summer scholarships to Parson's School of Design while in junior and senior high school. She received a scholarship to the Neighborhood Playhouse in New York to study acting with Sanford Meisner. She has appeared in several motion pictures and television shows. She has been writing for about five years and is currently working on her one-woman show. This is her first published work.

D. A. Roisler's short stories have appeared, or are forthcoming in *Hawaii Pacific Review*, *Heartlands Today*, *The Laurel Review* and *Passages North*.

Tom Ruschak makes his living as an economist.

Frances Kim Russell is currently a graduate student in East Asian Studies at Stanford University. Her poetry has been published in *Red Wheelbarrow*, and she has work in the anthology *InvASIAN: Asian Sisters Represent*.

Terry Savoie's work has been received by more than 85 literary journals, anthologies, and small press publications. These include *American Poetry Review, The Iowa Review, The North American Review, Poetry, The Sonora Review, The Black Warrior Review, Ploughshares* and *Another Chicago Magazine.* Others are in current or forthcoming issues of *Flyway, the minnesota review, Evansville Review, Tar River Poetry, Natural Bridge, Rattle, Many Mountains Moving* and *America.*

Leslie Schenk returned to his writing career late 1993 after a long hiatus in UN service around the world, and has since received over 100 acceptances for publication. Special honors include Honor Roll of *The Best American Short Stories,* and finalist for *Ernest Hemingway First Novel Contest* both 1997 and 1998. He was nominated for the Pushcart Prize in 1998, 1999, and 2000.

Patricia L. Scruggs was born in Colorado, grew up in Alberta, Canada, earned her B.A. and M.F.A. at Cal State Fullerton. She teaches high school art in Chino, California. Her work has appeared in *Caylx, Rattle, Spillway, ONTHEBUS* and *13 Los Angeles Poets.*

Nancy Shiffrin's second collection of poems *The Holy Letters* is available online from www.booksurge.com. Her most recent credits include *inside english, earth's daughters, Religion and Literature,* and *The Canadian Jewish Outlook.* Through Creative Writing Services: A Literary Arts Consultancy she helps aspiring writers achieve publication and personal satisfaction. She can be reached at nshiffrin@earthlink.net.

Dan Sicoli has worked in a variety of vocations including baker, district sales manger, letter carrier, housing coordinator, printer, cheese packer, and rhythm guitar player. He is co-founder and co-editor of *Slipstream Magazine,* which is in its 21st year of publishing and is one of the oldest active small press literary magazines in western New York. He is also an active member of the just buffalo literary center. In 1999 he was nominated for a Pushcart Prize.

Karol Siegel is an independent filmmaker and writer. She has worked in film, television, and theatre for the past twelve years and has an M.F.A. from the Yale School of Drama. She lives in L.A. with her husband, John.

Terrie Silverman is a performance artist, poet and playwright. She received an M.F.A. in the Professional Writing Program at USC. Her work has been presented at such venues as The HBO Workspace, KPFK Radio, the LA Poetry Festival, Highways and LATC. She is an Artist-in-Residence at Beyond Baroque literary Arts Center where she teaches autobiographical writing and performance.

Rick Smith is a clinical psychologist and co-directs Back in the Saddle, a residential program for brain-damaged adults in Apple Valley, California. His previous book is *Exhibition Game* (1973). He plays blues harmonica with the Hangan Brothers. Poems have recently appeared in *Rattle, Hanging Loose, New Letters, Poetry Motel,* and the anthology *So Luminous the Wildflowers* (Tebot Bach, 2003).

P. C. Spectre is a freelance journalist and paranormal investigator in Dade County, Florida. He is a frequent contributor to print and online journals dealing with the occult. His book, *Ghosts I Have Known,* will be published in 2005.

Dale Griffiths Stamos's poetry has appeared in *Rattle, The Lucid Stone, rivertalk, Into the Teeth of the Wind* and *Mothering.* A playwright as well, she has had short and one-act plays produced in Los Angeles, New York City and at Actors Theatre of Louisville, where she was named co-recipient of the 1997 Heideman Award. Her full-length play, *Blue Jay Singing in the Dead of Night,* was produced by Actors Alley in North Hollywood, California, and her newest full-length, *Dialects of the Heart,* won the Jewel Box Theatre's Original Playwrighting Competition. She was also Emmy-nominated in 1993 for her story credit on the afterschool special *Words Up!*

Dagmar Stansova was born in Czechoslovakia, raised in New York City and graduated from Brown University. She has performed in leading roles at the Public Theatre, LaMama and off Broadway. Her film credits include *Tick, Tick, Tick* which premiered at Sundance and *Dirty Money.* This poem is her first publication and is part of her chapbook, *Swoon.*

Paul Stebleton's works have appeared in *Poetry Motel*, *Blank Gun Silencer* and the anthology *Michigan Voices III*. He is a graduate of the University of Michigan and a Hopwood Award winner.

Mark Steinbeck is the webmaster for Website Designs and editor of *North County Online*. His writing and photography have appeared in *Santana*, *The San Diego Log*, and *Valley Roadrunner*.

Virgil Suárez was born in Havana, Cuba in 1962. At the age of twelve he arrived in the United States. He is the author of two new poetry collections, *Palm Crows* (University of Arizona Press) and *Banyan* (LSU Press). *Guide to the Blue Tongue*, his sixth collection of poetry, will be published by the University of Illinois Press. He is the co-editor of the anthologies *American Diaspora: Poetry of Displacement* and *Like Thunder: Poetry of Violence in America*, both published by the University of Iowa Press. His work continues to be featured in international and national literary magazine journals. He divides his time between Key Biscayne and Tallahassee, where he is professor of creative writing at the Florida State University.

Edward Michael O'Durr Supranowicz's poems have appeared in *mojo risin'*, *Nanny Fanny,* and *Spillway*.

Mario Susko, a witness and survivor of the war in Bosnia, left the city of Sarajevo in 1993 and, in fact, returned to the US in November of that year. He received his M.A. and Ph.D. from SUNY at Stony Brook and has lived in this country half of his past 30 years. He is the author of 18 books of poems, the most recent being *Versus Exsul* (Yuganta Press, 1998). His poems have appeared in *Borderlands*, *Seneca Review*, *Fence*, *Nassau Review*, *Poetry International*, *Bottomfish*, *Sulphur River Review*, *Kiosk*, *Potato Eyes*, and *Ellipsis*, among others. He is the recipient of several awards, including the 1997 *Nassau Review* Poetry Award, the 1998 "Nuove Lettere" International Prize for Poetry and Literature (Naples, Italy) for his English edition of *Mothers, Shoes and Other Mortal Songs*, and the 2000 Tin Ujevic Award (Zagreb) for the best book of poems, the Croatian edition of *Versus Exsul*, published in 1999.

Zahava Sweet was born in Poland in 1930 and survived the Holocaust. She emigrated to Israel in 1947, served in the army and was wounded in the Independence War in 1948. Julian Tuwim was "the beloved poet" of her childhood, one of the best poets in Poland, and she translated many of his poems into English. In 1958, she came to the U.S. to be with the rest of her family. She has written poems since her childhood. Her work has previously appeared in *ERGO*, the literary magazine of Bumbershoot Festival, *Port Towsead Gazette*, and *Semi-Dwarf*, to name a few. Her new poety collection is *The Return of Sound* (Bombshelter, 2004).

Holly Swick's poetry has appeared in *Love's Chance Magazine*, *The PEN*, *The Oak,* and *Scroll*.

Mark Terrill lives in Germany.

Susan Terris's book *Fire Is Favorable to the Dreamer* has just been published by Arctos Press. In 2004, Gary Metras at Adastra Press published a letterpress edition of her chapbook *Poetic License* and Marsh Hawk Press published *Natural Defenses*. Other recent books are: *Eye of the Holocaust* (Arctos Press, 1999) and *Nell's Quilt* (Farrar, Straus & Giroux). Her journal publications include *The Antioch Review*, *The Midwest Quarterly*, *Ploughshares*, *Shenandoah*, *Missouri Review* and *Southern California Anthology*. With CB Follett, she is co-editor of an annual anthology, *Runes, A Review of Poetry*.

Bill Thomas is a social worker, actor, improviser, and sketch comedy writer. He was a company member of Los Angeles Theatresports, Acme Comedy Theater, Improv Olympic, and Comedy Dojo. Bill is from Morro Bay on the central California coast. He has lived primarily in Los Angeles since he first attended UCLA. This is his first publication since he last wrote for the UCLA *Daily Bruin*.

Irene Thomas was born and raised in Palo Alto, California. She now lives in Los Angeles, where she graduated from UCLA with a major in sociology and is now studying various healing arts and methods. After her husband unexpectedly died, she started writing to move through her grief and regain her balance. This is her first published work.

Kathleen Tyler is a teacher in the Los Angeles public school system. Her poetry has appeared or is forthcoming in *Runes, Spillway, The Great American Poetry Show*, and *So Luminous the Wildflowers*, among other publications. A poem of hers was selected for the Common Prayers postcard project. At one time, she reviewed books of military history for the *Daily News*.

Nadia van de Walle is a high school poet who lives in East Lansing, Michigan.

Ryan Van Cleave is the Anastasia C. Hoffman Poetry Fellow at the University of Wisconsin-Madison's Institute for Creative Writing. New work is forthcoming in *The Journal, TriQuarterly* and *Ploughshares*.

Robert Vivian's work as an essayist, poet, and playwright has appeared in numerous journals throughout the United States, including *Creative NonFiction, Harpers, The New York Quarterly, River Teeth*, the *Sycamore Review*, and *Best American Monologues*. His collection of nonfiction, *Cold Snap as Yearning* is forthcoming from University of Nebraska Press.

Jasmine Dreame Wagner is a graduate of Columbia University. Her poetry and prose have appeared in *Agnieszka's Dowry, Obsessed with Pipework*, and *Konfluence*, and is forthcoming in *The North American Review*. She currently lives between Connecticut and Brooklyn, NY.

Farley Walker is studying to receive an M.A. in creative writing at the University of Southern Mississippi. This is Farley's first publication.

Lizzy Leaman Waronker published her first poem at the age of 17. She is currently working on her first novel. She lives in Los Angeles, California.

Paul Watsky is a Jungian analyst practicing in San Francisco, where he lives with his wife and twin sons. In 1996 and 1997 he was awarded Second Place in the Gerald Brady competition of the Haiku Society of America. His work has appeared in *Poetry Flash, The Cream City Review, Modern Haiku, Elysian Fields Quarterly,* and, currently, in the online journal *Pemmican* (Summer, 2003) at www.pemmicanpress.com. A chapbook, *More Questions than Answers*, was published by tel-let (2001), and his work has been included in *A New Resonance: Emerging Voices in English Language Haiku* (Red Moon Press, 2000), as well as four volumes of the *Red Moon Anthology*. Forthcoming are a book, *Counterofferings,* from Bloody Twin Press, and a chaplet in the New American Imagist series by Hermitage West. More of his writing can be found at his web site, www.paulwatskypoetry.com

Megan Webster is a founding member of San Diego Writers' Cooperative (www.sandiegowriters.org) and an English as a Second Language textbook writer and editor. Her recent poems appeared, or are forthcoming, in *Cedar Hill Review, Limestone Circle, Red River Review, Magee Park Poets Anthology 2002, Shoreline Poetry and Prose: Explorations in Mental Illness,* and *Decades of a Woman* (anthology).

Richard Weekley's poems have been widely published in literary journals, among them *Kansas Quarterly, Wisconsin Review, Midwest Review*, and *Crosscurrents*. He's had several collection of poems published, including *These Things Happen* (Inevitable Press, 1999), *The Scrubwoman and 231/3 Other Poems* (L.A. Poets Press, 2001) and *Not the Subject of Cocktail Parties*, which won first prize from Black Bear Publications International Chapbook Competition. He lives in Santa Clarita, California.

Joe Weil has had his reviews and poetry published in *Poet Lore, Red Brick Review, Rattle,* and many other small presses. His most recent book of poems is *The Pursuit of Happiness* (Iniquity Press/Vendetta Books). He is a three-time Pushcart Prize nominee and a Geraldine R. Dodge poet. His poetry has been anthologized in the Def-Jam poetry anthology *Bumrush the Page*, as well as *Identity Lessons*.

Lawrence Welsh is an award-winning journalist, writer and poet. He is the former director of publications for the county of Los Angeles and is one of America's leading writers on life in border towns. His previous books of poetry are *Rusted Steel and Bordertown Starts* and *Lenny Bruce in El Paso*.

Victoria Stern Whelan lives in Santa Monica with her husband and two sons. She received a B.A. from Smith College. An actress for many years, Victoria has performed in numerous off-Broadway and regional theatres. She appeared in several films and television shows including *Law & Order*, *Feds*, and *Boston Public*. Victoria is the star and producer of the award-winning short film, *Ladies Room, L.A.* She has co-authored two screenplays. Victoria recently completed her first children's book.

Gwenne Wilcox has been writing since the age of six. She was first published in *McCall's Magazine* in 1966. Currently, she is working on *Making Mahmool,* a novel. Ms. Wilcox lives in Los Angeles with her two children and three pets.

Anne Wilson was Nominated for a Pushcart in 2000, and has published widely in such award winning journals as *The Bitter Oleander, South Dakota Review, Sheila-Na-Gig, Rattle,* and *Comstock Review.* She has won awards in *The Muriel Craft Bailey Competition, Explorations 2000,* and *Center Press's Master Awards.* She teaches writing at several colleges and universities in San Diego and summer workshops on Whidbey Island (Washington). Her book *Solea* was recently released by Finishing Line Books.

Eliot Khalil Wilson currently teaches at the University of Alabama. His poems have appeared in or are forthcoming in *Willow Springs, Carolina Quarterly, Ploughshares, Many Mountains Moving, Beloit Poetry Journal,* and *The Journal.*

Sholeh Wolpé's poems have appeared and are forthcoming in *Grain, Green Hills Literary Lantern, Poetry Salszburg Review, Spillway,* and *California Poetry Anthology* (2003). She lives in Southern California, where she owns a small company, ZyQuest, and hosts Poetry at the Loft. She is also the project director and artistic designer for Tebot Bach's April–April calendar, *Poets of Southern California—The Swimsuit Issue,* where poets appear in mythological and surreal scenes in their swimsuits. She has just completed her first book-length manuscript of poems, *The Painted Sun.*

Carson Wu graduated from the University of Michigan. His work has been recognized with a Minnesota State Arts Board Fellowship in fiction and an inaugural Santa Fe Writers' Project Award. His stories appear or are forthcoming in *Confrontation, International Quarterly, Crab Orchard Review* and *Mississippi Review's* online edition. He is currently a journalist in Asia.

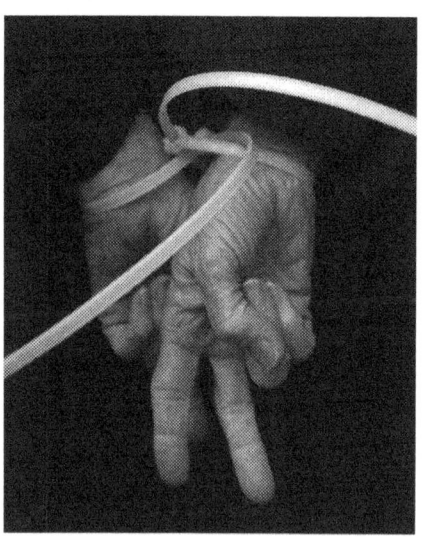

The Rev. Louis Vitale made a peace sign after his arrest during a demonstration in San Francisco against the war in Iraq. A police officer escorted Vitale from the site of the protest—Bechtel Corp. headquarters in the financial district. About 400 people marked the first anniversary of the conflict by demonstrating in San Francisco and Oakland in a prelude to nationwide antiwar rallies to commemorate the dead and decry the profits Bechtel Corp has earned in reconstruction contracts. Vitale was among about half a dozen protesters who were arrested. Some who congregated at the 7 A.M. protest wore pink tutus; some beat drums. Many vowed to risk arrest to condemn what they described as "war profiteering" by Bechtel, which has received about $3 billion in government contracts for Iraq reconstruction. Others—grandmothers, teachers, ministers and veterans—said they felt compelled to voice their opposition to a war they believe was draining resources from education and healthcare.

Native Californian Aaron Smith is a figurative painter who lovingly employs techniques and inspirations of 17th-century masters with his own skillfully subtle injection of modern connotation. Smith's warm palate reflects an intense emotional quality that each work strives to evoke, in the ultimate homage to the past.

Smith is continually influenced by his own ever-changing personal interests of 19th-century philosophy and culture. As earlier works were heavily steeped in a definite aura of Caravaggio, a handful of the other themes arising and influencing his work over the years have included the lives and works of Walt Whitman, the English pre-Raphaelite Simeon Solomon, the Finnish Symbolist painter Magnus Enckell and the Swiss painter Ferdinand Hödler.

Aaron Smith's work has been exhibited in museums and galleries nationwide, including the Frye Museum of Art in Seattle, the Arnot Art Museum in Elmira, NY, the Laguna Museum, Ann Nathan, and Koplin Del Rio Gallery in West Hollywood, California. He has been the recipient of many teaching awards and painting commissions since becoming a faculty member at the Art Center College in Pasadena since 1996, where he also received his B.F.A. in 1989.

BOMBSHELTER PRESS

Anthologies

Twelve Los Angeles Poets (224 pp) $14.95

13 Los Angeles Poets (160 pp) $13.95

Moving Pictures: Nine Los Angeles Poets (62 pp) $5.00

Raising the Roof: Poets Supporting Habitat for Humanity, Riverside (72 pp) $10.00

The New Los Angeles Poets (203 pp) $12.50

Two-Women Show (Haft/Laumeister) (62 pp) $10.00

After I Fall (Alexander/Kulikov/Lee/Wilson) (64 pp) $8.95

Books by Single Authors

A Lone Black Gull (Michael Andrews) (320 pp) $18.00

Coffin Lumber (Michael Andrews) (128 pp) $12.00

Breaking Down the Surface of the World (Jack Grapes) (62 pp) $10.00

Lucky Finds (Jack Grapes) (45 cards) $12.50

Chaos and Dancing Stars (Jean Katz) (140 pp) $15.95

Passion & Shadow (Judi Kaufman) (98 pp) $18.00

Crossing the Double Yellow Line (Stellasue Lee) (95 pp) $12.95

Corpses of Angels (Henry Morro) (72 pp) $12.95

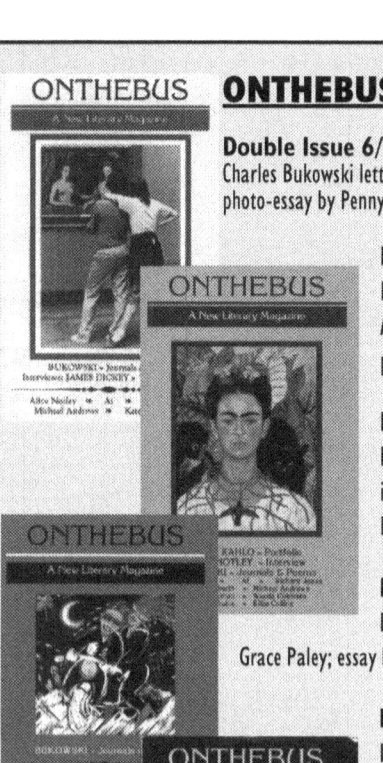